The 1960s on Film

Recent Titles in Hollywood History

The Vietnam War on Film
David Luhrssen

The American West on Film
Johnny D. Boggs

The Civil War on Film
Peg A. Lamphier and Rosanne Welch

World War II on Film
David Luhrssen

The Cold War on Film
Paul Frazier

Sports on Film
Johnny D. Boggs

The 1960s on Film

Jim Willis and Mark Miller

Hollywood History

BLOOMSBURY ACADEMIC
NEW YORK • LONDON • OXFORD • NEW DELHI • SYDNEY

BLOOMSBURY ACADEMIC
Bloomsbury Publishing Inc
1385 Broadway, New York, NY 10018, USA
50 Bedford Square, London, WC1B 3DP, UK
29 Earlsfort Terrace, Dublin 2, Ireland

BLOOMSBURY, BLOOMSBURY ACADEMIC and the Diana logo
are trademarks of Bloomsbury Publishing Plc

First published in the United States of America by ABC-CLIO 2021
Paperback edition published by Bloomsbury Academic 2024

Copyright © Bloomsbury Publishing Inc, 2024

For legal purposes the Acknowledgments on p. xiii constitute
an extension of this copyright page.

Cover photo: *Easy Rider*, directed by Dennis Hopper, 1969.
(Columbia Pictures/ScreenProd/Photononstop/Alamy Stock Photo)

All rights reserved. No part of this publication may be reproduced or
transmitted in any form or by any means, electronic or mechanical,
including photocopying, recording, or any information storage or retrieval
system, without prior permission in writing from the publishers.

Bloomsbury Publishing Inc does not have any control over, or responsibility for,
any third-party websites referred to or in this book. All internet addresses given
in this book were correct at the time of going to press. The author and publisher
regret any inconvenience caused if addresses have changed or sites have
ceased to exist, but can accept no responsibility for any such changes.

Library of Congress Cataloging-in-Publication Data
Names: Willis, Jim, 1946 March 19– author. | Miller, Mark, 1992– author.
Title: The 1960s on film / Jim Willis and Mark Miller.
Description: Santa Barbara, California : ABC-CLIO, [2021] |
Series: Hollywood history | Includes bibliographical references and index.
Identifiers: LCCN 2021024187 (print) | LCCN 2021024188 (ebook) |
ISBN 9781440868771 (hardcover) | ISBN 9781440868788 (ebook)
Subjects: LCSH: Nineteen sixties. | Motion pictures—United
States—History. | United States—In motion pictures. | United
States—History—1961–1969.
Classification: LCC PN1995.9.U64 W555 2021 (print) | LCC PN1995.9.U64 (ebook) |
DDC 791.43/6587392—dc23
LC record available at https://lccn.loc.gov/2021024187
LC ebook record available at https://lccn.loc.gov/2021024188

ISBN: HB: 978-1-4408-6877-1
PB: 979-8-7651-3092-6
ePDF: 978-1-4408-6878-8
eBook: 979-8-2160-4098-9

Series: Hollywood History

To find out more about our authors and books visit www.bloomsbury.com
and sign up for our newsletters.

To my dedicated colleagues at Azusa Pacific University

To Clay Lee Musselman

Contents

Series Foreword	ix
Preface	xi
Acknowledgments	xiii
Introduction	xv
Chronology	xix
1. *The Graduate* (1967)	1
2. *Easy Rider* (1969)	17
3. *The Deer Hunter* (1978)	37
4. *The Right Stuff* (1983)	55
5. *Mississippi Burning* (1988)	75
6. *JFK* (1991)	89
7. *Thirteen Days* (2000)	107
8. *Mad Men* (2007–2015)	125
9. *Selma* (2014)	145
10. *Hidden Figures* (2016)	163
Select Bibliography	183
Index	187

Series Foreword

Just exactly how accurate are Hollywood's film and television portrayals of American history? What do these portrayals of history tell us, not only about the events they depict but also the time in which they were made? Each volume in this unique reference series is devoted to a single topic or key theme in American history, examining 10–12 major motion pictures or television productions. Substantial essays summarize each film, provide historical background of the event or period it depicts, and explain how accurate the film's depiction is, while also analyzing the cultural context in which the film was made. A final resources section provides a comprehensive annotated bibliography of print and electronic sources to aid students and teachers in further research.

The subjects of these Hollywood History volumes were chosen based on both curriculum relevance and inherent interest. Readers will find a wide array of subject choices, including American Slavery on Film, the Civil War on Film, the American West on Film, Vietnam on Film, and the 1960s on Film. Ideal for school assignments and student research, the length, format, and subject areas are designed to meet educators' needs and students' interests.

Preface

The 1960s on Film analyzes how one of the most important decades of the twentieth century was depicted on the big screen and how close those framings came to real life.

Often remembered as the "counterculture decade," the 1960s was a decade of great change in America, as the nation awakened to the horrors of a hotly debated, undeclared war that would claim almost 60,000 American lives and to the realities of how racial discrimination and continued suppression of minorities was still being practiced a century after the Emancipation Proclamation. It was a decade that stripped away the pretense of serenity and hypocrisy and demanded action. And it was a decade in which experimentation occurred in pushing not only the boundaries of free speech, sex, music, and drugs but also the boundaries of space travel. It was the decade in which America landed the first human being on the moon. All of that has been recorded permanently in movies about the decade, which are still being made today. A few of the most recent films are *Once upon a Time in Hollywood* (2019), *Green Book* (2018), and *Bridge of Spies* (2015).

This book examines nine films and one television series that portrayed various aspects of life during the 1960s, showing the struggles faced by different demographics amid crisis, challenges, and change. In some cases, such as the race to the moon, these obstacles were navigated successfully; in others, such as the Vietnam War, they were not. The list of films and television series chosen by the principal author and editors is not meant to be definitive about the decade, but each is well made and depicts different aspects of life in the decade. Most of the films were nominated for Academy Awards or Golden Globes or both, and some were controversial in how they framed the events and characters as well as how close they came to reality.

As can be seen by their release dates, only two of the films were actually made during the 1960s (*The Graduate* and *Easy Rider*), and they came toward the end of the decade. Writers and filmmakers often like to have the perspective that time offers between an event and the telling of it. Given the value that time brings to an accurate reflection, it is notable how spot-on *The Graduate* was in presenting the ambiguities and emotions felt by young adults in the 1960s. The same can be said for *Easy Rider*, appearing in the concluding year of the decade and showcasing the search by two rebellious bikers and their disillusioned companion encountering an America often filled with hate and hypocrisy.

The Graduate, Easy Rider, The Deer Hunter, and *Mad Men* stand out from the rest of the films in another way: they are the only stories that are fictionalized (although certain characters are fictional or composites in some of the other films). The other six films either portray accurately or are based upon events that really happened involving people who really lived. Some films, like *Mississippi Burning* and *JFK*, drew some controversy for taking too much artistic license, while other critics noted their overall framing of the events was fairly accurate.

Films like these and many others are the work of storytellers, directors, and actors whose work educates as well as entertains. Their movies offer us a chance to reflect not just on the characters portrayed but also on who we are ourselves—how we might react to provocations such as those portrayed on screen. We see values such as grace, heroism, and love depicted as well as the baser values we would all like to avoid.

Acknowledgments

Any book, especially one analyzing the history of an era, is built upon at least three foundations: the discussions with others who lived that era, the insight put into writing by other researchers, and—if you're lucky—the chance to have lived the era yourself. This book could not have been written were it not for all these foundations. Research focused not just on these nine films and one television series but also on the decade of the 1960s itself. Because the films and the television series represented here have all won critical acclaim, much has been written about them by some very gifted film historians and critics.

My coauthor, Mark Miller, and I have also pored over the films and television series ourselves for meaning. One of the hallmarks of a good film is that it stays with you long after you leave the theater or change the TV channel; it teaches you something, and each time you see it, you find yourself learning something new—something you didn't see or think about before.

Having discussions with others who were there also helped, especially for Mark who missed living the 1960s by at least three decades. So, special thanks to William Carroll for his timely role in facilitating research for Mark on the civil rights movement and to Thomas Rapchinski for sharing valuable insights and resources that shed light on the sociocultural nuances of this earlier generation. As for myself, it helped to reminisce with friends who—like me—spent the 1960s traversing from teens to young adults.

We have endeavored to give credit to sources from where much of our information originated, and they are found in the references section of each chapter. Of special note, the online movie sites IMDB and Rotten Tomatoes have a wealth of reviews and behind-the-scenes information, facts, and trivia about the films and television series. *The New York Times, Los*

Angeles Times, and *The Washington Post*, as well as other notable newspapers and film industry publications like *Variety*, have been the source of a lot of information and perspectives on the films and television series.

For myself, I want to thank my talented wife, Anne, for (once again) sharing me with this writing project and for providing a soothing piano soundtrack at times in the next room. I also want to thank my sister C.J. who—like Annie—has always found a way to believe in me.

— *Jim Willis*

Introduction

When the adjective "iconic" is used, it usually describes something or someone that is considered a symbol or type of something else, often something larger such as heroism, virtue, deception, or maybe corruption. When "iconic" is used in connection with the decade of the 1960s, many would say it describes an era of protest and societal changes of great magnitude and impact. From the moment that a young and charismatic John F. Kennedy was elected president in 1960 to the moment that Neil Armstrong set his foot down on the moon's surface in 1969, this was a decade like no other in the history of the United States.

The two main flashpoints for protest and resulting impact were (1) the fight for civil rights and the resulting Civil Rights Act of 1964 and Voting Rights Act of 1965 and (2) America's plunge into the Vietnam War until that war became "Americanized" and resulted in more than 58,000 U.S. troops dying in combat for what many perceived as a useless cause. Before that death toll began mounting, however, there was another national tragedy when President Kennedy was assassinated in the streets of Dallas in 1963. Later, in 1967, Dr. Martin Luther King became the martyr of the civil rights movement when he was assassinated in Memphis. In 1968, the Democratic hopeful for the presidency, Robert F. Kennedy, would suffer the same fate just two months later while speaking at a rally in San Francisco.

Still, the 1960s also saw great advances in science and technology, and the most prominent of these was the conquering of space travel. From astronaut Alan Shepard's first suborbital flight on May 5, 1961, to the touchdown of the Apollo 11 Lunar Module Eagle on the moon on July 20, 1969, the American race into space provided points of anticipation and pride for most Americans.

All this and more took place in the span of these 10 years. If the decade were a movie, much of its soundtrack would feature a persistent drumming of protest chants directed at all these issues and events. The most audible of those protests came from two places: the streets of the American South and the campuses of American colleges and universities.

Although the civil rights movement was a national crusade, its most persistently vivid and bloody images came from protests and marches in places like Greensboro, North Carolina, where a group of four African American college students dared to sit in a whites-only portion of a Woolworths lunch counter, which set the stage for other similar sit-ins. In the following year, African Americans marched peacefully in Birmingham and Selma, Alabama, facing bloodshed, clashes with armed police, and jail time. Among those jailed was the most notable leader of the civil rights movement, Dr. Martin Luther King, who used his time behind bars to write his famed "Letters from a Birmingham Jail" that helped galvanize the resolve of other African Americans to achieve equal rights under the law. And then there was the tragic story of the three civil rights workers who used their summer college vacation in 1963 to head south into Mississippi and help Blacks get registered to vote. Instead of returning home safe and sound, the trio of James Chaney, Michael Schwerner, and Andrew Goodman were shot to death on a country road by Southern white supremacists.

The nation's college students raised their voices in loud protest to such abuses and to the growing threat of America's involvement in Vietnam. These protests began on the campus of the University of California at Berkeley during the 1964–1965 academic year, and this became the start of the Free Speech Movement (FSM) that swept across the nation's college campuses. It began as a ban by the administration of on-campus political activities and was under the informal leadership of Berkeley graduate student Mario Savio, who delivered a set of demands from the steps of the administration building, which led to a student sit-in inside administrative offices. The idealism of American college students, coupled with the very real threat faced by the military draft that would take many of them to fight in the Vietnam War, fueled nationwide campus protests against the policies of President Lyndon B. Johnson and President Richard M. Nixon. Organizations like the Students for a Democratic Society (SDS) would take the lead in furthering the protests and goals of this young counterculture generation of Americans. The musical soundtrack of protest songs by singers and groups like Pete Seeger, Joan Baez, Judy Collins, and Peter, Paul & Mary provided iconic phrases and melodies that further helped unite the dissident young. Many of them came from song titles such as "We Shall Overcome," "Eve of Destruction," "Give Peace a Chance," "R-E-S-P-E-C-T," "One Tin Soldier," "Where Have All the Flowers Gone?" and "Sounds of Silence."

The resulting mantras of "Question Authority" and "Don't Trust Anyone over 30" were heard and seen across the country and knitted many young Americans together during the 1960s. These came to symbolize their distrust of anything associated with the "establishment." That included traditional values like restricting sexual activities to married couples and the avoidance of mood- and mind-altering drugs. To show their resistance to such traditions, young Americans began experimenting en masse with sex and unions outside of marriage (which became known as "free love") and with drugs like marijuana and the hallucinatory LSD. Not to be overlooked in the changing culture were societal norms relating to gender roles. As the decade began, women were still largely relegated to a one-dimensional role of homemaker often subjugated to the dominance of men and therefore stunted in their quests for self-fulfillment outside the home. But that would change, and by 1970, the beginnings of the women's liberation movement were well underway. Women had entered the workforce and were starting to challenge men for jobs that traditionally had gone to men.

For both white and Black Americans, it is hard to overstate the physical threat of the Vietnam War, along with its ethical and philosophical questions, had in giving rise to and galvanizing the protests of the 1960s. Beginning on November 14, 1965, American military "advisers" in Vietnam became more than advisers and morphed into full-fledged soldiers in combat as 1,000 members of the Seventh Calvary Unit faced off against 2,500 battle-hardened North Vietnamese soldiers in the Ia Drang Valley. Hundreds of U.S. soldiers lost their lives during the four days of fighting. America was now involved, big time, in Vietnam, and the numbers of American troops there grew exponentially in the coming months and years. After that, the Vietnam War became the main flashpoint of the era and the main (but not the only) target of counterculture protest and wrath.

The 1960s version of the 1950s "beatniks" were the hippies and those who identified with that movement because of their own deep distrust of society's norms. Hippie communes were springing up around America, and they drew inspiration from the nineteenth-century farming commune, Brook Farm, visited by transcendentalists like Ralph Waldo Emerson and famed New York newspaper editor Arthur Brisbane. The commune was founded by Unitarian minister George Ripley and his wife Sophia Dana Ripley, and it covered 175 acres just outside of Boston, in West Roxbury. This experiment in communal living, where intellectual introspection was matched with manual farm labor in a socialist environment of sharing among its members, lasted from 1841 to 1847.

History is an endless labyrinth of stories, comprising both fact and legend. American history, and the 1960s in particular, overflows with rollicking, nail-biting, and otherwise controversial stories that many have undertaken to narrate in the years since that decade has passed. While written historical records provide an oftentimes objective lens through which the current generation may understand the nation's past, film, operating within the bounds of its own potentials and limitations, offers another lens by which people may interpret events in history. It has been said that "history is written by the victors"; one might just as well attach the addendum, "History is rewritten by the filmmakers." In any case, over half a century of film has attempted to portray the events of the 1960s with widely varying results—all of them colored by subjectivity, in one way or another, as they retell their respective historical narratives.

This book takes a look at the 1960s through the eyes of 10 filmmakers who found the decade to be a rich tapestry of individual stories showing what it was like to live in these turbulent times. For example, in thinking of what it was like to be young in the 1960s, one could picture Benjamin Braddock, the leading character from the 1967 classic film *The Graduate*, which was the signature film for the baby boomer generation as they were finishing college just as the counterculture movement got underway. When Ben was suffering through the college graduation party his upper-class parents were throwing for him at the start of the film, he personified both Ralph Waldo Emerson and Henry David Thoreau in his exasperation. When he was chafing at the suggestion by his dad's business friend, Mr. Robinson, that he would find success by entering the field of *plastics*, surely we could hear Emerson whispering in Ben's ear, "To be yourself in a world that is constantly trying to make you into something else is the greatest accomplishment" (Emerson, 2014). That one line from the script also made *plastic* the embodiment of the establishment world to the counterculture revolutionaries of the 1960s. And when Ben donned his new scuba gear and used it to dive to the bottom of the backyard pool and escape the throngs of his parents' friends high above, we could hear Thoreau whispering, "The mass of men lead lives of quiet desperation" (Thoreau, 2019). A myriad of other portraits of 1960s life emerged vividly through the other eight films—*The Right Stuff*, *Mississippi Burning*, *JFK*, *The Deer Hunter*, *Thirteen Days*, *Selma*, *Hidden Figures*, and *Easy Rider*—and the much-acclaimed television series *Mad Men* studied in this book.

Virtually every aspect of life was touched by this iconic decade: from traditions to experimentation, from politics to music, from war to peace, from authority to equality, from discrimination to civil rights, from literature to film, from business to pleasure, from love to hate. All these and other aspects of American life went under the microscope in the years between 1965 and 1975. And the legacy of these years has left a lasting imprint on America.

There has never been another decade like it.

FURTHER READING

Emerson, Ralph Waldo. 2014. *Ralph Waldo Emerson Essays*. Deadtreepublishing.com.
Thoreau, Henry David. 2019. *Walden*. New York: SDE Classics, p. 4.

Chronology

February 1, 1960	A group of college students stage a sit-in to protest segregation at the Woolworth's lunch counter in Greensboro, North Carolina, triggering national interest in the evolving civil rights movement.
May 1, 1960	An American U2 spy plane, piloted by Francis Gary Powers, is shot down by Russia over Soviet air space, and Powers is detained for what would be two years. Cold War tensions rise.
June 23, 1960	The Food and Drug Administration approves public use of Enovid, the first birth control pill that gives women control over their body's reproductive process. The door to the sexual revolution is open.
September 26, 1960	Presidential candidates Richard M. Nixon and John F. Kennedy hold the first nationally televised debate in history.
November 8, 1960	America goes to the polls and elects John F. Kennedy as president of the United States in the closest vote in 76 years.

December 15, 1960	A joint fighting force of insurgents and communists arises in South Vietnam, and the United States takes notice. This fighting force is named the Viet Cong.
April 17, 1961	The Central Intelligence Agency leads a small army of Cuban exiles in the Bay of Pigs to overthrow dictator Fidel Castro. It fails. Tensions between Cuba and the United States increase and Cuba looks to Russia for military aid.
May 4, 1961	A group promoting civil rights departs Washington, D.C., on buses to take their message to southern states. They are known as the Freedom Riders.
May 5, 1961	America sends its first man into space when astronaut Alan Shepard rides a rocket into a suborbital mission. The space race is on. The story of these original Mercury 7 astronauts will be chronicled in the 1983 film, *The Right Stuff*.
February 22, 1962	Following Shepard's pioneering mission, astronaut John Glenn becomes the first American to complete an orbit of the earth in space.
June 15, 1962	The newly formed Students for a Democratic Society (SDS) holds its first national convention in Michigan and drafts its Port Huron Statement, setting in motion a long student protest movement around the country.
August 1, 1962	Author Rachel Carson publishes her groundbreaking book, *Silent Spring*, warning of environmental disaster if conservation is not practiced. America's green movement begins.
October 1, 1962	The first African American student in history registers at the University of Mississippi, and the National Guard is called in to quell violent protests.
October 16, 1962	America and the Soviet Union begin a 13-day showdown in Cuba when President Kennedy demands that Russia remove its nuclear missiles from the island nation 90 miles from Key West, Florida. The world is on the brink of war until October 28. This will become the focus of the 1991 film *Thirteen Days*.

February 19, 1963	The modern-day women's rights movement is ushered in with the publication of author Betty Friedan's book, *The Feminine Mystique*.
August 28, 1963	Some 250,000 people hear Rev. Martin Luther King deliver his stirring "I Have a Dream" speech in Washington, D.C. It becomes a pivotal event in the civil rights movement.
October 11, 1963	Vatican II begins on October 11, called by Pope John XXIII. Its council sessions will cover two years and will change the Catholic Church, bringing it more in line with the modern era.
November 22, 1963	An assassin's bullet kills President John F. Kennedy in Dallas, plunging the nation into shock and ushering Vice President Lyndon Baines Johnson into the Oval Office. An alternative theory to the lone-assassin theory will be detailed in the 1991 film, *JFK*.
February 9, 1964	The Beatles makes the first of two appearances on the popular Ed Sullivan variety show on television, garnering 70 million viewers, on February 9 and 16. The group will change popular music history.
June 22, 1964	Three civil rights workers go missing while helping register Black voters in Mississippi. The FBI is called in, and the bodies are found in an earthen dam, victims of murder. The event accelerates the passage of the Civil Rights Act and forms the focus of a later 1988 movie, *Mississippi Burning*.
July 2, 1964	The Civil Rights Act is passed on July 2 by Congress and becomes the law of the land.
August 2, 1964	The Gulf of Tonkin Resolution is passed in Congress. It gives President Johnson permission to send troops into Vietnam against the North Vietnamese Communists without actually declaring war. America's involvement in Vietnam accelerates.
October 14, 1964	Martin Luther King is honored with the Nobel Peace Prize for his work in promoting civil rights in America.

November 3, 1964	Lyndon Johnson wins an easy victory for the White House as he beats GOP challenger Barry Goldwater in the presidential race to earn his first full term in office.
July 30, 1965	The Medicare Bill becomes law on July 30, establishing government health care for the elderly.
August 6, 1965	The Voting Rights Act is passed by Congress, extending equal voting rights to voters of all races.
August 11, 1965	Violence breaks out in the Watts section of Los Angeles during a summer of race wars in cities. Thirty-four die, and property damages total $200 million.
September 5, 1965	The word "hippie" is coined by a *San Francisco Examiner* writer, Michael Fallen. He uses it in a series of stories describing the beatniks who migrated into the Haight-Ashbury District of San Francisco in search of a communal lifestyle.
November 14, 1965	The Battle of Ia Drang is fought in Vietnam, and it is the first battle there pitting a U.S. ground brigade of soldiers against North Vietnamese regular soldiers. Hundreds of U.S. troops die over a four-day period.
June 16, 1966	Black militant Stokely Carmichael assumes leadership of the Student Nonviolent Coordinating Committee (SNCC) and pivots the group away from its philosophy of nonviolence. He coins the term "Black power," instead.
June 30, 1966	The National Organization for Women (NOW) is created with the purpose of bringing equality to women.
October 15, 1966	Under the leadership of militant activists Bobby Seale and Huey Newton, the Black Panther Party is formed to promote the use of violence in achieving civil rights goals.
November 8, 1966	Edward Brook, a Republican from Massachusetts, is elected the first African American U.S. senator in 85 years.

January 15, 1967	The First Super Bowl is played as the Green Bay Packers defeat the Kansas City Chiefs.
January 30, 1967	By now, the total number of American troops in Vietnam has hit nearly 400,000 as the Vietnam War becomes Americanized and as dissension and protest rises in America.
October 2, 1967	Thurgood Marshall is confirmed for the U.S. Supreme Court as the first African American to take a seat on the high court.
Summer, 1967	San Francisco's Haight-Ashbury District is ground zero for the "Summer of Love" that draws thousands of hippies celebrating free love and promoting peace.
November 9, 1967	Jann Wenner launches *Rolling Stone* magazine in San Francisco, uniting music, culture, and politics in what will become the flagship music magazine for decades.
December 22, 1967	The motion picture *The Graduate* premiers and becomes a classic. In many ways, it defines the generation that came of age in this decade.
January 30, 1968	Vietnam erupts as the Tet Offensive starts and lasts for two days as a resurgent North Vietnam enemy strikes at several targets in the country, and some 2,500 American troops are killed. The offensive belies the official statements from the military and White House that America was winning the war.
February 27, 1968	Walter Cronkite, named in polls as "the most trusted man in America," returns from a fact-finding trip to South Vietnam and tells his millions of viewers the war is "unwinnable." President Johnson decides not to seek reelection shortly after that.
June 6, 1968	Robert F. Kennedy, brother of John F. Kennedy and the leading Democratic candidate for the presidency, is assassinated in Los Angeles.
August 25, 1968	The Democratic National Convention boils over in anger and violent confrontations between protesters and police outside.

November 5, 1968	Shirley Chisholm is elected the first African American woman to Congress.
	Richard M. Nixon defeats Democratic challenger Hubert H. Humphrey and becomes president.
June 27, 1969	The Gay Liberation Movement is launched in the Stonewall Inn tavern in New York City when police raid the gay bar and a violent confrontation breaks out in the streets outside. It becomes known as the Stonewall Riot.
July 20, 1969	Astronauts Neil Armstrong and Buzz Aldrin walk on the moon, the first humans to do so. It is seen by many as the crowning achievement of the space race, launched by President Kennedy at the start of the decade.
August 15, 1969	More than 400,000 people gather and party in upstate New York on a farm near Woodstock between August 15 and 17 to hold what many believe was the most important pop music festival in history.
October 15, 1969	Some 2 million war protesters converge in cities across America, with 250,000 alone descending on Washington D.C. It is the largest such demonstration in history, and it is targeted at the Vietnam War.
November 17, 1969	The Strategic Arms Limitation Talks (SALT) begin between the United States and Russia as the two superpowers work toward curbing the spread of nuclear missiles.

Chapter 1

The Graduate (1967)

In 1967, a film appeared that featured a little-known actor and a first-time director in a story with a simple plot. For most films, that would mean a short run, but for this film—*The Graduate*—it would result in a classic, generation-defining film that would stand the test of time. *The Graduate* was directed by Mike Nichols and starred a very young Dustin Hoffman and Katharine Ross, alongside veteran actress Anne Bancroft as the iconic Mrs. Robinson. Within just the first three minutes of the film, the overall theme is presented metaphorically as young Benjamin Braddock arrives in LAX, transported over the last leg on a moving sidewalk. Braddock, as a type of so many young people of the tumultuous 1960s, is floating through life, being propelled by external forces and their rules, with no plan on how to deal with it on his own. He knows he will encounter others' expectations and plans when he gets home, but wonders how to respond to them. This young scholar and campus newspaper editor from one of the country's elite universities hasn't got a clue.

As for the film itself, all that's left is to flesh out the details of this theme and answer the question of whether Ben can find a way to walk for himself, toward an end goal that he decides he wants. Along the way, all the young baby boomers watching this coming-of-age film, set in this pivotal decade of the 1960s, go along for the ride vicariously and maybe even get some direction for their own life's journey.

The Graduate was only the second film directed by Nichols, the male half of the former comedy duo of Mike Nichols and Elaine May whose three of their social satire record albums hit the top 40 Billboard albums between 1959 and 1962. Having turned to directing, Nichols had just distinguished himself in 1966 with the film *Who's Afraid of Virginia Woolf?*, starring Elizabeth Taylor, Richard Burton, and George Segal. He was paired on *The Graduate* with humorist and satirist Buck Henry, who cowrote the screenplay with Calder Willingham who had done excellent screenplays for the earlier films *Paths of Glory* and *One-Eyed Jacks*. For *The Graduate*, the two writers adapted their screenplay from a novella of the same name written by Charles Webb in 1963. The 106-minute film was produced by Lawrence Turman and distributed by Embassy Pictures and United Artists, and it was made on a budget estimated at only $3 million. It wound up returning approximately $105 million in the United States and Canada. Adjusted for inflation, the film ranked 23rd in 2020 among the highest-grossing American films in those two countries. It premiered on December 21, 1967, and stayed in release for 106 weeks.

Nichols received the Best Director Oscar in 1968, while Willingham and Henry received a nomination for Best Adapted Screenplay. The film itself was nominated for Best Picture and Best Actor awards for Hoffman and Bancroft. Ross was nominated as Best Supporting Actress. Photographer Robert Surtees was also nominated for Best Cinematography.

The film traces the story of Benjamin through the first several months of his return to Los Angeles after completing his bachelor's degree. Upon his return, his parents immediately hold a graduation party for him that Ben is reluctant to attend. When his father enters his room, he finds Ben lying on his bed, leaning against an aquarium stocked with fish, a recurring shot in the early part of the film. Mr. Braddock says the guests are waiting to see Ben and asks him what's wrong, and his son replies, "Dad, could you explain to them I just have to be alone for a while? I'm just worried about my future. . . . I don't know. I want it to be different."

It will be the first of several references Ben makes about his future. Undaunted, his dad takes him downstairs into a sea of friends who are all Ben's parents' friends. There is not a young face in sight. He is pawed over and constantly congratulated and asked what he plans to do. That sets up one of the best remembered scenes in the film when one of his dad's friends, Mr. McGuire (played by Walter Brooks), hustles Ben aside and says, "I just want to say one word to you. Are you listening to me? *Plastics*. There's a great future in plastics. Think about it. . . . Enough said."

That one short exchange was enough for the word "plastics" to become the commonly understood word among young people of the late 1960s that defined everything that was wrong with America. It connoted hypocrisy, superficiality, and a threat to more important values. More on this later. Within the first two minutes of mixing with his parents' friends, Ben has had enough, and he darts back to the solitude of his bedroom and shuts the door to be alone with his fish who, like him, are the object of scrutiny in their glass house.

One of the recurring images in the early scenes of the film is of Ben's bedroom aquarium where he would spend time looking at the fish swimming around. That was the idea of production designer Richard Sylbert, who felt it would symbolize young Ben's feeling of living in a glass house while at his parents' home and that he was entrapped in a human aquarium. That motif was carried even further with scenes of Ben drifting in the family swimming pool, and especially with the scuba scene in the middle of his 21st birthday party. Sylbert felt these scenes also depicted what he saw as a narcissistic culture (Roberts 2017).

Mrs. Robinson (played by Anne Bancroft) enters Ben's bedroom, claiming to be looking for the bathroom. This attractive, but life-hardened, woman is twice Ben's age and is the wife of his father's business partner (played by Murray Hamilton). She asks Ben to drive her home, saying Mr. Robinson has taken the car and left the party. Ben is hesitant and confused, but does so. Arriving at her home, she waits for him to get out, come around, and open her door. She then invites Ben to come in and have a drink. Bewildered, he does, and the scene winds up with Mrs. Robinson undressing and telling Ben she is "available" for him anytime. Ben is even more confused and tries to escape when Mr. Robinson comes home unexpectedly before things go any further. Mr. Robinson doesn't see what's going on and, in a brief conversation downstairs, tells Ben he should have some fun before going on to graduate school and advises him to "sow a few wild oats and have a good time with the girls while you can." Mr. Robinson then suggests Ben should get to know his daughter, Elaine. Ben chokes, because Mrs. Robinson had just tried to seduce him in Elaine's room upstairs as Elaine's portrait hung over the whole scene.

Back at Ben's home the next week, another unwanted party—this one for his birthday—is set up by his parents. The classic scene here is of Ben having to model his new scuba gear for the guests. As he reluctantly appears, he is in a wet suit with tank, mask, and regulator, walking toward the family pool. The sounds go silent except for a loud breathing action heard through the air tank's regulator. He jumps in the water, then tries to surface, but his dad keeps pushing him back under. So Ben decides to go straight to the bottom, lie on his back, and try to wait out the gawking guests staring down from above the surface. All the while you hear him breathing heavily through the scuba air regulator. Benjamin has become one like the fish in his aquarium.

Abruptly, the scene shifts to Ben on the phone. Surprisingly, he's calling Mrs. Robinson and clumsily asking her out for a drink. She's way ahead of him, though, asking if he has reserved a hotel room. Sleeping with Mrs. Robinson becomes a routine thing for Ben over the next few months, although he has absolutely no idea what to do in their first encounter. He's also concerned about the propriety of the whole scene. As she draws him into bed, he resists at first by protesting, "For God's sake, can you imagine my parents? Can you imagine what they would think if they saw me here with you right now?" When she starts to put her dress back on, though, he quickly changes his tone, turns out the lights, and nature takes its course.

Over the next several weeks, there are more encounters. Ben soon realizes the relationship is entirely sexual; he feels it should be more than that, but his attempts to get to know her or even have any kind of conversation prove useless. He continues to call her "Mrs. Robinson" throughout all of the sex sessions. His parents become worried about his continual nightly disappearances, and his father is frustrated over his shiftlessness. "Do you mind telling me what those four years of college were for?" his father asks. Ben gives him a quick and simple "You got me!" His dad pushes him into asking Elaine Robinson out when she comes home from Berkeley for the summer.

The first date with her is awkward to say the least. Ben seems intent on making sure there is no second date, worried about the promise Mrs. Robinson exacted of him to never ask Elaine out. He humiliates her by taking her to a strip club, but he realizes he has gone too far, as she begins to cry. He apologizes and leaves with her. He takes her to a hamburger drive-in as he tells her about the trouble he's been having "playing a game" with his parents for which they had set the rules, one of which was forcing him to ask Elaine out. The evening ends with his telling Elaine how much he enjoys being with her, and he confides that he is messing up his life by having an affair with a married woman, although he doesn't tell her it is her mother. Elaine is attracted to Ben's vulnerability, and they decide to see each other again.

That's where Mrs. Robinson enters the picture once more, this time threatening Ben that she will tell Elaine about them just to keep her away from him. Ben rushes to tell Elaine himself before her mother can and blurts it out. Elaine is devastated. They both look up and see her mother has just entered the room.

Elaine leaves home and goes back to college, but Ben vows to his parents he is going to marry her even though she seems as if she's through with him. His mind is made up. For the first time, he knows what he wants, and that is to marry Elaine. He drives up the coast to Berkeley and embarks on efforts to soften Elaine into talking with him first and then marrying her. Although she has been told by her mother that Ben forced himself on her and raped her, Ben explains what really happened. She is considering his proposal of marriage when her father shows up in Ben's apartment and threatens him with legal action unless he stops seeing Elaine.

When Ben goes to the campus to see Elaine, he finds she has left school and has left him a note saying she loves him, but it would never work between them. She is going to marry a medical student, Carl Smith (played by Brian Avery). Ben then crisscrosses California two more times to find Elaine and discovers the wedding is to take place at a church in Santa Barbara. He is late in arriving, however, and watches from the glass-encased balcony as Elaine and Carl tie the knot and kiss at the altar below. He is frantic and starts pounding on the glass and screaming her name repeatedly. She hears and sees him, and realizing she has just married the wrong guy, she turns and goes to him in front of angry and hysterical families and guests. Ben and Elaine embrace in the church foyer, and Ben takes a cross and swings it in wide arcs at Mr. Robinson and the others trying to mob him and Elaine. The couple escapes through the front doors, with Ben cramming the cross through the outer door handles, effectively locking the others inside.

In the last scene, Ben and Elaine—she in full wedding gown regalia—sprint toward a passing city bus that has stopped at the corner, jump aboard, and make their way to the rear seats, all under the disbelieving gaze of a bus full of passengers. The couple flash smiles at each other, but, slowly, those smiles morph into a more sober expression of bewilderment as if they are silently asking, "What do we do next?" In some ways, it seems they are back to the beginning of the story where Ben is asking the same question about his life. The difference is, this time, he has taken control of his life, found what he wanted in life, went after it, and achieved it. Although confused now about the rest of his journey, he is in better shape to figure it out, and now he has a partner to help him do it.

When *The Graduate* premiered, it found a very receptive audience among young people. Remembering its initial New York preview in an 86th Street theater (with Hoffman present), Nichols recalled, "In the last five minutes—starting with the melee in the church—everyone stood and cheered. . . . And it wasn't even a finished print. . . . Poor Dustin was white as a sheet. It was his first time seeing the movie and he was stunned by the reaction. We all were" (Fear 2012).

On the 50th anniversary of the movie, Hoffman himself looked back on the night Nichols described and called it unbelievable. He said most people associated with the film didn't expect it to do that great at the box office. "If my memory is correct," he said, "it was a slow build in terms of people going to see it. The first time I saw it—Mike didn't allow any of us to see rushes—I was in New York on unemployment and they said they were going to have a sneak of it on 86th Street and I went to see it. I couldn't tell if the audience was liking it or not. By the time we got to the church [scene], something happened to the audience and the next thing I knew they were all standing up and cheering and I thought, 'Oh my God.' I was the waiter for most of these people's tables the year before" (Tapley 2017).

The *Los Angeles Times* also looked back on the film 50 years later and continued to issue the same kind of praise it did when the movie premiered in 1967. "*The Graduate* charmed most everyone when it arrived in theaters 50 years ago, topping the 1967 box office . . . and becoming an evergreen generational touchstone" (Chang 2017).

Critics like Chang see in Benjamin Braddock a kind of everyman—or everywoman in today's cultural era—who is baffled by what to do with life, so he winds up shifting into the neutral gear for a while. "His rootlessness and uncertainty about who he is and what he wants in life—and . . . his willingness to own and assert that uncertainty—seem to anticipate each new generation's crises of identity, career and purpose," Chang writes. "An imaginative cine-sociologist might sketch a plausible throughline from Benjamin to the unorthodox postgraduate heroes of movies like 'Into the Wild' and 'Adventureland.' . . . Which is not to suggest that the Braddocks of the millennial era are exclusively young men. On the contrary, in an era where young women enjoy far greater social, sexual and vocational freedom, some of Benjamin's restlessness lives on in the awkward, indecisive heroines of 'Frances Ha' and 'Funny Ha Ha,' to say nothing of the collected works of Lena Dunham including the just-concluded HBO series, 'Girls'" (Chang 2017).

HISTORICAL BACKGROUND

The Graduate is not a film that chronicles a particular event or persons in history. Instead, it presents and analyzes a cultural history of the decade of the 1960s. It uses a story and a few fictional characters and their situations to symbolize larger cultural distinctions—the zeitgeist—of the era. When Ben Braddock seems clueless about his future or what he wants out of life, he is a stand-in for so many young people of an era who questioned most traditional norms and values of their parents' generation. Among those were values related to sex, marriage, and drugs. In a larger vein, they were values related to peace instead of war, and to equality among races and economic classes rather than discrimination and cutting people out of the American dream. But there was also a striking preference for individualism as opposed to corporate thinking and behavior.

It is worth knowing that there have never been more college students in America than there were in the 1960s, thanks to the baby boom following World War II. The number had doubled between 1940 and 1960 to 3.6 million, so there was a huge cadre of young people who were intent on exploring social issues and pursuing idealism. That pursuit often took the form of activism in this tumultuous decade, and there were plenty of college students with the time and motivation to push for change. It was, in fact, a very loud decade. Adding to this phenomenon was the fact that the American economy had pivoted from one dominated by industry to one dominated by service, innovation, and white-collar jobs. It was a time of ideas, many of which resulted in technological breakthroughs that gave birth to the digital revolution to follow.

Sociologist Todd Gitlin summed up the 1960s in the title of his book: *The Sixties: Years of Hope, Days of Rage* (1987). Citing the uniqueness of that era, he also noted that it has carried its legacy to today's culture. In 2010, writer Kenneth Walsh quoted Gitlin as saying, "The genies that the sixties loosed are still abroad in the land, inspiring and unsettling and offending, making trouble. For the civil rights and anti-war and countercultural and women's and the rest of that decade's movements forced upon us central issues for Western civilization—fundamental questions of value, fundamental divides of culture, fundamental debates about the nature of the good life" (Walsh 2010).

Indeed, the catch phrase that became a main rallying cry for young people of the decade was "Don't trust anyone over 30!" It quickly caught on with young people and became a unifying rallying cry among teens and 20-somethings. The man who actually coined that phrase was named Jack Weinberg, a student in the Free Speech Movement at the University of California at Berkeley at the time. When interviewed in 2000, Weinberg said he was surprised the phrase became so famous. "I was being interviewed by a newspaper reporter, and he kept asking me who was 'really' behind the actions of students, implying that we were being directed behind the scenes by the communists or some other sinister group," he said. "I told him we had a saying in the [free speech] movement that we don't trust anybody over 30. It was a way of telling the guy to back off, that nobody was pulling our strings." A *San Francisco Chronicle* writer called attention to that quote, which was then picked up by other newspapers around America. "It went from journalist to journalist, then leaders in the movement started using it because they saw the extent it shook up the older generation," Weinberg recalled. The spirit of his statement remained with him, however, as he continued working throughout his life as an activist for environmental issues (Daily Planet Staff 2000).

Every generation of young people want to carve out their own identity, and many see themselves avoiding the traps of conformity that ensnared their parents and caused them to wind up in jobs or careers they didn't like or even married someone they couldn't get along with very well. The youthful rebellion may take the form of different music, different hairstyles, different clothing, and different slang. What made the 1960s unique in creating what was called the "generation gap," which is depicted vividly in *The Graduate*, was the difference in values that teens and 20-somethings had in the 1960s. And much of the impetus for those different values was the external context and pressure of this era. America in the 1960s and early 1970s was taking on social issues that past generations long ignored. Chief among the issues were inequality and discrimination, especially as these were directed at minority races. The days of "separate but equal" treatment of Blacks was proving not to be equal at all, and the overt hatred and racism—still there in parts of the country—had just gone below the surface in other parts. Its effects were still seen in the separate entrances for Blacks in movie theaters and the whites-only restaurants and restrooms of the South. It was there also in many voting places. The Civil Rights Act of 1964 and the Voting Rights Act of 1965 may have legally changed those conditions, but, in practice, they still remained and the new federal civil rights laws were unenforced in parts of the South.

The whole protest era began in earnest in 1964 when a group of students at the University of California at Berkeley started demanding rights of free speech on campus, and thus the Free Speech Movement (FSM) was born. It grew in numbers geometrically around the country and came to encompass many problems these protestors identified as needed fixing.

Many protest groups emerged out of the FSM were largely populated and led by young people. Before long, these groups would divide into those who favored nonviolent protests and those who favored taking militant action to right the wrongs. Among the latter were the Black Panthers and the Weatherman (which became the Weather People). Those favoring nonviolence were led by Martin Luther King and the Students for a Democratic Society, which had chapters on nearly all major campuses during the 1960s.

To all of these young people, the real threat America faced was its own government, whose leaders were taking the country down the wrong road and endangering tens of thousands of American lives in the process by failing to enforce civil rights violations and by sending some hundreds of thousands of troops annually to fight in Vietnam. Certainly a strong motivation for many protestors was warding off the threat of being sent to Vietnam themselves. Because of the military draft, they felt they would likely have to go and be killed in a war they didn't support. The military draft was in place for most of the 1960s, and every able-bodied young man became eligible at age 18. It was not an experience they looked forward to, and it put a damper on what had been a birthday most young men looked forward to.

There were other societal pressures young people had to deal with, but Vietnam and civil rights activism alone accounted for much of their angst and much of their distrust of an older generation they blamed for producing them. Many young people felt they could not conform to a society that had handed them such a mess, and the inner cry became a public one when they started to dissent with newfound voices. The 1960s was similar in spirit to the words of Charles Dickens who wrote in an earlier era: "It was the best of times, it was the worst of times, it was the age of wisdom, it was the age of foolishness, it was the epoch of belief, it was the epoch of incredulity, it was the season of light, it was the season of darkness, it was the spring of hope, it was the winter of despair" (Dickens 1998, 1).

This era of Vietnam and the fight for civil rights—that also produced the beginnings of the modern fight for women's equality and LGBTQ rights—was loud and violent, and it often tested whether we were—in fact—a United States of America. To be sure, some of a young college graduate's angst over what to do with their lives is present in every generation. But the 1960s was a time that welcomed unconventional thinking about charting lives that went against mainstream thinking. For many young people in this decade, it was all about going against mainstream thinking.

Societal change doesn't happen in a vacuum, and it helps to understand that the decade of the 1960s followed the postwar 1950s when America was getting back on its feet from the devastation of World War II. This so-called "feel good" decade was when families reunited and began new lives in the growing suburbs of America. But while the decade of *Father Knows Best* and *Leave It to Beaver* was peaceful on the surface, underneath there were tensions growing. Prosperity was not being shared by all. In the segregated neighborhoods and schools, Blacks were living much harsher lives, out of view of the whites and unentitled to the opportunities whites had. Two other films that pointed out this dichotomy of surface life and the reality underneath were *Far from Heaven* (2002) and *The Help* (2011).

The sexual revolution—the idea of having sex freely outside of marriage if two people desired doing so—was ushered in when the first birth control pill, Enovid, hit the market in 1960. Unlike the condom, which was the man's decision to use or not, the pill was controlled by the woman herself, and it was considered safe and reliable. Further, the woman could use it without the man's knowledge and—more importantly as the age of gender equality was dawning—without his consent. By 1964, some 6 million American women were using the pill, and all it required was that a woman make one appointment with her doctor to get the prescription. With the advent of the pill, women—for the first time in history—had sole power over her fertility. "The Pill made possible the sexual revolution of the 1960s. . . . If not for women's self-determined sexual liberation, the sexual revolution might have been another unremarkable episode in the long and varied sexual history of humankind," wrote Nancy Cohen (Cohen 2012).

Sex without strings attached was the center of the "playboy philosophy," espoused by Hugh Hefner, who as early as 1953 had founded and published what became the very successful *Playboy* magazine. Originally seen as another "skin" magazine, *Playboy* would become something more than that. The *Playboy* "interview" was something the magazine touted and which many readers agreed were good. Important and influential people in the news were often the object of intensive questioning, especially regarding the culture of America. But there was more than that; Hefner became known for espousing a philosophy of individual liberation from societal norms, especially when it came to having sex. It was a controversial theory as this 1966 reaction by conservative commentator William F. Buckley pointed out:

> Mr. Hefner's *Playboy* is most widely known for the raciness of its prose and the total exposure of the female form. It is more than that, Mr. Hefner insists—and many agree, including professors and ministers and sociologists. It is a movement of sorts, and its bible is an apparently endless series, published monthly by Mr. Hefner, entitled, "The *Playboy* Philosophy," the key insight of which is that "a man's morality, like his religion, is a personal affair best left to his own conscience." The phrase sounds harmless enough, and the tendency is to cluck-cluck one's agreement to it. The trouble with Hefner's law is that society is composed of nothing more than a great number of individuals, and if each man's morality is defined merely to suit himself, then everyone will endure the consequences of the individual's autonomously defined ethics. (Buckley 2017)

In *The Graduate*, Mr. Buckley's conclusion about the inevitable consequences of sex without moral boundaries proved true: Someone could get hurt. Such sex was not always a victimless, amoral act as both Benjamin and Mrs. Robinson discovered. The consequences included Ben nearly losing his true love Elaine, the Robinsons getting divorced, Elaine and her mother having to confront an unbelievably difficult problem in life, and perhaps his own father losing a business partner in Mr. Robinson. Unrestrained sex, the movie seemed to be saying, was problematic, and it was not going to get Benjamin any closer to what he wanted out of life.

As noticeable as the sexual revolution theme was in *The Graduate*, the era's generation gap was just as front and center. The idea that a gap in thinking, orientation, and values is always present between younger and older generations was not new to the 1960s. Sociologists like Karl Mannheim had been proposing such a theory since the early twentieth century. Mannheim, a German, produced a book in 1928 called *Das Problem der Generationen*, translated as *The Problem of Generations*. He said young people are heavily influenced by their own socio-historical environment and are especially affected by the distinctive and singular issues, events, threats, and opportunities that pertain to them directly. For these young adults, these influences create shared experiences that provide the glue that cause their social cohorts to form and stay together. The thinking and behavior of these cohorts influence events of their day and even affect future generations (Pilcher 1994).

The 1960s brought the sociological theory of a generation gap to the forefront as the younger generation, typified by Benjamin in *The Graduate*, appeared to go against most of the things that the so-called Silent Generation of their parents believed in. That included career and lifestyle values, politics, music, and other cultural tastes like clothing and hairstyles. Sociologists often refer to the "generation gap" now as "institutional age segregation." That phenomenon occurs when either generation isolate themselves from members of older or younger generations in pursuing their lifestyle activities. In so doing, little or no cross-generation interaction occurs apart from the nuclear family level.

It would be hard not to see the 1960s as the decade that produced so many unique influences on young people to cause them to form the kind of social cohort that Mannheim and other sociologists speak of as central to generation gaps. Certainly the threat of Vietnam and the military draft—directed squarely at young people who didn't want to fight in a war they didn't support—was enough to cause bonds to be formed among them. Add in the appealing idealism and charisma of equal-rights champions like Martin Luther King, John Kennedy, and Robert Kennedy, and there was much to hold youth together in the 1960s. The hypocrisy they saw in their parents' generations caused them to segregate from the older generation.

DEPICTION AND CULTURAL CONTEXT

Some saw 1960s America as a country adrift, cut off from the norms that had once made sense. Surveying her San Francisco surroundings after immersing herself in a hippie community to write about it, novelist Joan Didion characterized larger problems of the era this way in her book, *Slouching Towards Bethlehem*, which first appeared as an article in the magazine, *The Saturday Evening Post*: "The center was not holding. . . . Adolescents drifted from city to torn city, sloughing off both the past and the future as snakes shed their skins, children who were never taught and would never now learn the games that had held the society together. People were missing. Children were missing. Parents were missing. Those who were left behind filed desultory missing-persons reports, then moved on themselves. It was not a country in open revolution. It was not a country under enemy siege. It was the United States of America in the year 1967" (Didion 1967).

Didion's description of the era serves as a good cultural context for *The Graduate*, which released in the same year as Didion's book. Although Didion wrote about her observations and experiences up the California coast in San Francisco, and although she observed young people who had "tuned in, turned on, and dropped out," as the saying of the day went, her observations captured the bewilderment, disillusionment, shiftlessness, and resistance that upper-class young people like Benjamin often exhibited. They were caught in the same web of the generation gap and credibility gap that confronted young people everywhere in the 1960s. As a 20-year-old college graduate, Ben had reached the point where he no longer believed in many of the values that his parents and their friends espoused. When he was urged to pursue a future in "plastics" because it was an up-and-coming industry, he perceived it as a career in hypocrisy. Ben was a rebel, but his rebellion was passive. He was an infidel who didn't believe in traditional societal values, but he had not found anything yet to take the place of those values. In quick sequence, when he first chided Mrs. Robinson for seducing him, and then apologized profusely for being so disrespectful, he wasn't sure what was right any more.

Like Ben, young people of the 1960s wanted a future that was "different," as he tells his dad. When Ben turns his back on the advice of his dad's business partner to go into plastics, he is saying he wants something real and genuine. And when presented with a "plastic" relationship defined only by sex with Mrs. Robinson, he chooses a relationship built on love with Elaine instead. Most of all, though, Ben wants his future to be one of his own choosing and not one someone else chooses for him. In other words, in the vernacular of the 1960s, he wants to do his own thing.

Looking back on his creation 45 years after directing *The Graduate*, Mike Nichols said he and his friend Buck Henry worked very closely for months on the script, adapting Charles Webb's novella for the big screen. The script had made the rounds of a couple of writers, one of whom was Calder Willingham who, Nichols said, provided little more than the characters' names that Henry would end up using. The final script was Henry's work, with a little of his own touches worked in, Nichols said. Reflecting on one of the most memorable scenes from the script, Nichols recalled, "Buck did the heavy lifting. I still remember the one place where he sort of aced me: I read it and said, 'Buck, really? Plastics? The guy says plastics to Benjamin? That joke is already 20 years old.' Buck said, 'Let's try it, Mike.' When we had the first public preview screening, Mr. McGuire says the line, and the place went nuts. So, you know . . . smart Buck!" (Fear 2012).

Nichols said Hoffman got the part of Ben after hundreds of actors were tested for the role. The fact that Hoffman underplayed the role so well, and so much of the humor came out of his understatement, set him apart from the others. "They had to move me to a different soundstage when we shot because I would ruin takes by laughing too loud," Nichols said. "I'm not kidding, I had to eat handkerchiefs during some scenes to keep from cracking up. He could be absolutely hilarious while hardly moving a muscle—which was exactly what I was after, without being able to specifically describe it before I saw him do it" (Fear 2012).

One thing in the film that may have seemed odd to moviegoers is that none of the characters older than Ben, Elaine, and Carl (her jilted fiancé) was called by their first name. It was always Mrs. Robinson, Mr. Robinson, etc. But the younger characters were all called by their first names. The filmmakers felt this added to the theme of the generation gap.

The character of Mrs. Robinson was the subject of some moviegoer debate who had differing ideas about what caused her to behave in the way she did with Benjamin. To the director, Nichols, Mrs. Robinson was a woman who harbored deep anger with herself over trading who she really wanted to be in exchange for material wealth. Anne Bancroft agreed with that description, and that persona came out in the scene where Ben gets her to reveal a tiny bit about herself, and she tells him she studied art in college. She then tries to convince him (maybe herself) that she has no interest in it anymore and knows nothing about the subject. Nichols believed that was an important scene in conveying her regret and anger over bargaining away her life and dreams.

A montage sequence that alternated between Ben bedding Mrs. Robinson and then drifting on an air mattress back home in his swimming pool was the creation of Nichols and Henry. They felt it depicted the affair as a non-relationship with Mrs. Robinson. "It was really just a way for Ben to become the mindless object that his parents wanted him to be," Nichols said (Fear 2012).

The cross-generational affair also depicted the sexual liberation theme of the 1960s, in large part made possible by the development of the birth control pill, Enovid. Certainly Mrs. Robinson felt sexually liberated as she embarked on a sustained and successful campaign of seducing Benjamin, who was half her age, even though she was married with a college-aged daughter. But, once into it, Ben felt the liberation himself and was happy to keep it going, despite having no romantic feelings toward Mrs. Robinson, and vice versa. That was another hallmark of the 1960s' sexual revolution: that sex did not have to mean two people were in love with each other; it was more of a recreational activity that did not connote commitment in a relationship.

Executive Producer Joseph E. Levine wanted the film taken first to college campuses to be previewed. The first question many young viewers had was why the Vietnam War—or fear of it—was not featured in the film since the story was about a young college graduate in 1967. Worry over being drafted upon graduating from college was on the minds of most young men in that year. The all-inclusive draft (every eligible man between 18 and 26 could be called) did not end until December 1, 1969, and even then it was replaced by the equally anxiety-producing lottery that remained in place until 1973. Although all young men were eligible to be called to service when they turned 18, they could obtain a student deferment for at least four years to graduate from college, assuming their grade point average remained at least a 2.0 (on a 4.0) system. There were only a few ways to legally avoid the draft. Among the most popular were as follows:

- Go through ROTC and enter the service voluntarily as an officer.
- Enlist for two years and hope for a noncombat position.
- Join the military Reserves or National Guard and do six months of active duty, followed by seven years of monthly drills and two weeks of summer camp.
- Obtain a medical deferment. They were not easy to obtain.
- Obtain a ministerial deferment, go to seminary for three or four years, and be ordained.

With the statistics of American troops killed in action in Vietnam rising every year (the number reached 58,000 by war's end in 1975), it was easy to see why young men were worried about this possibility. To produce a movie about a young college graduate in 1967 who didn't seem to worry about that seemed odd to young viewers of the time.

While *The Graduate* did not tackle Vietnam or civil rights, it did tackle the generation gap head-on, as young Benjamin spent a lot of time resisting the expectations of his parents and their friends who kept thrusting them upon him. The famed "plastics" advice Ben got from a very sincere Mr. McGuire was the most vivid example of that. The film also tackled young people's confusion over the standards of sexual conduct and marriage and whether to challenge the thinking and behavior of older generations on marriage and sex outside of marriage. The scenes of the 40-something Mrs. Robinson seducing 20-year-old Benjamin depicted beautifully his naivety and awkwardness over how to respond to his unbelief that an older married person could be doing this. Premarital sex, which had by then become commonplace among his friends in college, was one thing. But sex with an older, married woman who was thrusting herself on you? Something else entirely. How could this square with what his parents' generation had tried to pass off as the traditional norms of adulthood and marriage?

The Graduate was an especially meaningful film for those college seniors eagerly waiting graduation in the spring of 1968. Since the film premiered in December 1967, it caught the attention of those college students who—like Benjamin—realized they didn't know what they would do when they graduated. It was a serious question for them, but the humor in *The Graduate*, coupled with the young Hoffman and Ross, made considering that question a pleasurable experience. Many theaters showing the film were packed with college students, and spontaneous applause arose in many of them as Ben shoved the cross through the church door handles, keeping the angry mob at bay while he and Elaine made their escape from her wedding.

Some critics and audiences pointed to some inaccuracies with the film, such as *New Yorker* critic Jacob Brackman, seven months after it premiered. While duly noting the popularity of the film and the good filmmaking touches of Mike Nichols, Brackman noted several problems with *The Graduate*, including the decision to exclude any mentions or visualizations of the major divisive threat of the day to young people, which was Vietnam. In leaving that, civil rights, and drugs out of the film, Brackman argues, Benjamin's restlessness and resistance seem to operate in a vacuum for unidentified reasons.

On one hand, Brackman understands Nichols's decision to forego fleeting images of these overarching issues of the day and to just focus on Benjamin, but he counters, "Yet, in another sense, what Nichols is talking about is precisely these things, for which the suburban void is no metaphor at all. He has not simply denied attention to drugs or politics; he has created a world in which they play no part, a world still obsessed with that old hang-up sex. *The Graduate* has to do with an outstanding young man who finds himself turned off by the society he has been preparing to ensconce himself in. Yet all the readily available images to justify a turn-off far more compelling than Benjamin's have been declined" (Brackman 1968).

One could counter Brackman's critique, however, by understanding that there was no need to remind young Americans of what they already knew. They were living every day within the culture that Ben was a part of. They knew the stressors that Vietnam and the fight for civil rights produced. They were witnessing a lot of hypocrisy that they blamed the older generations for. They understood they were in the midst of a sexual revolution. They understood the generation gap was a real thing between their parents' values and their own. And, in knowing all of this firsthand, they could understand how that culture contributed to the kind of angst and behavior they were witnessing in Benjamin Braddock.

FURTHER READING

Brackman, Jacob R. 1968. "The Graduate." *The New Yorker*, July 27, 1968. https://www.newyorker.com/magazine/1968/07/27/the-graduate

Buckley, William F., Jr. 2017. "The Playboy Philosophy." *The National Review*, September 28, 2017 (originally published October 1, 1966). https://www.nationalreview.com/2017/09/hugh-hefner-dies-playboy-philosophy-william-f-buckley-jr-criticism-sexual-revolution/

Chang, Justin. 2017. "Commentary: 50 Years after 'The Graduate,' Restless Benjamin Braddock Still Speaks to Young Men—And Women." *Los Angeles Times*, April 20, 2017. https://www.latimes.com/entertainment/movies/la-et-mn-the-graduate-justin-chang-20170420-story.html

Cohen, Nancy. 2012. "How the Sexual Revolution Changed America Forever." Alternet, February 6, 2012. https://www.alternet.org/2012/02/how_the_sexual_revolution_changed_america_forever/

Daily Planet Staff. 2000. "Don't Trust Anyone over 30 Unless It's Jack Weinberg." *The Berkeley Daily Planet*, April 6, 2000. https://www.berkeleydailyplanet.com/issue/2000-04-06/article/759

Dickens, Charles. 1998. *A Tale of Two Cities*. New York: Dover. Originally published in 1859.

Didion, Joan. 1967. "Slouching Towards Bethlehem." *The Saturday Evening Post*, September 23, 1967, as republished in June 14, 2017. https://www.saturdayeveningpost.com/2017/06/didion/

Evans, Bradford. 2012. "The Lost Roles of 'The Graduate.'" Vulture.com, December 20, 2012. https://www.vulture.com/2012/12/the-lost-roles-of-the-graduate.html

Fear, David. 2012. "Mike Nichols on The Graduate." *Time Out*, February 9, 2012. https://www.timeout.com/newyork/film/mike-nichols-on-the-graduate

Holland, Bill. 1996. "'50s Trailblazers Brought Social Satire to the Masses." *Billboard*, September 28, 1996.

Lawrence, T.E. 1991. *Seven Pillars of Wisdom: A Triumph*. New York: Anchor. Originally published in 1922.

Pilcher, Jane. 1994. "Mannheim's Sociology of Generations: An Undervalued Legacy." *The British Journal of Sociology*, Vol. 45, No. 3 (September): 481–495.

Roberts, M.B. 2017. "19 Things You Didn't Know about 'The Graduate.'" *Parade*, December 21, 2017. https://parade.com/626910/m-b-roberts/19-things-you-didnt-know-about-the-the-graduate/

Tapley, Kristopher. 2017. "50 Years Later: Dustin Hoffman Recalls Mike Nichols' Vision for 'The Graduate.'" *Variety*, October 8, 2017. https://variety.com/2017/film/news/dustin-hoffman-the-graduate-50th-anniversary-1202583845/

Walsh, Kenneth T. 2010. "The 1960s: A Decade of Promise and Heartbreak." *U.S. News and World Report*, March 9, 2010. https://www.usnews.com/news/articles/2010/03/09/the-1960s-a-decade-of-promise-and-heartbreak

Chapter 2

Easy Rider (1969)

As the 1960s unfolded, more and more of the nation's youth went in search of America and of a set of values that seemed to jibe better with their understanding of the country's founding principles. So when a pioneering movie came out in 1969 about two bikers on the road looking for that freer America, it's no wonder it was a hit. The story was *Easy Rider,* a film about two companions, Wyatt and Billy, who peddle some drugs in Southern California, hide their cash in their motorcycle gas tanks, and turn their souped-up bikes east for a cross-country ride.

During their trek toward the Mardi Gras celebration in New Orleans, Louisiana, the pair encounters not only the beauty of the American landscape but also the ugliness of hatred among many who still aren't ready to acknowledge the value in hippies or their culture. Along with these, however, Wyatt and Billy find a fair number of people like themselves who are attempting alternative lifestyles, sometimes in hippie communes and sometimes alone or in pairs living off the land. One friend who helps them on their way, an alcoholic lawyer named George Hanson, decides to join the free-spirited twosome on their way to New Orleans, becoming acquainted with marijuana on the way there. Following a nighttime murder, revelry at Mardi Gras, and a bad LSD trip in a cemetery, the journey reaches a tragic end for all three, who never quite find what they are searching for.

Dennis Hopper directed *Easy Rider* and starred in the film alongside Peter Fonda, the son of legendary movie star Henry Fonda. The film premiered on July 14, 1969, and was distributed by Columbia Pictures. Filming was naturally done in several states along the old Route 66, including California, Arizona, New Mexico, and Louisiana. Written by Fonda, Hopper, and Terry Southern, the movie follows two freewheeling motorcyclists on their countercultural journey across America in the late 1960s. Fonda served as producer, and Jack Nicholson, Antonio Mendoza, and Robert Walker Jr. played supporting roles. The film was shot on a $360,000 budget and returned a domestic total gross of $41,728,598, finishing third in revenue rankings of 1969 films.

Even with a low budget, *Easy Rider* achieved breathtaking success in the box office and drew much attention from movie critics, carving out a place in history as "the most expressive movie of the sixties counterculture" (Hamilton 1997, 93). *The Hollywood Reporter*'s John Mahoney declares, "*Easy Rider* is very likely the clearest and most disturbing presentation of the angry estrangement of American youth to be brought to the screen, played against the barren and bountiful beauties of a cross-country pilgrimage that is at once a search for freedom and a tragic encounter with the intolerance that corrupts the ideals of freedom" (Mahoney 1969). The film served as the Unites States' official entry at the 1969 Cannes Film Festival, where Hopper won the Prize for the First Work, awarded for the best film by a new director. *Easy Rider* received two nominations for the 42nd Academy Awards: Best Original Screenplay and Best Actor in a Supporting Role (Jack Nicholson). Film critic Roger Ebert asserted, "Nobody went to see 'Easy Rider' only once. It became one of the rallying-points of the late '60s, a road picture and a buddy picture, celebrating sex, drugs, rock 'n' roll, and the freedom of the open road. It did a lot of repeat business while the sweet smell of pot drifted through theaters" (Ebert 2004).

Indeed, the film's protagonists resonated with audiences who found kindred spirits in an easygoing team of nonconformists. Gene Moskowitz writes, "Fonda exudes a groping moral force and Hopper is agitated, touching and responsive as the sidekick, hoping for that so-called freedom their stake should give them. Nicholson is excellent as the articulate alcoholic who fills in the smothered needs in a verbal way that the others feel but cannot express" (Moskowitz 1969). In her 1969 review, Pauline Kael explains how *Easy Rider* was able to communicate directly to the present-day counterculture: "What is new about *Easy Rider* is not necessarily that one finds its attitudes appealing but that the movie conveys the mood of the drug culture with such skill and in such full belief that these simplicities are the truth that one can understand why these attitudes are appealing to others. *Easy Rider* is an expression and a confirmation of how this audience feels; the movie attracts a new kind of 'inside' audience, whose members enjoy tuning in together to a whole complex of shared signals and attitudes" (Kael 2011).

Set to a soundtrack of popular 1960s rock bands, the film was one of the first to make use of already existing music as opposed to creating a brand-new score for the production. The movie also gives ample space to the drug use and promiscuity pervading the counterculture, and accordingly it ruffled some feathers. In October 1969, Vice President Spiro Agnew assigned blame to *Easy Rider*, as well as the band Jefferson Airplane, for promoting the sort of permissive countercultural lifestyle that was gaining traction near the close of the turbulent decade (Patterson 1996, 736). Vincent Canby of *The New York Times* calls the movie "a motorcycle drama with decidedly superior airs about it," ending his review with the conclusion: "Hopper, Fonda and their friends went out into America looking for a movie and found instead a small, pious statement (upper case) about our society (upper case), which is sick (upper case). It's pretty but lower case cinema" (Canby 1969).

While the film is full of young countercultural vibes, the story does not depict the countercurrent as an idealistic fantasy. Instead, *Easy Rider* leaves its viewers with ambiguity in the final scene, "implying that excesses, even countercultural ones, can be harmful" (Hamilton 1997, 93). An interview in *Rolling Stone* shares Fonda's take on the movie, with emphasis on the title chosen: "'Easy Rider' is a Southern term for a whore's old man, not a pimp, but the dude who lives with a chick. Because he's got the easy ride. Well, that's what's happened to America, man. Liberty's become a whore, and we're all taking an easy ride" (Campbell 1969).

Following in the wake of films such as *Bonnie and Clyde* and *The Graduate* (both 1967), *Easy Rider* figured prominently at the start of the Hollywood Renaissance, or the New Hollywood era, in which an array of cutting-edge productions broke with the classical norms in film and instead embraced a grittier, more experimentative style. A younger generation of filmmakers was rising to prominence in the late 1960s and into the 1970s, as they defied long-standing taboos and unraveled motion pictures that were innovative, raw, and unapologetically antiestablishment. Hopper and Fonda's highly lucrative film enticed others to follow their example: rounding up a cast and crew with young blood and creating a movie expressive of "youthful alienation and struggles with a repressive know-nothing society." Thus Hollywood experienced a fresh "movie gold rush," writes Sklar, "for a few noncommercial filmmakers, television directors, free-lance screen writers and off-Broadway performers. It lasted until the imitations of *Easy Rider* nearly all turned out to be box-office disasters" (Sklar 1975, 302).

With a story, soundtrack, and camerawork that helped to set a new standard in filmmaking, in 1998, the United States National Film Registry added *Easy Rider* to its titles esteemed "culturally, historically, or aesthetically significant." *Easy Rider* also holds a place among the American Film Institute's list of 100 Years, 100 Movies, at number 84.

HISTORICAL BACKGROUND

In 1968, when a *New York Times* writer conducted a survey of parents, teachers, and school counselors, the participants unanimously shared the belief that the youth of America presently held conventional values in disdain. The activities manifesting this youthful, rebellious spirit included "sexual libertarianism, angry politicism, vehement rejection of adult authority, and a widespread disposition to experiment with drugs" (Hamilton 1997, xi). A wide gambit of countercultural movements progressed in great part due to the unprecedented number of young people living in the United States. In 1966, *Time* magazine named "People Twenty-five and Under" as its "Man of Year." These baby boomers accounted for over one-third of the population, so their voice was sure to create shockwaves across the sociopolitical landscape.

While the nation's young rebels were indeed catalysts for the counterculture, the variety of challenges that emerged in the 1960s were products of the messy mix of both culture and politics, as Americans across generational and racial lines started to accept wholesale change during this tempestuous decade. The counterculture essentially took form in the groups and individuals who contested mainstream practices in American culture (Hamilton 1997, xi–xii).

Several countercultural movements gained momentum in the early 1960s and set the tone for the decade as a whole. After the Greensboro sit-ins of 1960 and the emergence of the Student Nonviolent Coordinating Committee, the civil rights movement gained a firm grip on America's attention, shifting the nation's focus toward the budding counterculture. Simultaneously, political activism started to surge, spurred on by the 1962 Port Huron Statement, which painted the American mainstream in uncaring and undemocratic terminology. Students for a Democratic Society, responsible for the statement, arose as an organization of the New Left and compelled college students to "take an active role in creating a participatory democracy, not run by technocrats but by the people" (Hamilton 1997, xiii).

Influenced by the New Left, the 1964–1965 Free Speech Movement (FSM) at the University of California at Berkeley provided the first spark for mass civil disobedience on college campuses. Voicing fiery discontent with the status quo, FSM leader Mario Savio decried the perceived machinations of university bureaucracy in his December 2, 1964, speech: "There's a time when the operation of the machine becomes so odious . . . you can't even passively take part! And you've got to put your bodies upon the gears and upon the wheels, upon the levers, upon all the apparatus, and you've got to make it stop" (Willis 2015, 8). The antiestablishment vocabulary in Savio's speech resonated with many young idealists frustrated with the conformity, censorship, and racism experienced in the 1950s. Using the same tactics as the civil rights movement, the FSM prepared the way for large student demonstrations opposing the war in Vietnam (Cohen 2009, 1–3).

More than anything else, perhaps, the anti-war movement weighed down the scales in favor of generating the 1960s counterculture. America's youth was fed up with lies from the government and the increasing death toll in Vietnam, and they rallied to denounce the corruption and oppression that the establishment represented (Hamilton 1997, xiii). "The campus unrest of the late 1960s," writes William Pierce Randel, "was a culmination of the frustration that generation felt at having its individual identity suppressed, its voice ignored" (Randel 1978, 197). In direct response to this alienation, Americans protested and reexamined the nation's values connected to manifold important issues: free speech, the Vietnam War, civil equality for African Americans and for women, the country's stance on LGBTQ Americans, and its relationship to migrant workers and to the indigenous peoples of America.

As American society experienced new rifts and shifts in its very fabric, the style of music changed accordingly. "At first, young people flocked to folk music with its social and political consciousness and to the early Beatles with their innocent lyrics and happy tone; then they listened to psychedelic rock with its distorted sounds and hallucinogenic imagery, then to a harsher, politicized rock as anti-war protests grew heated and the gulf between counterculture and straight society widened" (Hamilton 1997, xiii). While the boomers submerged themselves deeper into the anti-war and civil rights activities, lyrics hardened and matured. The 1960s left behind a barrage of political protest music, most notably by folk-rock song-poet Bob Dylan and followed up by bands belonging to the "L.A. sound" and the Laurel Canyon scene. Groups like The Byrds, Buffalo Springfield, and Crosby, Stills & Nash (and, later, Young) seemed to fuse the political messages of the times with fine musical artistry evolving in the contemporary popular culture.

As heralded by the discerning lyrics in Dylan's "The Times They Are A-Changin'," the music of the 1960s served as vehicles for advocating a different future for America. Randel describes the songs as "polemics" that express "political ideas of peace, love, and brotherhood. When this idealism met head-on with the entrenched system, frustrations boiled over, and drugs and dropping out of society became popular" (Randel 1978, 194). With its origins in the 1950s youth culture, rock music was the most drastic barrier between the younger and older generations. "Part romantic escape, part physical reaction, and part cultural anthem, rock music served as the steady underbeat of much of the political activity of the times" (Bloom and Breines 2011, 225). Translated into both words and emotion, the content carried clear messages. John Sinclair, manager of the rock group MC5, went so far as to proclaim, "Rock and roll music is a weapon of cultural revolution" (Sinclair 2007, 97).

Morphing out of the pessimism of San Francisco's beatnik culture, hippiedom and all of its idealism appeared as a new manifestation of rebellion around the halfway point of the decade. Pulsating with colors and buoyancy, the hippie culture attempted to construct a new type of society that embraced mysticism and a strong sense of community in place of the self-interest and materialism of mainstream American life. Hippies stood at the forefront of countercultural groups expressing a strong displeasure with technocracy, the dependence of society on powerful scientific authorities that issue their verdicts while remaining aloof and indifferent to everyday citizens (Hamilton 1997, xiii). In a 1967 essay, Guy Strait called attention to "the straight community's angry, sometimes violent reaction to the hippies," which he attributes to their intentional disregard of middle-class ideology. This overt choice to rebel created a perceived sense of "danger" in direct opposition to the commonly accepted notions of the American way (Strait 2011, 269).

With their emphasis on passionate, harmonious living, hippies communicated rebelliousness most demonstrably by the way they dressed. Long hair, denim work shirts, and blue jeans were typical of both men and women. This "uniform of nonconformity" was accompanied by a high regard for naturalness, simplicity, and homemade items, including love beads and primitive accessories, peasant shirts and skirts, Indian shirts, and Mexican serapes (Randel 1978, 200). The hippies also used the American flag and military-themed attire to voice contempt with the government and the Vietnam War; the flag appeared on shirts or the back of leather jackets, disgruntling any "straight" Americans who saw the spectacle. "Hippies dressed for the public and their attire became an identifier for who they were, as clothes became costumes and costumes became clothes. To conventional eyes the hip look reflected slovenliness and sexual ambiguity; to hippies their dress represented freedom from the uptight, cramped, and contrived, to the loose and natural" (Moretta 2017, 47).

Another aspect of style that shifted in the counterculture was speech. Peppered with newer expressions like "far out" and "groovy," the slang of the 1960s hippie communities recycled lingo originally belonging to the beats and hipsters that came before them. The collective vocabulary absorbed language stemming from various underground milieus, including the realms of rock 'n' roll and jazz musicians, drug circles, circuses and carnivals, and the Black and homosexual communities. As a form of inside language, the countercultural vocabulary expressed opposition and distrust toward orthodox ideas and behavior, creating a sense of belonging for the estranged and marginalized individuals while simultaneously creating distance between them and the outsiders. Provocative language, as evident in the use of the word "revolution," frequently showed up in the speech of the nonconformists (Moretta 2017).

While the counterculture was gaining traction, the 1960s also saw a conservative movement growing in direct correlation to the feelings of alienation and frustration that large portions of the populace shared. Americans who held to more traditional elements of society watched from the sidelines as counterculturists rejected long-standing values—exchanging them boisterously for various forms of revolution. Student demonstrations embodied an apparent political "anarchy," a rebelliousness rivaled by the sexual revolution that advocated premarital sexuality, gender equality, and free love (Bloom and Breines 2011, 287). "In a nation where, as late as 1969, more than two-thirds of all people believed that premarital sex of any kind was wrong, the hippies' anthem of 'Free Love!' resounded, as it was meant to be, like a war cry" (Farber 1994, 182). The questioning of established mores across the continent sparked a polarized effect: upsetting some while attracting others.

The counterculture's public affection for drugs also catalyzed polarization. Marijuana and LSD, as prime examples, served as the drug culture's pathways to enlightenment and freedom from inhibitions, all the while enraging and frightening occupants of the mainstream. In 1967, San Francisco's Human Be-In and Summer of Love were emblematic of the countercultural embrace of mind-altering drugs, as seen in the context of large, collective experiences where peace and love ruled and "acid rock" broke on to the music scene. Thrill-seeking teenagers and LSD users packed out concerts where acid rock musicians played, such as the Grateful Dead, the Jefferson Airplane, Janis Joplin, and the MC5. Also during the Vietnam era, New Orleans's annual Mardi Gras extravaganza, another regional thermostat for social conflict, displayed the confrontation between the counterculture of the hippies and the "Squaredom" of the straights, overflowing in an excess of music and movement, drugs and alcohol, brazen sensuality, and an overwhelming sense of cultural diversity (Mitchell 1999, 4).

Formerly found primarily in African American and Mexican American circles, marijuana extended its reach toward young white citizens looking for pleasure. In fact, the higher an individual's social class, the more likely he or she was to have smoked marijuana in the 1960s. "Young underground drug manufacturers and dealers, many operating out of the protected enclaves of America's counterculture, would at first supply the new drugs" (Farber 1994, 174–176). As time passed, various age groups and demographics tried the substance. Part of the hype stemmed from the influence exerted by rock musicians who promoted marijuana. America's youth wanted to emulate their rock stars, who were, for their part, following the pattern of the previous generation's hip African American jazz musicians claiming that getting high improved their music. The use of marijuana was commonly paired with the notion of joining a nondiscriminatory and accessible community of fellow users, and the effects of the substance were relatively mild. "Joints were typically passed around a circle and people who got stoned together often shared a gentle amusement over the 'power trips' so many people 'laid on one another'" (Farber 1994, 175–177).

Lysergic acid diethylamide (LSD), on the other hand, was a psychedelic drug that turned people's minds inside out and left a much deeper impression in their lives. Acid was more likely to be found in the possession of hippies and college-aged individuals, and the drug often carried with it spiritualized implications in its ability to expand one's consciousness to fresh realities. Psychologist and LSD guru Timothy Leary started the 1967 Human Be-In with the famous instructions: "Tune in, turn on, and drop out." Acid rocker

John Sinclair was one who ceased seeing a logical distinction between reality and illusion. In the musician's words, LSD produced full-color visions, or hallucinations, that people could embrace as they chose to challenge traditional ideas and continue to chemically "unlock" or "unblock" their unconscious minds (Bloom and Breines 2011, 226; Farber 1994, 178). From the streets of Haight-Ashbury to the rural homesteads across the Midwest, young Americans tried their luck with acid and attempted to give life to the products of their imagination. "Along the way, a few people died and others lost their minds. Though LSD often just provided simple euphoric feelings and a pleasant buzz at low doses, at hallucination-producing doses of 250 micrograms or more LSD often played for keeps" (Farber 1994, 178).

Only when the criminal and violent repercussions of the drug culture came to a head in the late 1960s did the hippie communities leave their city havens and seek a new setting for their ideal-driven lifestyle. Communes in rural and urban areas popped up with minimalistic infrastructure for people to work the land and benefit from cooperative undertakings. Herds of hippies were attracted to relatively remote patches of land, relocating to regions of northern California, Colorado, Oregon, New Mexico, and other places. "This back-to-the-earth movement came from a desire to escape crowded, impersonal, polluted cities and live close to nature, peacefully and harmoniously," writes Hamilton. "In rejecting middle-class materialism and trying to live off the land, some back-to-earth hippies formed communes, others established homesteads" (Hamilton 1997, 15). Figuring among the counterculture's most defiant members, academic dropouts likewise chose to abandon formal education (whether high school or college) to pursue their own way in life. Some college graduates, too, were part of the flocks dropping out of society, as they packed up their belongings and moved to rural or stark regions of the country. In accordance with the ideas of Henry David Thoreau, these young members of the back-to-the-land movement embraced Eastern philosophy and mysticism, shunning all forms of materialism and doing without many modern conveniences (Randel 1978, 198).

Thousands of America's youth, primarily whites, banded together in communal living as they attempted to forge a new identity for themselves. Some constructed teepees, farmhouses, and geodesic domes as their dwellings, while others lived in buses or apartment buildings. Subsistence agriculture was adopted by various such communities. Other communards took up endeavors such as selling marijuana, printing newspapers, and running medical clinics, bookstores, day-care centers, garages, or health-food eateries. "The settlements were motivated by a wealth of inspirations and ideologies: Christian, Buddhist, the spiritual beliefs of Native American tribes, anarchism, pacifism, feminism, and a ferocious desire to end the war in Vietnam," write Isserman and Kazin. "By the early 1970s, some 30,000 communes—large and small, rural and urban—served as home and, often, workplace for over three-quarters of a million people" (Isserman and Kazin 2012, 155).

For all of its diversity, the back-to-the-earth movement was marked by unity. Most notable was the demonstrative definition of equality. Almost all commune dwellers supported the idea of both men and women working together; they constructed their living spaces, took care of the infants, and brought new members into their fold. Men and women collectively shared the responsibility of rearing children, who were allowed to voice their concerns and assist with whatever chores they could reasonably accomplish. In their unified laboring and sharing of resources, communards derided American orthodoxy and indulged in uninhibited drugs and free love. It was ultimately the "tension between personal freedom and the collective ideal" that fated many communes to "a short, if compelling, existence" (Isserman and Kazin 2012, 155–156).

The changes that came at the end of the decade seem to point to three different stages of the counterculture: "an early stage, prior to 1968, when the civil rights movement worked its greatest influence and young people expressed optimism about change; a middle stage, from 1968 to 1970, when polarization intensified and the core both within the counterculture and society at large no longer held; and a late stage, after 1970, when new activist groups came to the fore, stirred by previous developments" (Hamilton 1997, xiv). In its broad strokes, the 1960s counterculture was revolutionary, idealistic, perceptive, self-aware, and often indicative of larger political issues even when not directly addressing them. Sometimes hedonism seemed to take the stage, but in other countercultural expressions, a deep concern about the quality of life in America was seen at the forefront, touching on areas like race, ecology, personal fulfillment, and the sociocultural status quo. "[B]eneath it all was the notion that how one lived one's life and the power of art in the world were as crucial to an emerging social transformation as any political activity—and, more important, that they were all one" (Bloom and Breines 2011, 227).

DEPICTION AND CULTURAL CONTEXT

The late 1960s saw the gradual emergence of countercultural sensibilities in Hollywood. With *Bonnie and Clyde* in 1967, the traditional understanding of criminals and authorities was questioned as outlaws stole the center stage. That year *The Graduate* also presented a rebellious outlook through its satire of suburbia conformity. Geoff King wrote that "*Easy Rider*, in a sense, takes up the story where *The Graduate* leaves off. It offers a paean to the freedoms of life on the road, 1960s style, fuelled not so much by gasoline as by marijuana, LSD, and the anthems of contemporary music" (King 2002, 16).

Premiering less than a week before the first moon landing and one month before the Woodstock Music Festival, *Easy Rider* was released on to a volatile threshold of American history. In the words of Roger Ebert, the film "captures so surely the tone and look of that moment in time" (Ebert 2004). King describes the way in which *Easy Rider*'s depiction of America was a historical snapshot: "The landscape traversed by Billy and Wyatt is undoubtedly that of the 1960s. The commune in which a group of city kids attempt sincerely, but somewhat desperately, to create a pastoral idyll in semi-desert. The southern small-town café where a group of teenage girls are bursting with attraction to the passing bikers while the adults are all crew-cuts, innuendo and menace; an outpost of the redneck world whose flarings of racial violence were regularly thrust onto television screens across America in the 1960s" (King 2002, 17).

The America of 1969 was a land of extremes. "The headlines were filled with body counts, protests and demonstrations, drug busts and overdoses, trials, bombings, kidnappings, and police shootouts," recounts McGilligan. "In this context *Easy Rider* seemed (to some extent, it *was*) a watershed film for the Woodstock Generation" (McGilligan 2015). During the same year that the number of U.S. troops in Vietnam ballooned to over half a million, nearly that same number of young Americans gathered for four days at a 600-acre farm in Bethel, New York, a milieu steeped in rock music, drugs, sex, and (incidentally) rain—all while *Easy Rider* was making its debut. Hopper reflected, "When we were making the movie, we could feel the whole country burning up—Negroes, hippies, students. I meant to work this feeling into the symbols in the movie, like Captain America's Great Chrome Bike—that beautiful machine covered with stars and stripes with all the money in the gas tank is America—and that any moment we can be shot off it—BOOM—explosion—that's the end" (Biskind 1998, 74).

Regardless of political or ethical persuasion, *Easy Rider* definitely struck a chord in 1969 American culture, as Kael explained in her review, "Although one may be uneasy over the satisfaction the audience seems to receive from responding to the general masochism and to the murder of Captain America, the movie obviously rings true to the audience's vision. It's cool to feel that you can't win, that it's all rigged and hopeless" (Kael 2011). "Those of us who reject the heroic central character and the statements of *Easy Rider* may still be caught by something edgy and ominous in it—the acceptance of the constant danger of sudden violence. We're not sure how much of this paranoia isn't paranoia" (Kael 2011). In that same vein, Hoberman calls *Easy Rider* "a generational statement and outlaw vision of the Great Society," opining that the film's "sense of narcissistic paranoia is clinched by Roger McGuinn's rendition of Bob Dylan's 'It's Alright Ma (I'm Only Bleeding)' moments before outlaws Wyatt and Billy are dispatched to oblivion by their vigilante doppelgängers" (Hoberman 2003, 235–237). For many moviegoers, the bikers' doom likely triggered images of the all-too-recent assassinations of Martin Luther King Jr. and Robert Kennedy in 1968.

A salient feature of *Easy Rider* is its keen ability to give expression to the multifaceted counterculture of America's disenchanted youth. The movie "captured the imagination of young audiences who identified the cyclers' rootlessness and alienation from American society with their own" (Sklar 1975, 302). Mahoney points to the bridge of angst connecting naivete and realism in the 1960s: "If *Easy Rider* succeeds in illustrating a manifest disillusionment with the land of the free, it is because it simultaneously and clearly chronicles the idealism of its youth. It presents as well their anguished recognition that one group's freedom to conform to one mode of expression encourages that group to presume to discriminate against, even justify liquidation of those who would freely choose a different style" (Mahoney 1969). The countercultural themes in *Easy Rider* sparked a wide spectrum of responses from moviegoers depending on the specific geographic location. Hopper recollects reactions in theaters following the film's release: "If you're in New Orleans, they applaud the guys that shoot you at the end. *Applaud*, OK? And if you're in Los Angeles, they get up screaming, 'Kill the pigs!'" ("Making-of Documentary" 1999).

During the shooting of *Easy Rider* in 1968, Hopper attempted to translate into his storyline the blaze of discrimination present in the American south. In the Southern jailhouse scene, Nicholson's line "They used rusty razorblades on the last two longhairs that they brought in here" derived its substance from real-life accounts of bigotry and violence in Texas that Hopper and production manager Paul Lewis had heard. The filmmakers, many of them "longhairs" themselves, accordingly chose to bypass Texas when filming ("Making-of Documentary" 1999). Regarding Nicholson's death later in the film, Hopper said he did not cast a Black man as the character George to prove that prejudice ran much deeper than racial differences: "In point of fact, we didn't need to be different. We didn't need to be black. We just needed to have long hair.... I wanted them to kill one of their own. I wanted America to kill their own son when they kill Jack Nicholson. The worst thing he's done is get drunk and work for the ACLU" ("Making-of Documentary" 1999).

The grittiness of *Easy Rider* seemed to set it apart from the rest of 1960s Hollywood fare. Based on the iconic figures Wyatt Earp and Billy the Kid, Fonda and Hopper embodied the next generation of Wild West legends as two pot-smoking bikers in the film. "Because of smoking marijuana and the kind of things we were doing in the '60s, it seemed like everyone was outside of the law at that time," said Hopper ("Making-of Documentary" 1999). The actors are seen actually smoking marijuana in the movie, although in Fonda's opinion that detail shouldn't be the make-or-break determiner of the film's authenticity. "It's just a publicity gig, to talk about it," Fonda said in a September 1969 interview. "We just turned on because that's the way we wanted to do it. It was also fun" (Campbell 1969).

Yet the protagonists' drug-dependent existence speaks to something beyond the simple fact that the two fellows like marijuana. "Wyatt and Billy don't seem particularly free, not if the only way they can face the world is through a grass curtain," opines Canby. "As written and played, they are lumps of gentle clay, vacuous, romantic symbols, dressed in cycle drag" (1969). *Easy Rider* seems to be all about freedom, but the story's heroes share an experience stymied by a paradoxical freedom. Fonda had specific motives for spinning the narrative the way he did: "I am representing everybody who feels that freedom can be bought, who feels that you can find freedom through other things, like riding motorcycles through the air or smoking grass. . . . My movie is about the lack of freedom, not about freedom. My heroes are not right, they're wrong" (Campbell 1969).

Likewise, the criminal actions portrayed in *Easy Rider* present an intentional social critique formulated by the filmmakers. "At the start of the movie," explains Hopper, "Peter and I do a very American thing—we commit a crime, we go for the easy money. That's one of the big problems with the country right now: everybody's going for the easy money. Not just obvious, simple crimes, but big corporations committing corporate crimes" (Biskind 1998, 74). The opening scenes of Wyatt and Billy smuggling cocaine from Mexico present a twofold reality: According to Ebert, the outlaws "specifically break with the establishment" by stuffing their gas tanks "full of bribes from the establishment" (Ebert 1969). "Victims can sell out just as well as their persecutors. They sold out because what they were trying to be was the mirror image of the rednecks in the truck, and neither life-style is healthy" (Ebert 1969).

Moreover, the lawless deeds of *Easy Rider*'s ill-fated heroes possess a twinge of irony in regards to the general perception of drugs in the late 1960s. "Cocaine was at the time still somewhat beyond the pale, a 'hard' drug dealt by non-countercultural criminals and thus unsuited for the gentler cravings of the hippies, who conveniently ignored the fact that marijuana was imported by the same criminals who trafficked in heroin and cocaine" (Walker 2006, 156). Hopper emphatically took credit for popularizing cocaine among hippies and nonconformists: "The cocaine problem in the United States is really because of me. There was no cocaine before *Easy Rider* on the street. After *Easy Rider* it was everywhere" (Biskind 1998, 74). In 1968, predating the official launch of "Crosby, Stills & Nash," David Crosby and Stephen Stills made a three-track acetate disc using the name Frozen Noses. Crosby recounts, "Stills and I were just starting to become cokeheads at the time, so the name Frozen Noses was, well, it spoke for itself" (Zimmer 2000, 69–70). Once cocaine reached new levels of popularity, however, the substance was a surefire way to ruin any sense of innocence or charm in those who used it. "Whereas pot and acid were seen as tools of enlightenment, encouraging collaboration and damping, as much as was possible, the egos raging beneath the tie-dye and buckskin, coke magnified and amplified the worst qualities of nearly everyone who became heavily involved with it" (Walker 2006, 156).

Less than a year after *Easy Rider* was released into theaters, *The New York Times* presented an article about the present state of Mardi Gras, which had around 500,000 participants in its yearly festivities. The February 11, 1970, edition describes a spike in unsavory behavior in New Orleans and points to a cause-and-effect relationship between the 1969 film and the city's current activities:

> This has been, by all accounts, the drunkest and the most violent carnival season in many years. . . . In addition to the violence and accidental bloodshed, New Orleans is contending with what the local newspapers refer to as a "hippie herd" and "thousands of the undesirable element." Many of the young say they were inspired to come by the movie "Easy Rider." . . . They came to grief. So have many of this year's visitors. The police have arrested more than 200 young persons for the crime of sleeping in the open air on the banks of the Mississippi River and Lake Pontchartrain. (Reed 1970)

Touching a variety of previously taboo subjects, *Easy Rider* was characteristic of the nascent New Hollywood, which attempted to use film artfully "to engage the culture in all its dimensions and to provide a source for cultural and social renewal" (Girgus 1998, 211). The Hollywood Renaissance was part and parcel of the gradual dissolution and replacement of the Production Code Association (PCA) governing the self-regulation and approval of films in the classical Hollywood studio era. "Few of the films associated with the Renaissance could have existed within the confines of the PCA in the forms that made them so striking, precisely as something new and innovative" (King 2002, 32). The drugs, sex, and violence appearing in these new films effectively attracted some demographics, primarily young men, while alienating many other Americans who then decided to refrain from going to the cinema altogether (Krämer 2005, 66).

Easy Rider enjoyed unforeseen success and influence in the industry after being picked up by a large studio, Columbia Pictures. When looking for the finances to make his dream a reality, Dennis Hopper consulted with his buddy Jack Nicholson, who connected him to Bert Schneider, a partner in BBS Productions. With its films released through Columbia Pictures, BBS then jumped aboard and financed the budget for *Easy Rider* ("Production Notes" 1999). Originally the film had been slated for release through the low-budget American International Pictures, known for its teenager-intended "exploitation" material that typically involved bikers, beaches, horror, and the like. "*Easy Rider* marked a point at which this kind of filmmaking crossed over into the Hollywood mainstream. Money flowed more freely, if not in huge amounts, to a new generation of filmmakers who . . . made considerable inroads into the culture and business of Hollywood"

(King 2002, 12–13). *Easy Rider* had substantial impact on Hollywood's years to come. According to film historian Joseph McBride, "The old Hollywood was dying. The studio system was really collapsing by about 1966. The major studios were in big trouble and they seemed to be out of touch. The older guys around the studios didn't understand the youth market" (King 2019).

In his August 1969 review of the film, the *Los Angeles Times* Charles Champlin dubbed *Easy Rider* "an astonishing work of art" and projected, "If there is an American New Wave, film historians may well one day cite 'Easy Rider' as early evidence of it." Likened to the avant-garde products of the French New Wave of the 1950s and 1960s, Hopper's film came to fruition on a tight budget and reflected the current filming style of Europe more than that of Hollywood. In a knee-jerk reaction, the big studios tried to copy the film's success regardless of whether they actually understood it. "Suddenly all the studios were approving films with young directors, usually with stories related to rebellious, drug-using, sexually-active young people" (Brueggemann 2019). Most turned out to be flops.

When filmmakers departed from classical conventions, they often employed expressive stylistic devices to elicit a sense of subjectivity and uncertainty (King 2002, 41–42). At times, the New Hollywood-era films present viewers with the clashing juxtaposition of the "expressive" and the "realistic." Breaches in continuity editing, linked to the perceived coherency in space and time, surface in *Easy Rider*, such as Wyatt's ominous flash-forward near the end of the story. Hopper's use of shaky camerawork and stutter cuts combines with his "unflinching portrayal of life in the late 1960s" to make his film, in the words of one writer, "feel just a shade shy of a documentary" (Scott 2010). Moreover, the graveyard acid trip scene is colored by an extended sequence of "experimental" techniques: "rapid discontinuous montage editing, the use of a distorting 'fish-eye' lens, unstable 'subjective' camera-work and non-realistically motivated sound effects" (King 2002, 41). The novel techniques throughout the film (before, during, and after the LSD) may even act as an interpretation of the psychedelic experience through the cinematic arts. "LSD did create a frame of mind that fractured experience," notes film historian and cultural critic Peter Biskind. "And that LSD experience had an effect on films like *Easy Rider* and *Head*, which are essentially experimental movies" (Whalen 1998).

In addition to the cinematography, the movie's soundtrack diverged from the status quo by featuring popular rock beats from the 1960s. The way in which the film unravels each of the songs forms "a celebration of the counterculture reduced again, primarily, to a freewheeling spirit of freedom, motion and style" (King 2002, 16–17). The filmmakers were among the first to set a new trend, as they used a majority of original recordings by hip musicians of the day (although they would have to shell out an estimated $1 million to use these songs in the film) (Tzioumakis 2018). Accompanying the sounds of The Byrds, Jimi Hendrix, and The Electric Prunes are The Band's "The Weight" and Steppenwolf's "Born to Be Wild," which had reached the No. 2 spot in 1968's charts. The Byrds front man Roger McGuinn also sung the closing number, "Ballad of Easy Rider," part of which Bob Dylan wrote but subsequently did not want credit for ("Making-of Documentary" 1999). The soundtrack would wind up climbing to No. 6 in the best-selling albums of 1970.

Another stylistic choice that characterizes *Easy Rider* is its sparse use of dialogue, with background music filling many of the gaps between words. Fonda commented to *Rolling Stone*, "We don't give out any information through dialogue. We have a very loose plot, nothing you can follow. You can't predict what's going to happen, and that puts everybody off. People want it predicted for them" (Campbell 1969). Through a heady use of visuals, the movie communicates the themes central to the counterculture's worldview: "a desire for the open road, a longing for simplicity and companionship as an antidote to scientific technology and impersonal relations, and a belief that mainstream society will destroy anything unconventional" (Hamilton 1997, 93).

The exception in the film is Nicholson's George Hanson, who Fonda described as a "mouthpiece" for the central characters ("Making-of Documentary" 1999). While serving as a supporting actor, Nicholson garnered widespread praise for his breakout performance, which secured him an Oscar and led to celebrity status. Canby asserts, "Nicholson is so good, in fact, that 'Easy Rider' never quite recovers from his loss, even though he has had the rather thankless job of spelling out what I take to be the film's statement (upper case). This has to do with the threat that people like the nonconforming Wyatt and Billy represent to the ordinary, self-righteous, inhibited folk that are the Real America" (Canby 1969). In his biography on Nicholson, Patrick McGilligan accurately unpacks the actor's role in *Easy Rider*: "Nicholson had the character few took issue with and everybody liked. As much as people identified him with Easy Rider (as much as he identified himself with the Sixties), Nicholson was the equivocal presence in the film. Neither redneck nor hippie, Jack's character seemed a stand-in for the audience, the proverbial Everyman. In a movie that dared to suggest the death of the American dream, Jack seemed to personify a more resilient America, offering hope—and humor—despite troubled times" (McGilligan 2015).

In the fireside exchange between George and Billy, the lawyer's twangy voice offers the clearest articulation of the film's takeaway message. "They're not scared of you. They're scared of what you represent to them," George tells Billy. "What you represent to them is freedom." The perpetually stoned biker responds, "What the hell is wrong with freedom, man? That's what it's all about." In a swift foreshadowing of his own death, George declares, "It's real hard to be free when you're bought and sold in the marketplace.

Of course, don't ever tell anybody that they're not free, 'cause then they're gonna get real busy killin' and maimin' to prove to you that they are. Oh, yeah, they're gonna talk to you, and talk to you, and talk to you about individual freedom. But they see a free individual, it's gonna scare 'em."

Through tragedy, then, *Easy Rider* compels audiences to reflect on its sometimes-obscured themes. "In all great Greek tragedies, the innocents die first," states Fonda. "George is only killed because he is with us, not because he has done something wrong" (King 2019). The demise of the main characters seemed to pack the kind of punch that would connect with audiences while simultaneously leaving them unsettled. "I knew how it was going to end when I started writing it," Fonda recalled half a century after the film's debut. "That the end would be mine and Dennis' death and nothing beyond that. People would wonder and ask themselves what was that? They would have to come back again to figure it out" (King 2019).

In the movie's final fireside chat, the laconic Wyatt counters Billy's naive buoyancy with a dose of realism (though, apparently, too late in the game). "We're rich," affirms Billy. "We're retired in Florida now, mister." Wyatt responds, "You know, Billy, we blew it." Billy tries to make his point by saying, "That's what it's all about, man. You go for the big money, man, and then you're free." But the only response that comes: "We blew it." Leaving movie viewers with a type of poetic mystery, Fonda commented on the dialogue: "I intended it to be enigmatic and applicable to all kinds of things. When asked today if it's still relevant, go look out the window and tell me we haven't blown it" (King 2019).

With all of its original character, *Easy Rider* occupies a significant place in American history. Instrumental in paving a new pathway for Hollywood, the film stands out in particular with its content, camerawork, and soundtrack. Most recently, in recognition of the "mythical" movie's 50th anniversary, the 2019 Cannes Film Festival included a restored version of *Easy Rider* in its Cannes Classics section. This timeless motion picture continues to spark discussion among cultural commentators, international film critics, and everyday U.S. citizens. "In 1969, I went looking for America," Fonda intimated in a 2019 interview. "Fifty years later, I'm still looking" (Amos 2019).

FURTHER READING

Amos, Jim. 2019. "Rev Up The Harley, 'Easy Rider' Celebrates Its 50th Anniversary by Rolling Back into Cinemas." *Forbes*, May 8, 2019. https://www.forbes.com/sites/jamos/2019/05/08/rev-up-the-harley-easy-rider-celebrates-its-50th-anniversary-by-rolling-back-into-cinemas/#92654cc1123b

Biskind, Peter. 1998. *Easy Riders, Raging Bulls: How the Sex, Drugs, and Rock 'n Roll Generation Saved Hollywood*. New York: Simon & Schuster.

Bloom, Alexander, and Wini Breines, eds. 2011. *"Takin' It to the Streets": A Sixties Reader*. New York: Oxford University Press.

Brueggemann, Tom. 2019. "In 1969, Dennis Hopper and Peter Fonda's 'Easy Rider' Pushed Hollywood into the '70s." *IndieWire*, July 12, 2019. https://www.indiewire.com/2019/07/easy-rider-1969-dennis-hopper-jack-nicholson-50-year-anniversary-70s-1202157254/

Campbell, Elizabeth. 1969. "Easy Rider," *Rolling Stone*, September 6, 1969.

Canby, Vincent. 1969. "'Easy Rider': A Statement on Film." *The New York Times*, July 15, 1969. https://www.nytimes.com/1969/07/15/archives/easy-rider-a-statement-on-film.html

Caryl, Sue. 2014. "Jan 14, 1967 CE: Human Be-In." *National Geographic*, December 12, 2014. https://www.nationalgeographic.org/thisday/jan14/human-be-/

Champlin, Charles. 1969. "Dennis Hopper, Peter Fonda and 'Easy Rider'." *Los Angeles Times*, August 10, 1969. Republished May 29, 2010. https://latimesblogs.latimes.com/thedailymirror/2010/05/charles-champlin-on-dennis-hopper-peter-fonda-and-easy-rider.html

Cohen, Robert. 2009. *Freedom's Orator: Mario Savio and the Radical Legacy of the 1960s*. New York: Oxford University Press.

Dreisbach, Tom. 2014. "Behind the Motorcycles in 'Easy Rider,' A Long-Obscured Story." *NPR*, October 11, 2014. https://www.npr.org/2014/10/11/354875096/behind-the-motorcycles-in-easy-rider-a-long-obscured-story

"Easy Rider." n.d. American Film Institute. Accessed on July 30, 2019. https://catalog.afi.com/Catalog/moviedetails/19428

Ebert, Roger. 1969. "Easy Rider." September 28, 1969. https://www.rogerebert.com/reviews/easy-rider-1969

Ebert, Roger. 2004. "Easy Rider." October 24, 2004. https://www.rogerebert.com/reviews/great-movie-easy-rider-1969

Farber, David. 1994. *The Age of Great Dreams: America in the 1960s*. New York: Hill and Wang.

Fleming, Charles. 2014. "'Easy Rider's' 'Captain America' Bike Sold for $1.35 Million." *Los Angeles Times*, October 19, 2014. https://www.latimes.com/business/autos/la-fi-hy-easy-rider-captain-america-bike-sold-20141019-story.html

Girgus, Sam B. 1998. *Hollywood Renaissance: The Cinema of Democracy in the Era of Ford, Capra, and Kazan*. New York: Cambridge University Press.

Hamilton, Neil A. 1997. *The ABC-CLIO Companion to the 1960s Counterculture in America*. Santa Barbara, CA: ABC-CLIO.

Harpaz, Beth J. 2018. "Drawing 200K Visitors a Year, a Rare Free Tour at One of New Orleans' Famous Cemeteries." *NOLA*, July 31, 2018. https://www.nola.com/entertainment_life/article_ec9ff54d-3d33-5b86-a2b6-caa16ae15c96.html

Higgins, Bill. 2019. "Hollywood Flashback: 'Easy Rider' Was Filmed Guerrilla-Style at 1969 Mardi Gras." *The Hollywood Reporter*, March 5, 2019. https://www.hollywoodreporter.com/news/easy-rider-was-filmed-guerrilla-style-at-1969-mardi-gras-1190587

Hill, Sarah. 2016. *San Francisco and the Long 60s*. eBook. London: Bloomsbury Academic.

Hoberman, J. 2003. *The Dream Life: Movies, Media, and the Mythology of the Sixties*. New York: The New Press.

Isserman, Maurice, and Michael Kazin. 2012. *America Divided: The Civil War of the 1960s*. New York: Oxford University Press.

Kael, Pauline. 2011. "The Bottom of the Pit." In *The Age of Movies: Selected Writings of Pauline Kael*, edited by Sanford Schwartz. New York: Library of America.

King, Geoff. 2002. *New Hollywood Cinema*. New York: Columbia University Press, 2002.

King, Susan. 2018. "Classic Hollywood: Nearly 50 Years after 'Easy Rider,' Peter Fonda Plays—What Else?—A Pothead in New Film." *Los Angeles Times*, June 13, 2018. https://www.latimes.com/entertainment/movies/la-ca-mn-classic-hollywood-peter-fonda-20180613-story.html

King, Susan. 2019. "'Tell Me We Haven't Blown It': Peter Fonda Reflects on 'Easy Rider' and Its Unanswered Question." *The Hollywood Reporter*, July 12, 2019. https://www.hollywoodreporter.com/news/making-easy-rider-peter-fonda-reflects-films-unanswered-question-1223889

Krämer, Peter. 2005. *The New Hollywood: From Bonnie and Clyde to Star Wars*. London: Wallflower Press.

Mahoney, John. 1969. "'Easy Rider': THR's 1969 Review." *The Hollywood Reporter*, June 26, 1969. Republished July 12, 2019. https://www.hollywoodreporter.com/review/easy-rider-review-movie-1969-1221117

"Making-of Documentary." 1999. *Easy Rider*. Columbia Pictures.

McGilligan, Patrick. 2015. *Jack's Life: A Biography of Jack Nicholson*. eBook. New York: W. W. Norton & Company.

Miller, Timothy. 1999. *The 60s Communes: Hippies and Beyond*. Syracuse, NY: Syracuse University Press.

Mitchell, Reid. 1999. *All on a Mardi Gras Day: Episodes in the History of New Orleans Carnival*. Cambridge, MA: Harvard University Press.

Moretta, John Anthony. 2017. *The Hippies: A 1960s History*. Jefferson, NC: McFarland & Company, Inc.

Moskowitz, Gene. 1969. "Easy Rider." *Variety*, May 14, 1969. https://variety.com/1969/film/reviews/easy-rider-1117790631/

Patterson, James T. 1996. *Grand Expectations: The United States, 1945–1974*. New York: Oxford University Press.

"Production Notes." 1999. *Easy Rider*. Columbia Pictures.

Randel, William Pierce. 1978. *The Evolution of American Taste*. New York: Crown Publishers.

Reed, Roy. 1970. "New Orleans Ends the Most Violent Mardi Gras Season in Years with 600 in Its Jail." *The New York Times*, February 11, 1970. https://www.nytimes.com/1970/02/11/archives/new-orleans-ends-the-most-violent-mardi-gras-season-in-years-with.html

Robinson, Lisa. 2015. "An Oral History of Laurel Canyon, the 60s and 70s Music Mecca." *Vanity Fair*, February 8, 2015. https://www.vanityfair.com/culture/2015/02/laurel-canyon-music-scene

Scott, Mike. 2010. "Big Easy Rider: Dennis Hopper's Legacy Inextricably Intertwined with New Orleans." *The Times-Picayune*, June 2, 2010. https://www.nola.com/entertainment_life/movies_tv/article_13589950-2683-581c-a22c-0ca3269cf62f.html

Simpson, Dave. 2018. "How We Made Steppenwolf's Born to Be Wild." *The Guardian*, July 31, 2018. https://www.theguardian.com/music/2018/jul/31/how-we-made-steppenwolf-born-to-be-wild

Sinclair, John. 2007. *Guitar Army: Street Writings/Prison Writings*. Los Angeles: Process.
Sklar, Robert. 1975. *Movie-Made America: A Cultural History of American Movies*. New York: Random House.
Strait, Guy. 2011. "What Is a Hippie." In *"Takin' It to the Streets": A Sixties Reader*, edited by Alexander Bloom and Wini Breines, 269. New York: Oxford University Press.
Tzioumakis, Yannis. 2018. "From Exploitation to Legitimacy: *Easy Rider* (1969) and Independent Cinema's Journey into Hollywood." In *The Hollywood Renaissance: Revisiting American Cinema's Most Celebrated Era*, edited by Yannis Tzioumakis and Peter Krämer. New York: Bloomsbury Publishing.
Walker, Michael. 2006. *Laurel Canyon: The Inside Story of Rock-and-Roll's Legendary Neighborhood*. New York: Faber and Faber, Inc.
Weller, Sheila. 2012. "Suddenly That Summer." *Vanity Fair*, June 14, 2012. https://www.vanityfair.com/culture/2012/07/lsd-drugs-summer-of-love-sixties
Whalen, John. 1998. "The Trip." *LA Weekly*, July 1, 1998. https://www.laweekly.com/the-trip/
Willis, Jim. 2015. *1960s Counterculture: Document Decoded*. Santa Barbara, CA: ABC-CLIO, LLC.
Zimmer, Dave. 2000. *Crosby, Stills & Nash: The Authorized Biography*. Cambridge, MA: Da Capo Press.

Chapter 3

The Deer Hunter (1978)

The Deer Hunter is a 1978 Vietnam War film directed by Michael Cimino and starring Robert De Niro, Christopher Walken, and John Savage. Premiering on December 8, 1978, with a wide release on February 23, 1979, Universal Pictures distributed the film domestically, and EMI Films handled international distribution. The movie tells the fictional story of three Pennsylvanian steelworkers who confront deep personal challenges both in the midst of Vietnam and back on their home terrain. John Cazale, Meryl Streep, and George Dzundza filled supporting roles. Filming took place in Ohio and Pennsylvania for the hometown scenes, Washington for the hunting sequences, and Thailand for scenes portraying Vietnam. The screenplay was composed by Cimino and Deric Washburn, who reworked a script by Louis Garfinkle and Quinn K. Redeker. Cimino, Michael Deeley, John Peverall, and Barry Spikings produced the film. Shot on a $15-million budget, the film returned a domestic total gross of $48,979,328, finishing ninth in revenue in 1978.

Vietnam changes everything for Michael (De Niro), Nick (Walken), and Steven (Savage), three down-to-earth steelworkers who find themselves at home in a Russian-speaking community in Western Pennsylvania before enlisting in the military. The film begins in the latter half of the 1960s as the three friends enjoy their final days before leaving for Vietnam. Along with three other pals, they band together at the local bar, celebrate Steve's ornate wedding in a Russian Orthodox Church (and the festive reception that follows), and then take a final jaunt into the mountains to hunt deer together.

The roaring fires of the steel plant are exchanged for the fiery explosions of battle as the trio plunges into the midst of wartime chaos—soon taken captive by the enemy. As the communist soldiers force their prisoners to play Russian roulette, the American infantrymen barely escape certain death, thanks to Mike's quick thinking and heroics. Afterward, Nick is lost to the dark gambling world of Saigon, while Mike goes home emotionally detached, yet more functional than Steve, who survives with only one arm intact and takes refuge in the isolation of a veterans hospital. Concluding after the fall of Saigon in 1975, the movie focuses on the veterans trying to cope with the hardships that they experienced in Vietnam, redefining friendship and life itself during one of America's most tumultuous eras.

Opening with strong support from film critics and flocks of moviegoers, *The Deer Hunter* went on to win five Oscars at the 1979 Academy Awards: Best Picture, Best Director, Best Supporting Actor (Christopher Walken), Best Editing, and Best Sound. Four additional nominations included Best Actor (Robert De Niro), Best Supporting Actress (Meryl Streep), Best Original Screenplay, and Best Cinematography. Cimino won a Golden Globe for Best Director, and the film was nominated for five other Golden Globes, collecting multiple other film awards that year. The *Hollywood Reporter*'s Arthur Knight made the clear claim: "For me, *The Deer Hunter* is *the* great American film of 1978. . . . I can't imagine anything more timely, more important, more uncompromising" (Knight 1978). Vincent Canby of *The New York Times* called the movie "a big, awkward, crazily ambitious, sometimes breathtaking motion picture that comes as close to being a popular epic as any movie about this country since 'The Godfather'" (Canby 1978).

Following less than four years after the close of the Vietnam War, the film gained attention due to both acclaim and controversy. In her critique of the 183-minute-long film, Kathleen Carroll highlighted the story's social commentary: "In ferociously intense, chillingly brutal scenes, this bravely innovative, kingsized movie . . . enables one to fully understand why this particular war not only destroyed the hopes and dreams of America's young men, but why it left so many of them permanently shattered and alienated from society" (Carroll 1978). The historicity of the movie's portrayal of Vietnam became a key point of debate, as the story ventures freely from established fact in its lengthy narrative. In April 1979, publications such as the *Los Angeles Times*, *Harper's*, *Seven Days*, and *L.A. Weekly* criticized the movie as butchered history and "a criminal violation of the truth," dubbing it a "racist" production that only shows Asian individuals as "sweaty, crazy, vicious, and debauched" (Harmetz 1979). On the very night of the film's fivefold Oscar triumph, a band of Vietnam Veterans Against the War protested outside the Los Angeles Music Center, decrying *The Deer Hunter*'s misinterpretation of history. After clashing with the picketers, police arrested 13 members of the group for inciting to riot. A few weeks prior, Soviet delegates at the 1979 Berlin Film Festival, accompanied by other socialist Eastern Europeans, protested the screening of the American film and eventually withdrew their own films from the festival.

A common conclusion among movie critics was that *The Deer Hunter* proved to be a cinematic masterpiece despite its historical inconsistencies. Peter Arnett, a Pulitzer Prize-winning Associated Press reporter who covered the Vietnam War extensively, wrote, "The sheer power of the film's photographic imagery, particularly the agonizing torture scenes, stunned me into mute acceptance of the divine right of the Hollywood dream-machine operators to drench us in fictional nightmares if they wish" (Arnett 1979). Prominent film critic Roger Ebert called the movie a successful, haunting work of fiction set within a historically war-torn era: "'The Deer Hunter' is said to be about many subjects: About male bonding, about mindless patriotism, about the dehumanizing effects of war, about Nixon's 'silent majority.' It is about any of those things that you choose, if you choose, but more than anything else, it is a heartbreakingly effective fictional machine that evokes the agony of the Vietnam time" (Ebert 1979).

HISTORICAL BACKGROUND

It can be said that the 1960s were years full of turmoil for America, and one of the central catalysts for societal upheaval was the Vietnam War. Set within the larger backdrop of the Cold War, the "American War" (as it was known in Vietnam) was a conflict of peoples and ideologies, which had geographically split the Asian nation into two. The communist North Vietnamese were allied with the Viet Cong, their supporters dispersed throughout the south, pitted against the South Vietnamese government and its great Western ally, the United States of America. After supporting France's interests in the First Indochina War (1946–1954), American military advisers were increasingly sent to Vietnam by 1961, and the United States was willing to invest active combat units in 1965, in a heated effort to keep the spread of communism at bay. Meanwhile, North Vietnam was receiving arms, advisers, and supplies from the Soviet Union and China—unrelenting in the fight to unite a communistic Vietnam.

It wasn't until the mid-1960s when Americans started to find their curiosity sparked by Vietnam, a distant land about which few had any prior knowledge. The homeland began to focus its attention on East Asia, as more troops were departing and national investment in the success of the war grew. Moreover, reporters and objective observers were beginning to depict the conflict in ways that greatly diverged from the narrative issued by the American government. During the latter half of the 1960s, the nation's interest in the Vietnam War turned into an obsession, demarcating what became "the central political issue of the era" (Bloom and Breines 2011, 152).

More than half a million U.S. military forces were present in Vietnam by 1969. While every area of America was represented in the military servicemen and women, disproportionate numbers came from small towns, inner cities, and farms. Unlike in previous wars, the more well-to-do young men in America tried to avoid being drafted and often did not enlist voluntarily for Vietnam. Around four out of five enlisted U.S. troops in Vietnam had their roots in poor and working-class families, and many of them had only graduated from high school, not choosing to pursue higher education. The average age of an American soldier was 19—seven years less than the average in World War II (1939–1945); only a few hundred American casualties in Vietnam were older than 30 years of age. "The war was generally fought by those baby boomers whose families' hold on the postwar prosperity was weakest" (Farber 1994, 147).

During the 1960s, approximately two out of three men serving in Vietnam had volunteered for service in the army or Marines. According to surveys done in 1964 and 1968, the number of volunteers who enlisted to avoid the draft rose from 37.6 percent to 47.2 percent over those four years. "By volunteering they hoped to have at least some control over the timing and type of their military service" (Farber 1994, 148). Almost all U.S. recruits spent a single year of duty in Vietnam. During the peak concentration of American men and women on Vietnamese soil, less than 20 percent were involved in combat. Many spent their time working in milder conditions removed from the violent fray: handling mounds of paperwork, transporting supplies, tending to wounded men, repairing battle equipment, and moving the bodies of the fallen. The shock that struck most Americans on foreign soil originated in the stark contrast between the affluent life they knew and the hectic world of poverty belonging to the native Vietnamese.

The typical experience of a soldier in Vietnam was concentrated on sheer survival, detached from an understanding of the war or any particular cause behind it. One veteran went on the record as saying, "Almost all of us were more concerned with staying alive and doing our job than we were with any philosophical investigation into the rights and wrongs of the war" (Farber 1994, 150). In the latter half of 1967, George Skakel, a college student in California who had been stationed in Vietnam, wrote that common conditions for U.S. troops were "miserable," often wearing "unwashed, dirty clothes for weeks on end" and living in a state of nervousness and loneliness (Skakel 2011, 167).

By the close of the war, around 2.7 million American military personnel had served in the Vietnam War during the 1960s and early 1970s. They fought a dual-pronged war: by air and by foot. As commenced with Operation Rolling Thunder, the airborne war was intent on eradicating the northern enemies; putting pressure on the communist government; halting the southbound movement of troops, supplies, and weapons from North Vietnam; and providing support for U.S. ground troops. The ground war was one of slowly chipping away at enemy forces, as American soldiers conducted "search and destroy" missions. The men would leave their base and hunt down their adversaries, marking their progress by "the body count" of dead enemies. Robert Cagle, a Vietnam veteran, shared with fellow veterans and other American travelers on a tour of Vietnam in 2001: "[Our mission] was 'search and destroy.' What does it mean to you? . . . to find it, and kill it. *Anything!* A village, a deer, water buffalo, some poor sonofabitch out in the rice paddy, you know, trying to work. It didn't matter. . . . And the big thing is that we didn't know who the V.C. [Viet Cong] were—we figured they were everybody. And the martial law was, 'If it moves at night, you shoot it.' Period" (Cagle 2011, 222).

The setting for most skirmishes was South Vietnamese territory, an area that America's enemies knew much more intimately and thus gave them an edge in guerrilla warfare. In late 1968, as U.S. presence in Vietnam was greatly inflated, a report by the Central Intelligence Agency found that U.S. combat patrols, on average, were successful in finding and engaging their adversaries less than 1 percent of the time. During the statistically few encounters, American troops annihilated their opponents, particularly when fighting in larger numbers. Yet the remainder of the time was consumed in traversing the Vietnamese countryside and villages, waiting, punctuated by a mixture of boredom, anger, and fear (Farber 1994, 151–152): "The troops saw peasants, grim-faced and seemingly indifferent to them. The war they fought rarely took place on set battlefields or against enemy fortifications but in the villages and rice paddies where the majority of Vietnamese people lived and worked. As a result, American soldiers often died not in firefights but in ones and twos, picked off by snipers, blown up by booby traps, emasculated by mines laid on paths villagers walked down every day. Identifying the sniper or saboteur or nighttime assassin among the blank-faced peasantry was beyond the capacity of most Americans."

Many of America's fighting men were restrained and did not aim for civilians, even ones who were certainly helping the adversaries. Even so, war crimes did occur, and military leaders decided to push atrocities underneath the carpet. Already the region had suffered thousands upon thousands of innocent casualties and injuries due to the carpet bombing, napalm, and cluster bombs rained down from American airplanes. Into a milieu filled with the inherent cruelty of war there erupted infrequent bouts of savagery. Cagle recounted the horrors that he witnessed in South Vietnam: "Every Wednesday afternoon in Saigon they had three stakes out there. They had sandbags, they had three stakes, and that's where they had public executions. They shot all V.C. or NVA [North Vietnamese Army] that they'd caught. Especially the ones they caught in Saigon. It didn't matter if they were children, men, women . . . didn't matter. Every Wednesday afternoon, doesn't matter if there were one or there were twenty. With people standing around cheering. How the hell can you cheer when somebody dies? . . . It's sick as hell" (Cagle 2011, 223).

Wartime brutalities were not limited to just one side of the battle. Former U.S. Representative Samuel Robert Johnson spent nearly seven years as a prisoner of war in Vietnam. The Viet Cong held him in the "Hoa Lo Prison," notoriously dubbed the "Hanoi Hilton," as well as another prison called "Alcatraz" located behind the North Vietnamese Ministry of National Defense. Johnson recalls: "I was 35 years old, a husband and father of three small children. Forty-two of those months were spent in solitary confinement with 10 other fine American patriots because the Vietcong labeled us 'diehard' resistors. And let me tell you, those years of physical and mental torture, away from my family, were hell" (Johnson 2015). The POW said he remembers sleeping on slabs of cement and remaining in leg stocks or cuffs for years in solitary confinement. "Starvation, isolation and torture were constant companions. There was no news from home, and the enemy worked hard to make us feel alone and forgotten" (Johnson 2015). Another Vietnam POW, air force pilot David Gray was captured at the start of 1967 and also spent time imprisoned in Hoa Lo. Gray described his experience as "23 hours of boredom a day and one hour of terror," during which he routinely endured torture and interrogations—sometimes suspended in the air with his hands and feet bound unbelievably tight, dangling from a meat hook (Olson 2013).

The Vietnam War sent America spiraling into a crisis in the late 1960s. Under the watch of President Lyndon Baines Johnson, public opposition and suspicions were ever increasing; nevertheless the government only amped up U.S. commitment in more legions of soldiers and billions of dollars, believing that a final push was necessary to conquer the communists' resolve. "Journalists reported in word and picture the brutal destruction of Vietnam and the price being extracted from the Vietnamese people, as well as the perpetual instability and corruption of the South Vietnamese government. Violence, confusion, and cruelty became staples of American news—on television as well as in print" (Bloom and Breines 2011, 153–154). As the first so-called television war, this conflict was the first to enter the living rooms of practically the entire nation, due to the newly advancing technology of television broadcasts. Not only was the news hitting home sooner than it ever had before, but more everyday citizens were turning into activists caught up in an unparalleled anti-war movement, propelled by the zealous charge to see America's soldiers returned home from what was widely seen as a senseless battle.

The events of 1968 were critical in turning the tide of the war. On January 31, the Viet Cong launched a massive surprise attack on all of South Vietnam's major cities, even striking the American embassy in Saigon, the southern capital. Headed by the communist leader Ho Chi Minh, the Tet Offensive left the North Vietnamese with severe casualties and in a much weaker position. Yet it succeeded strategically, as the news stunned Americans and "ended a grand American illusion" that the culmination of the war was near (Isserman and Kazin 2012, 211–212). Then on March 16, 1968, U.S. infantrymen engaged in a dark and bloody massacre that would only be uncovered late the following year: The December 5, 1969, issue of *Life* magazine displayed photos of My Lai, a hamlet in the Quang Ngai Province of South Vietnam, where American troops had slaughtered more than 500 civilians—mainly children, women, and older men.

Eyewitnesses recounted that the soldiers had raped women, killed herds of livestock, and burned down the town of huts, without a single bullet fired back at them. "There was no expression on the American faces," said Ronald Haeberle, an army photographer who witnessed My Lai. "I couldn't believe it. They were destroying everything. They were doing it all very businesslike. The Vietnamese saw the Americans but didn't run. . . . The GIs were opening up with M16s, machine guns and grenade launchers" (Eszterhas 1969, 42). After being concealed by military officials for over a year and a half, the coverage of the My Lai carnage ignited the indignation of countless Americans and added more momentum to the anti-war movement: "The debate over the war grew increasingly bitter. Already existing societal divisions . . . were more deeply exacerbated. The dreadful experience of many GIs in Vietnam, coupled with their often poor treatment upon returning home, added fuel to the anger, bitterness, and frustration. Some of these returning veterans organized the Vietnam Veterans Against the War (VVAW), a movement unprecedented in U.S. history. Never before had the soldiers returning from war organized into a large-scale organization to oppose the very war in which they had just fought" (Bloom and Breines 2011, 154).

In 1969, hundreds of America's sons were dying in Vietnam each week, even as President Richard Nixon now was gradually bringing them home. That year alone, 11,780 Americans were casualties of the war, just above the number in 1967 and roughly 5,000 less than the record year of 1968. The number of casualties decreased as the troops withdrew: only 6,173 in 1970 and 2,414 in 1971 (National Archives 2019). However, the morale of the troops dropped drastically, and many turned to drugs as a coping mechanism. Most used marijuana, but a 1971 study found that 15 percent of U.S. soldiers in Vietnam were addicted to heroin. Thousands of others abandoned their posts or went absent without leave for lengthy intervals. In 1970 and 1971, there were newfound hundreds of incidents in which enlisted men even tried to kill their own officers (Isserman and Kazin 2012, 256).

The strain of the war grew too much for America to handle, and on January 27, 1973, President Nixon signed the Paris Peace Accords along with representatives of North and South Vietnam as well as the Viet Cong, officially concluding America's military presence in Vietnam. "There were no victory parades in American cities, but 591 POWs returned home from Vietnam shortly afterward to a tumultuous welcome" (Isserman and Kazin 2012, 271). While the last of America's soldiers left South Vietnam in March 1973, around 7,000 civilian employees from the U.S. Department of Defense stayed in Saigon to continue helping the South Vietnamese in what would continue to be a severe conflict. Despite the formal peace treaty, communist forces immediately violated the agreed-upon ceasefire, and the Vietnamese were back to all-out war the following year. Authorities in South Vietnam counted 80,000 casualties in 1974, turning it into the most tragic year in the war's duration.

It was only a matter of time before South Vietnam succumbed to the communist onslaught. The North Vietnamese kept pushing forward, attacking the highlands just to the north of Saigon, and then firing on the capital's airport on April 28, 1975. That action sparked the decision from President Gerald Ford Jr. to evacuate the rest of the Americans and at-risk Vietnamese from Saigon. During the next two days, Operation Frequent Wind removed some 7,000 people from specified locations throughout the city, such as the U.S. Embassy and the Defense Attaché Office compound—the biggest helicopter evacuation in history. As pilots from the South Vietnamese Air Force ended up taking part in the airlift, helicopters whisked native Saigon residents above the seawaters, hoping to find refuge on some U.S. vessel. Others tried to flee the imminent enemy invasion by boat.

Edward "Ed" Bradley Jr., a former CBS reporter, was present in Saigon on April 29 and 30, 1975. His evening news report highlighted the desperation in many South Vietnamese families swimming toward departing vessels if no other means of escape was attainable. The pilots encircling Saigon were able to unload their passengers onto moving ships, but the prospect of landing the choppers thereupon was an entirely foreign maneuver. Thus, many Vietnamese pilots bailed out of their helicopters, which helplessly hurtled into the waters below, while a few crash-landed onto the deck of the USS *Blue Ridge*. Marines and sailors ended up pushing off the helicopters in order to create space essential for the American aircraft still en route carrying evacuees from the city (Haoues 2015).

As the final American chopper departed, South Vietnam's transitory President Duong Van Minh offered an unconditional surrender to the North. The name Saigon would fade into the history books, as Ho Chi Minh City was born. When the dust finally settled, it was evident that the Vietnam War had left giant wounds in all people groups involved. The total number of U.S. armed forces who had died or were missing as a result of the war came to 58,200. Only in 1995 did Vietnam officially publish its estimate of the toll on human life: up to 2 million civilian casualties from both north and south, in addition to 1.1 million North Vietnamese and Viet Cong troops. According to U.S. military estimates, somewhere between 200,000 and 250,000 South Vietnamese fighting men perished during the Vietnam War (Spector 2019). Besides the extreme losses of life, the United States wound up spending upward of $141 billion in South Vietnam between 1961 and 1975 (Associated Press 1975). America would not soon forget such a hefty investment.

DEPICTION AND CULTURAL CONTEXT

Hollywood largely kept the Vietnam War at arm's length until the latter half of the 1970s. When *The Deer Hunter* reached mainstream America, it was one of the first box-office successes related to the war, following *Rolling Thunder* (1977) and the Oscar-winning *Coming Home* (1978). The timeliness of the film's arrival and its central themes certainly struck a chord with American audiences and reviewers, who were still reeling in the aftershock of the war. In the words of Arthur Knight, "[*The Deer Hunter*] has much to tell us about a war that produced no heroes, even though individual actions may have been heroic. It has more to tell about a generation that went into that war trusting the rightness of our being there, and the disillusion that followed" (Knight 1978). Even though it deals with a politically charged subject, *The Deer Hunter* seems to exchange any interest in politics with a dream-like focus on brotherhood between common countrymen. "Although many will view it as a reactionary movie, 'The Deer Hunter' makes no attempt to come to grips with the political realities of Vietnam. Cimino is mostly concerned with the special camaraderie that exists between men, the deep bonds of affection that tie men together in times of pleasure and in times of crisis" (Carroll 1978).

Creating a primal focus on character development in the narrative, director Cimino said the movie "addresses itself to the question of the ordinary people of this country who journeyed from their homes to the heart of darkness and back. How do they survive that? . . . And how do they go on with some sense of hope, with their spirits intact? . . . That, to me, is what is important. The specific details of the war are unimportant. Because this is not a film of the intellect, it's a film of the heart—I hope" (Kent 1978). The down-to-earth characters and qualities in the story played a crucial role in getting the film off the ground: De Niro found inspiration in the script after being initially disinterested in taking on the movie. "I liked the story and the dialogue. It was so simple and it seemed so real to me," said the star, whose attachment to the film made it a more attractive prospect for EMI Films ("Production Notes" 2001).

The story arc, then, gravitates to each man's personal fight for courage and the question of communities grappling with daunting circumstances in a disenchanted moment in American history. Carroll of the *New York Daily News* writes, "Cimino's young men are just ordinary guys who face such bleak futures that guzzling beer in a local gin mill will always be their prime escape. They do not question the fact that they must go to Vietnam. The way is simply a test of their courage and moral character. And when those who are left sing 'God Bless America' during the movie's jarring final sequence, they do so instinctively because not to do so might cost them their sanity. 'The Deer Hunter' is ultimately a movie about the importance of survival" (Carroll 1978).

In telling a moving story on the nature of friendship and survival, Cimino described the film as a "very personal" undertaking. The director cited his experience in a Green Beret medical unit as key inspirational material for the movie: "My characters are portraits of people whom I knew. During the years of controversy over the war, the people who fought the war, whose lives were immediately affected and damaged and changed by the war, they were disparaged and isolated by the press. But they were common people who had an uncommon amount of courage" (Kent 1978). However, in contrast to Cimino's claim, records from the Pentagon and Defense Department show Cimino enlisting in the U.S. Army Reserve in 1962 and spending half a year on active duty, primarily stationed at Fort Dix in New Jersey (Hillstrom and Hillstrom 1998, 82–83). Whatever his motive, Cimino misrepresented his own service record upon recounting the formation of his film, and detractors readily jumped on the occasion to contradict his words.

For better or for worse, Cimino explicitly chose to make the Vietnam War the centerpiece to the action in *The Deer Hunter*. Yet the way in which he decided to portray the war drew heavy criticism from far and wide. In his last public appearance, John Wayne, who starred in the 1968 pro-Vietnam film *The Green Berets*, presented the 1978 Oscar for Best Picture to Cimino, although he personally expressed deep dissatisfaction in the movie and its message (McAdams 2005, 395). That same evening—while VVAW members demonstrated outside—the passionate anti-war activist and actress Jane Fonda reportedly criticized Cimino backstage for creating "a racist, Pentagon version of the war" (Biskind 1998, 372).

Perhaps in an effort to deflect criticism, Cimino attempted to keep his film aloof from political commentary. "My film has nothing to do with whether the war should or should not have been," the director asserted (Kent 1978). Moreover, Cimino said that he was not interested in keeping his film synchronized with the facts of history: "Look, the film is not realistic—it's surrealistic. Even the landscape is surreal. . . . And time is compressed. In trying to compress the experience of the war into a film, even as long as this one, I had to deal with it in a non-literal way" (Kent 1978). In an early 1979 interview, Walken echoed the same sentiment, saying the movie's "great virtue and its power are that it tells the story in a dramatic way. So, in a sense, equating it with anything real is maybe a mistake. . . . It's a story, and it's a piece of theater" (Reelin' 1979).

Despite artistic license, the film nevertheless specifically addresses the effects of Vietnam on the American people. In a 1978 interview with *The New York Times*, Cimino conceded, "You're right, I used events from '68 [My Lai] and '75 [the fall of Saigon] as reference points rather than as fact. But if you attack the film on its facts, then you're fighting a phantom, because literal accuracy was never intended" (Kent 1978). In *Guts and Glory*, Lawrence H. Suid confronts Cimino's apparent indifference to historic accuracy:

> Consequently, to the extent that Cimino ignored the historical and factual aspects of the conflict to suit his dramatic purposes, his "reference points" lost their ability to guide thought and feelings. . . . It may not matter that Cimino has placed a ten-thousand-foot snow-capped mountain in the heart of the Alleghenies. Audiences may not even become confused or bothered when they see

that the sequence of events does not adhere to the history of the U.S. involvement in Vietnam. To some it may not matter, as it did to the Army, that the film shows the United States withdrawing from Vietnam in "a Dunkirk-type bug-out" that was "associated with the fall of the South VN government" even though the United States had completed its troop withdrawal two years before the fall of Saigon. (Suid 2002, 356–357)

The surrealism expressed by *The Deer Hunter*, while departing from a historical basis, does represent a sense of the surrealistic memories that many veterans took with them from Vietnam. This surrealism stems from Americans' often contradictory realities during the war: One soldier might have been enjoying the comforts of air-conditioning in his compound while another, only a small trek away, suffered horrible wounds in a firefight. The infantrymen who actively patrolled were also able to spend ample time in relative ease in the rear—some with swimming pools and other recreational activities. Even on foreign ground, all Americans had access to the Armed Forces Vietnam Network, which offered them radio and television programs from their homeland. Then at the close of a year's worth of duty, the troops hopped aboard a plane and were able to touch U.S. soil again within a single day's journey. "The paradoxes inherent in fighting a war in this manner, in fighting a war that might provide entirely different experiences to soldiers thirty miles apart, six weeks earlier or later in time, created the surrealism that characterized Vietnam" (Suid 2002, 336).

As the director of the film affirmed no intent for "literal accuracy," *The Deer Hunter* often upholds the relevance of his words. The epic movie speeds through a disheveled chronology of the Vietnam War, whose events and conclusion appear superficial at best. What is more problematic is the way in which a massacre attributed to Viet Cong forces eerily resembles the atrocities committed by U.S. soldiers at My Lai. "I don't dispute the accounts of My Lai 4," Cimino commented, "but I think that anyone who is a student of the war, or anyone who was there, would agree that anything you could imagine happening probably happened" (Kent 1978).

The power of the imagination took on one particularly controversial form in *The Deer Hunter*'s nail-biting scenes of Russian roulette. The tense sequences tied to the bloody game are emblematic of the film in its entirety, recurring three times throughout the storyline. First, Mike, Nick, and Steve are forced to play Russian roulette as POWs for the Viet Cong's own twisted amusement. Later, Mike has a brief encounter with Nick in the red-light district of Saigon, where unfortunate souls bet large amounts of money on the outcome of the game. Near the climax of the film, Mike returns to Vietnam during the fall of Saigon and finds Nick still gambling his life away in the same dark milieu. There the two friends face each other in yet another round of Russian roulette, as Mike goes to any length to save his lifelong buddy from an empty, tormented existence.

Cimino stated that his clear purpose for the Russian roulette scenes was to "mix subconsciously with one of the world's worst images of Vietnam": the February 1968 photo of South Vietnam's national police chief, Nguyen Ngoc Loan, firing a bullet at point-blank range at Nguyen Van Lam, a captured Viet Cong fighter ("Production Notes" 2001). In his review of the movie, Ebert affirms the suitableness of the metaphor: "Anything you can believe about the game, about its deliberately random violence, about how it touches the sanity of men forced to play it, will apply to the war as a whole. It is a brilliant symbol because, in the context of this story, it makes any ideological statement about the war superfluous" (Ebert 1979). Resonating with *The Deer Hunter*'s visceral gun-to-the-head imagery, one Vietnam veteran gravely pronounced, "I've picked up a gun so many times to blow my brains out I can't even tell you. I couldn't do it. Why? Damned if I know. Sixty thousand other G.I.s have done it, that came over here! To get some relief from this s—. You can't imagine, you can't imagine what it's like. . . . You don't know what it's like to point a gun at someone's head and pull the trigger—and I thank God you don't know" (Cagle 2011, 223–224).

Despite its potency in the narrative, the inclusion of Russian roulette ultimately was a fanciful decision made by the moviemakers, who had no historical evidence to back up their portrayal of Vietnam. "Cimino's film failed to capture the essence of the American tragedy in Vietnam not only because it distorted or ignored history," Suid opines, "but also because its central metaphor, the recurring game of Russian roulette, portrayed a fiction" (Suid 2002, 357). The original screenwriters Louis Garfinkle and Quinn Redeker acknowledged the lack of historicity in the storyline, but even so, Garfinkle said he thought Russian roulette would serve "as a perfect metaphor" for the Vietnam War: "It seems to me that we can develop something that will perfectly delineate the problem Americans have living with a gun at their heads. This is a condition that man should not have to live with" (Suid 2002, 352).

Completely rejecting the notion that Russian roulette had any possible connection to the real-life experiences of Vietnam, Arnett wrote in a 1979 edition of the *Los Angeles Times*:

> I have found that enthusiasts are genuinely surprised and hurt when I tell them that while Vietnam had all manners of violence, including self-immolating Buddhist monks, fire bombings, rapes, deception and massacres like My Lai in its 20 years of war, there was not a single recorded case of Russian roulette, not in the voluminous files of the Associated Press anyway, nor in my experience either. The central metaphor of the movie is simply a bloody lie. The Deer Hunter is no more a historically valid comment on the American experience in Vietnam than was The Godfather an accurate history of the typical Italian immigrant family. (Arnett 1979)

The moviemakers likely did not anticipate the repercussions that the film's violent scenes would have in the days to follow. In retrospect, Redeker said

The Deer Hunter could have been "the heaviest movie ever made," in light of the fact that by 1981 upward of 27 young Americans had died engaging in Russian roulette after seeing the film (Suid 2002, 355). In 1986, Senator Paul Simon updated that statistic to 35 individuals (McLaughlin 1986). Furthermore, Garfinkle admitted that "the portrayal of the Vietnamese forcing prisoners to play the Russian roulette and later gambling reinforced the negative images and worst fears that most Americans have of Orientals" (Suid 2002, 353). In her review of the film published in *The New Yorker*, Pauline Kael wrote, "The impression a viewer gets is that if we [Americans] did some bad things over there we did them ruthlessly but impersonally; the Vietcong were cruel and sadistic. The film seems to be saying that the Americans had no choice, but the V.C. enjoyed it" (Kael 1978).

In contrast, the real Vietnamese on both sides of the war were just as human as any of America's young heroes. Tran Van Thinh, who earned several medals of honor as a North Vietnamese soldier, recalled his wartime experience in a 2015 interview: "I was very young. All I knew at that time was that I had to fight the Americans to reunify my country. . . . My most disturbing memory was killing two American soldiers" (Coomes 2015). Even decades after the war's conclusion, Pham Thanh Hung, a northerner who sustained severe injuries in combat, disclosed, "Sometimes I still have nightmares about being under an air strike" (Hastings 2018, 849). Another Vietnam native, Tran Thi Thon served the communists from 1965 until 1975 as a supply deliverer. "The day I remember most vividly was the day we found a downed American pilot," she recounted. "I saw that he had lost his shoe, so I took my shoe off and strapped it on his foot. Then, I took my handkerchief out and wiped the blood off his face. I felt very sympathetic because he was just another human and he didn't want to be in this war just like I didn't" (Coomes 2015).

In response to criticism regarding racism in *The Deer Hunter*, the Universal Pictures president, Ned Tanen, said, "I'm proud of the movie. It makes me feel good that people will sit through something that isn't intended as pure entertainment. And I know Cimino didn't intend the movie to be racist. His thrust was to make a film about comradeship among the people who volunteer to fight our wars" (Harmetz 1979). One young American who fought—and died—in Vietnam wrote home with relevant words that touch on the tense dynamic between wars as portrayed in film and the cold reality of battle: "The American voting public does not really appreciate what war is. If the average American housewife or truck driver could see movies of a real firefight or just hear one, they might be less inclined to send young men, other men's sons, into combat for contended and uncertain causes. Americans are quite familiar with war movies. The antics of combat heroes and the sound of machine gun fire. But they never hear the popping sounds of rounds, nor do they smell the horror" (Skakel 2011, 170).

The Deer Hunter made waves not only with its detailed depiction of violence but also in its commentary on the postwar lives of veterans. "More terrifying than the violence—certainly more provocative and moving—is the way each of the soldiers reacts to his war experiences," writes Canby. "Not once does anyone question the war or his participation in it. This passivity may be the real horror at the center of American life. . . . The big answers elude them, as do the big questions" (Canby 1978). Arnett chides the filmmakers for distorting the portrait of America in the Vietnam era: "Absent are the disillusion at home, the bitterness of those who served, the destruction of a country and any other factors that might lessen [Cimino's] epic theme" (Arnett 1979). Maj. Don Hudson, who led a company of infantrymen in 1970, said of the veterans returning from Vietnam, "They thought they were going home with their uniforms on and their little medals and everybody would be really happy to see them. They found out that was not true" (Hastings 2018, 849).

The movie shows nothing of the politics or protests that characterized those years in America under the war's lengthy shadow. The everyday citizens in the small town of Clairton receive their veterans with warmth and vitality, even without a deep understanding of their struggles. The only blatant anti-war statement in the film comes from the lips of a Green Beret who curiously wanders into the American Legion, where the rowdy wedding reception is underway. The three Vietnam-bound friends offer the silent veteran a drink and try to engage him in simple conversation about his war experience, but the only response they are able to elicit from the man is the twice-repeated phrase, "F— it."

Perhaps above all else, the heaviest consequence that followed the Vietnam War was the trauma inflicted on America's veterans. David Rogers, one of the 2.7 million to serve in Vietnam, described his postwar experience of feeling socially detached in terms of the guilt that the war produced in him: "I had a lot of trouble coming home and going to church. I couldn't confess. I felt dirty. I'd been part of killing" (Hastings 2018, 849). "Relationships are difficult. Jobs are difficult," relates Cagle. "Most of us feel dead inside" (Cagle 2011, 224). Australian Justice Philip Evatt, who formed a nine-volume report on Agent Orange in the 1980s, proposed that alcohol, post-traumatic stress, and tobacco "were the most convincing and widespread causes of veterans' difficulties" (Hastings 2018, 353).

The Deer Hunter attempts to paint a vivid picture of the damage done to U.S. troops who served in the war. While held captive in a waterlogged cage in Vietnam, Savage's character hyperventilates and shows signs of severe psychological distress while overhearing the other prisoners participate in Russian roulette in the enclosed area above his head. Steve winds up physically and emotionally debilitated back in the States: After having his legs and one arm amputated, the man succumbs to a reclusive existence in a Veterans Administration hospital, trying to avoid reliving the painful memories from the war. Consequently, his wife, Angela (Rutanya Alda), remains in a nonverbal state for a long time and only communicates to Mike through a written note when asked for Steve's whereabouts. When Mike comes to rescue his friend from isolation, Steve resists going home and repeats, "I don't fit," before finally acquiescing to Mike's wishes.

Set on his own emotional trajectory in the film, Nick's personage breaks down while at the U.S. Army Hospital in Saigon, unable to coherently hold a conversation with a medic. He then tries to place a phone call back home but hangs up before the operator makes a connection. Nick then submerges himself deeper in despair in the capital's dark recesses, where drinking, prostitution, and gambling are rampant. There the traumatized steelworker reaches another level of mental instability as he witnesses Russian roulette being played in a gambling den. Nick picks up a gun and fires two empty chambers, first aiming at a Vietnamese contestant and next at his own head. This causes chaos, and Nick flees into the night, going AWOL and eventually becoming a heroin addict.

As the story's protagonist, Mike displays the most physical and emotional fortitude throughout the entire film, attempting to console Steve while their fate is uncertain as POWs and later putting his life on the line in hopes to redeem his long-lost friend, Nick. But even the resilient Mike shows signs of emotional volatility. When first returning to Clairton, the veteran purposefully avoids his coming-home celebration and spends his first night alone in a motel; he only chooses to greet his friends gradually over the following days. Mike first assures Linda (Meryl Streep), "I'm fine," but later reveals to her a glimpse into his emotional struggle: "I feel a lot of distance. I feel far away." On the movie's second deer hunting trip, Mike comes to terms with his newfound unwillingness to shoot a deer and then returns to the cabin, where he confronts Stan (John Cazale) about flaunting his handgun in prideful banter with Axel (Chuck Aspegren). At this point, Mike snaps: He puts a bullet inside the gun, spins the chamber, shoves it against Stan's forehead, and pulls the trigger. The chamber is empty, and Mike storms outside, leaving his friends speechless.

The film rings true considering the hosts of U.S. veterans diagnosed with post-traumatic stress disorder (PTSD). As mandated by Congress in 1983, the government conducted the National Vietnam Veterans Readjustment Study to obtain a firmer grasp on the spread of PTSD among Vietnam veterans, in addition to other issues. The study found that by the mid- to late-1980s, around 15 percent of males and 9 percent of females who served in Vietnam had PTSD. Roughly, 3 out of 10 men and almost the same number of women showed signs of PTSD in at least some stage of their life following the war. Even after a decade had passed, many of these veterans were found to have a chronic case of PTSD (Tull 2019).

Traumatic wartime experiences tend to produce a variety of ill effects on veterans, although results vary considerably depending on the person. As highlighted in *The Deer Hunter*, depression and substance abuse commonly show up in conjunction with PTSD. Almost 50 percent of individuals with

PTSD experience clinical depression, and around one-third of men with PTSD grapple with alcohol or drug abuse (Tull 2019). Yet, trauma in itself does not ruin a veteran; each individual's unique response to trauma can help swing the balance toward a brighter future. In 2012, the Robert E. Mitchell Center for Prisoner of War Studies released its findings from a 37-year study, which centers on the lives of over 400 repatriated Vietnam POWs. The study concludes that dispositional optimism played a larger role in predicting resilience in these individuals than the severity of trauma that they experienced. "The results indicate that among this group, it was not merely the type of trauma that occurred which explained how one fared afterwards, but in addition, what type of person who experienced the trauma" (Olson 2013).

Vietnam stayed in the minds of Americans long after the soldiers came home. The disillusion and cynicism tied to the war, often illustrated by the battered lives of veterans, would impact the nation for years to come. One U.S. general declared, "The Vietnam war did more to change this country than anything in our recent history" (Hastings 2018, 847). America's self-image and its vision for the future felt dramatic shifts due to Vietnam (Bloom and Breines 2011, 154). *The Deer Hunter* represents one piece of the complex puzzle that is the United States' postwar experience, and as such, the film still holds great relevance for discussion today.

FURTHER READING

Aneja, Arpita, and Lily Rothman. 2015. "Eyewitness to the Fall of Saigon." *Time*, April 30, 2015. https://time.com/3838802/fall-of-saigon-memories/

Anthony, Scott. 2018. "A Film to Remember: 'The Deer Hunter'." Medium, December 23, 2018. https://medium.com/@sadissinger/a-film-to-remember-the-deer-hunter-1978-bfeda4139406

Arnett, Peter. 1979. "*The Deer Hunter*, Vietnam's Final Atrocity." *Los Angeles Times*, April 8, 1979.

Associated Press. 1975. "U.S. Spent $141-Billion in Vietnam in 14 Years." *The New York Times*, May 1, 1975. https://www.nytimes.com/1975/05/01/archives/us-spent-141billion-in-vietnam-in-14-years.html

Biskind, Peter. 1998. *Easy Riders, Raging Bulls: How the Sex, Drugs, and Rock 'n Roll Generation Saved Hollywood*. New York: Simon & Schuster.

Biskind, Peter. 2008. "The Vietnam Oscars." *Vanity Fair*, February 19, 2008. https://www.vanityfair.com/news/2008/03/warmovies200803

Biskind, Peter. 2016. "Peter Biskind on Michael Cimino's Twisted, Tortured Legacy: 'A Mystery in Death as He Was in Life'." *The Hollywood Reporter*, July 13, 2016. https://www.hollywoodreporter.com/features/peter-biskind-michael-ciminos-twisted-910101

Bloom, Alexander, and Wini Breines, eds. 2011. *"Takin' It to the Streets": A Sixties Reader*. New York: Oxford University Press.

Brigham, Robert K. n.d. "Battlefield Vietnam: A Brief History." PBS. Accessed on June 26, 2019. https://www.pbs.org/battlefieldvietnam/history/index.html

Cagle, Robert. 2011. "One Vet Remembers." In *"Takin' It to the Streets": A Sixties Reader*, edited by Alexander Bloom and Wini Breines, 220–224. New York: Oxford University Press.
Canby, Vincent. 1978. "Screen: 'The Deer Hunter'." *The New York Times*, December 15, 1978. https://www.nytimes.com/1978/12/15/archives/screen-the-deer-hunter.html
Carroll, Kathleen. 1978. "'Deer Hunter' Tells Vietnam War Horrors." *New York Daily News*, December 15, 1978. Republished February 18, 2015. https://www.nydailynews.com/entertainment/movies/archives-deer-hunter-tells-viet-war-horrors-article-1.2034791
Carucci, Mark. 1978. "Stalking *The Deer Hunter*: An Interview with Michael Cimino." *Millimeter*, March 1978, 34.
Coomes, Phil. 2015. "North Vietnamese Veterans Stories." *BBC*, July 9, 2015. https://www.bbc.com/news/in-pictures-33408096
Ebert, Robert. 1979. "The Deer Hunter." March 9, 1979. https://www.rogerebert.com/reviews/the-deer-hunter-1979
Eszterhas, Joseph. 1969. "The Massacre at Mylai." *Life*, December 5, 1969. https://books.google.com/books?id=mFAEAAAAMBAJ&printsec=frontcover
Farber, David. 1994. *The Age of Great Dreams: America in the 1960s*. New York: Hill and Wang.
Gilbey, Ryan. 2014. "After 36 Years, The Deer Hunter Remains One of the Most Fascinating Films on Vietnam." NewStatesman, August 5, 2014. https://www.newstatesman.com/culture/2014/08/after-36-years-deer-hunter-remains-one-most-fascinating-films-vietnam
Haoues, Rachid. 2015. "1975 CBS News Footage Shows Dramatic Evacuation of Saigon." *CBS News*, April 30, 2015. https://www.cbsnews.com/news/1975-cbs-news-footage-shows-the-dramatic-evacuation-of-saigon/
Harmetz, Aljean. 1979. "Oscar-Winning 'Deer Hunter' Is Under Attack as 'Racist' Film." *The New York Times*, April 26, 1979. https://www.nytimes.com/1979/04/26/archives/oscarwinning-deer-hunter-is-under-attack-as-racist-film-among-the.html
Hastings, Max. 2018. *Vietnam: An Epic Tragedy, 1945–1975*. New York: Harper. Kindle.
Hillstrom, Kevin, and Laurie Collier Hillstrom. 1998. *The Vietnam Experience: A Concise Encyclopedia of American Literature, Songs, and Films*. Westport, CT: Greenwood Publishing Group.
Isserman, Maurice, and Michael Kazin. 2012. *America Divided: The Civil War of the 1960s*. New York: Oxford University Press.
Johnson, Rep. Sam. 2015. "I Spent Seven Years as a Vietnam POW. The 'Hanoi Hilton' Is No Trump Hotel." *Politico*, July 21, 2015. https://www.politico.com/magazine/story/2015/07/i-was-vietnam-pow-donald-trump-120436
Kael, Pauline. 1978. "The God-Bless-America Symphony." *The New Yorker*, December 18, 1978. https://archives.newyorker.com/newyorker/1978-12-18/flipbook/066
Kent, Leticia. 1978. "Ready for Vietnam? A Talk with Michael Cimino." *The New York Times*, December 10, 1978. https://www.nytimes.com/1978/12/10/archives/ready-for-vietnam-a-talk-with-michael-cimino-cimino.html
Knight, Arthur. 1978. "'The Deer Hunter': THR's 1978 Review." *The Hollywood Reporter*, December 1, 1978. Republished December 8, 2018. https://www.hollywoodreporter.com/review/deer-hunter-review-1978-movie-1161827

McAdams, Frank. 2005. *The American War Film: History and Hollywood*. Los Angeles: Figueroa Press.

McLaughlin, Neil. 1986. "Simon Offers Bills to Pave Way for TV Violence Curbs." Associated Press, April 17, 1986. https://www.apnews.com/16ad59f8744a0266ccee57384e7736d9

National Archives. 2019. "Vietnam War U.S. Military Fatal Casualty Statistics." The U.S. National Archives and Records Administration, April 30, 2019. https://www.archives.gov/research/military/vietnam-war/casualty-statistics

Olson, Wyatt. 2013. "40 Years after Release, POWs at Hanoi Hilton Reflect on Experience." *Stars and Stripes*, February 10, 2013. https://www.stripes.com/news/pacific/40-years-after-release-pows-at-hanoi-hilton-reflect-on-experience-1.207382

"Production Notes." 2001. *The Deer Hunter*. Universal Studios.

Rasmussen, Karen, Sharon D. Downey, and Jennifer Asenas. 2003. "Trauma, Treatment, and Transformation: The Evolution of the Vietnam Warrior in Film." In *War and Film in America: Historical and Critical Essays*, edited by Marilyn J. Matelski and Nancy Lynch Street, 148–149. Jefferson, NC: McFarland & Company, Inc., Publishers.

Reelin' in the Years Productions. 1979. "Christopher Walken- Interview (The Deer Hunter) 1979." Filmed January 23, 1979. Published March 7, 2019. Video, 5:01. https://www.youtube.com/watch?v=cu4dcJV_AmM

Skakel, George. 2011. "One Soldier's View: Vietnam Letters." In *"Takin' It to the Streets": A Sixties Reader*, edited by Alexander Bloom and Wini Breines, 167–170. New York: Oxford University Press.

Spector, Ronald H. 2019. "Vietnam War." Encyclopaedia Britannica, May 23, 2019. https://www.britannica.com/event/Vietnam-War

Spiegel, Alix. 2012. "What Vietnam Taught Us about Breaking Bad Habits." *NPR*, January 2, 2012. https://www.npr.org/sections/health-shots/2012/01/02/144431794/what-vietnam-taught-us-about-breaking-bad-habits

Suid, Lawrence H. 2002. *Guts & Glory: The Making of the American Military Image in Film*. Lexington: The University Press of Kentucky.

Tull, Matthew. 2019. "The Long-Term Impact of PTSD in Vietnam War Veterans." Verywell Mind, March 15, 2019. https://www.verywellmind.com/ptsd-from-the-vietnam-war-2797449

Walsh, Kenneth T. 2015. "The U.S. and Vietnam: 40 Years After the Fall of Saigon." U.S. News, April 30, 2015. https://www.usnews.com/news/articles/2015/04/30/the-us-and-vietnam-40-years-after-the-fall-of-saigon

Chapter 4

The Right Stuff (1983)

The 1983 film *The Right Stuff* tells the story of the pilots who trained for the United States' first six manned space flights from 1961 to 1963. Written and directed by Philip Kaufman (*Invasion of the Body Snatchers*, *The Wanderers*), *The Right Stuff* starred Sam Shepard, Fred Ward, Dennis Quaid, Ed Harris, Scott Glenn, and Barbara Hershey. The film was distributed by Warner Bros. and premiered on October 21, 1983, with wide release on February 17, 1984. To portray an authentic sense of historicity, the movie was shot in various locations throughout California, including Edwards Air Force Base. The story shows an adaptation of Tom Wolfe's 1979 best seller of the same name, chronicling the feats of U.S. test pilots and the Mercury Seven astronauts with some dramatic license taken in the making of the film. Irwin Winkler and Robert Chartoff were the producers, and Levon Helm served as narrator as well as costar (cast as air force test pilot Jack Ridley). Supporting roles were filled by Lance Henriksen, Scott Paulin, Charles Frank, and Veronica Cartwright.

The date is October 14, 1947. Chuck Yeager (played by Sam Shepard), an Air Force captain and war hero, nimbly shoots to the skies in his bullet-shaped Bell X-1 rocket plane. This maverick aviator tests his luck and maneuvers his aircraft to an altitude of 42,000 feet—coolly defying naysayers as he shatters the sound barrier for the first time in history. A champion among the locals at Muroc Army Air Field in California's Mojave Desert, Yeager embodies the essence of the autonomous American hero (even accomplishing his first supersonic flight with broken ribs). Without doubt, this man has the right stuff. Flash-forward to 1953, and more rising pilots show up at what is now Edwards Air Force Base, including Captains Gordon Cooper (played by Dennis Quaid), Gus Grissom (Fred Ward), and Deke Slayton

(Scott Paulin). The stark reality for the test pilots stationed at Edwards is readily apparent with their scant accommodations and their wives' constantly suppressed anxiety about whether or not their husbands will survive their particular duties of the day.

Four years later, the looming terror of *Sputnik* is announced, and the United States scrambles to put together a space program with its very first selection of astronauts. With the Soviet threat becoming increasingly real and the final frontier of outer space coming within arm's reach, a large group of military men undergo an unparalleled variety of physically and mentally rigorous tests, weeding out all but the crème de la crème. Thus Cooper, Grissom, and Slayton join ranks with John Glenn (Ed Harris), Alan Shepard (Scott Glenn), Wally Schirra (Lance Henriksen), and Scott Carpenter (Charles Frank) to form the illustrious Mercury Seven in early 1959. America needs to break ahead in the race to space, and therefore, the public eye is fixated on the newborn NASA preparing tirelessly to launch its new "star navigators" into spaceflight with Project Mercury. As the Select Seven train with mind-boggling simulations (and as NASA successfully sends primates into space ahead of them), the USSR secures an early lead with its pioneering activity in space—silently taunting the United States and sparking swift reaction. It is at such a time that these overnight heroes rise to the occasion and pilot America's first six manned flights into space from May 1961 to May 1963.

The film was shot on a $27-million budget and returned a domestic total gross of $21,192,102, finishing 33rd in revenue rankings of 1983 films. Contrasted with a notable deficit in the box office, *The Right Stuff* picked up considerable acclaim from critics and secured eight Oscar nominations at the 56th Academy Awards, including Best Picture, Best Actor in a Supporting Role (Sam Shepard), Best Cinematography, and Best Art Direction. The film ended up winning four Oscars: Best Film Editing, Best Sound, Best Sound Effects Editing, and Original Score (Bill Conti). The movie received nomination for the Hugo Award for Best Dramatic Presentation in 1984, and Scott Glenn received nomination for the New York Film Critics' Award for Best Supporting Actor. In 2013, the Library of Congress chose to preserve the film in the United States National Film Registry due to its qualities as "culturally, historically, or aesthetically significant."

Critics lauded the film for its bravado in celebrating the high-flying heroes of America's past. Renowned movie buff Roger Ebert called *The Right Stuff* "a great film," accurately forecasting its historical weight as "likely to be a landmark movie in a lot of careers. It announces Kaufman's arrival in the ranks of major directors" (Ebert 1983). As a snapshot into U.S. history, the film stays largely on target throughout its epic 192-minute duration. "In all important respects, the movie is true to what really happened at those fighter jock heavens, the runways and bars of Edwards Air Force Base in the high desert of California and the launching pads and bars of Cape

Canaveral," wrote John Noble Wilford. "The booze, bravado and women are all there, as well as the quiet courage and fear of failure. This is the way it was in the 1940's and 1950's when pilots were pushing the outside of the envelope, as they said, to fly higher and faster, and in the early 1960's when the first American astronauts were venturing into space" (Wilford 1983).

The Right Stuff caught immediate attention among official critics but lacked on-the-ground support from moviegoers. Around the time of its release, famed astronaut and Ohio senator John Glenn was pursuing a nomination for presidency from the Democratic Party, and media coverage capitalized on the coinciding events, including the October 3, 1983, *Newsweek* cover showing Ed Harris (who played Glenn) and the words "Can a Movie Help Make a President?" In an attempt to explain this "puzzling flop at the box office," Ebert wrote, "Some blamed confusion in the public mind between the movie and John Glenn's run for public office. More likely, even then, audiences were not ready for a movie that approached the program with skepticism, comedy and irony" (Ebert 2002).

Reviewers tended to uphold the movie's narrative substance while still noting the irreverent reality behind the celebrities in the spotlight. "In a brash, beautiful, deeply American film, Kaufman has combined the resources and ingenuity of movie making with the freewheeling, damn-the-conventions style of the New Journalism and come up with a generous, high-spirited look at the bravery and lunacy that was that era," wrote the *Los Angeles Times*' Sheila Benson on the day of the film's release (Benson 1983). Although primarily historical in nature, the film uses Hollywood's theatrics to narrate a rollicking story, sometimes straying from facts to heighten emotions. Vincent Canby opined in *The New York Times*, "Philip Kaufman's rousing, funny screen adaptation of Tom Wolfe's book about Project Mercury and America's first astronauts [is] probably the brightest and the best rookie/cadet movie ever made, though the rookies and cadets are seasoned pilots and officers. . . . 'The Right Stuff' is full of short-term pleasures that yield to doubts only after the film is over" (Canby 1983).

HISTORICAL BACKGROUND

The open skies above California's desert lands proved to be the perfect arena for aeronautical research, and Edwards Air Force Base was home to some of America's best test pilots. Originally named Muroc Army Air Field, the high-desert milieu was unassuming, with meager living conditions for low-paid military men. One of these pilots was Charles Elwood Yeager, an air force captain in his early twenties who had been chosen for a particular research project overseen by National Advisory Committee for Aeronautics (NACA) engineers and technicians. "We didn't know if we could break the sound barrier, but it was our duty to try," said Yeager of the days leading up to his first supersonic journey (Clash 2017). In nine separate flights, he incrementally closed in on Mach 1, overcoming the excessive shock-wave turbulence present at Mach 0.94 with the plane's movable horizontal stabilizer.

It took the unprecedented rocket power of the orange-hued Bell X-1, coupled with Yeager's unparalleled zeal to fly, to surpass Mach 1. The deed was accomplished on October 14, 1947: "I noticed that the faster I got, the smoother the ride," Yeager wrote in his autobiography. "Suddenly the Mach needle began to fluctuate. It went up to .965 Mach—then tipped right off the scale. I thought I was seeing things! We were flying supersonic! And it was as smooth as a baby's bottom" (Yeager and Janos 1986, 164). After breaking the sound barrier, Yeager was promptly celebrated with a free steak dinner at Pancho's Happy Bottom Riding Club, the usual spot where the experimental test pilots congregated (Wolfe 2008, 45). Located on a dude ranch and flying resort (Rancho Oro Verde and Pancho's Fly Inn), the bar and grill displayed photographs of the regulars who would fly supersonic over the years that followed (Yeager and Janos 1986, 181).

To fly at Edwards during the 1950s, a pilot was joining "the greatest era in research flying in the history of aviation" (Yeager and Janos 1986, 221). Within half a decade, dozens of new airmen came to be a part of the flight testing at the base, as the air force was pushing millions of dollars into research and development for supersonic aircraft. "By the mid-1950s, the one hundred twenty test pilots working for General [Albert] Boyd had tested more than 50 prototype fighters, interceptors, deep penetration fighters, all-weather fighters, day fighters, medium and heavy bombers, helicopters, heavy-lift cargo planes, and fuel tankers" (Yeager and Janos 1986, 222). On November 20, 1953—almost 50 years to the day after the Wright Brothers' historic flight—NACA research pilot Scott Crossfield flew his D-558-II Skyrocket at twice the speed of sound. Not to be undone, Yeager hopped into the Bell X-1A on December 12 and rose 70,000 feet in the air to reach Mach 2.4—when suddenly the plane started tumbling out of control. Knocked semiconscious and "spinning down through the sky like a frisbee," Yeager somehow pulled out of the spin at 25,000 feet, living to fly another day and persistently set the standard for aeronautic feats (Yeager and Janos 1986, 250–256).

The incredible technological breakthroughs leading into the 1960s would perhaps only be rivaled by the radical changes taking place in American society. Cold War America was under a cloud of geopolitical tensions, which would leave their indelible mark on the decade. As the United States and the Soviet Union were locked in a battle between global superpowers, the two vied for supremacy—capitalist democracy effectively warring against communism—each claiming its military power and technology superior to the others. This conflict affected the lives of everyday citizens in both countries, due to looming nuclear threats amidst the arms race, international espionage, and much debate in the mainstream media.

By the close of the 1950s, space itself turned into an impressive new battleground for the Cold War competitors, who now had a compelling incentive to conquer "the final frontier" while being observed by a global audience. On October 4, 1957, the Soviet Union's R-7 intercontinental ballistic missile delivered the first man-made satellite, Sputnik 1, into Earth's orbit. This launch sent shockwaves into America's collective consciousness and elicited an urgent response from the U.S. government: "increased spending for aerospace endeavors, technical and scientific educational programs, and the chartering of new federal agencies to manage air and space research and development" (Garber and Launius 2005). The result of such an impassioned competition was a pair of remarkable space programs, each bolstered by a keen correlation to foreign policy and national security (Sagdeev and Eisenhower 2008).

On January 31, 1958, the United States launched its own 30-pound satellite, *Explorer 1*, the first to carry scientific instruments into space, which discovered the existence of radiation belts encircling the Earth (Loff 2017). On October 1 that same year, President Dwight David Eisenhower signed into existence the National Aeronautics and Space Administration (NASA), "a civilian agency of the government charged with the exploration of space for peaceful and scientific purposes" (NASA 1961). NASA hit the ground running with its predecessor NACA's $100-million annual budget, 8,000 employees, three large research laboratories—Langley Research Center, Ames Aeronautical Laboratory, and Lewis Flight Propulsion Laboratory—and two additional test facilities. NASA would soon take on more organizations like the Naval Research Laboratory's space science group in Maryland, the army-sponsored Jet Propulsion Laboratory in California, and the Army Ballistic Missile Agency in Alabama (Garber and Launius 2005).

NASA began to launch America's first missions into space within just months of its inception. Spurred on by an ever-increasing political and technological rivalry, NASA began recruiting for its $400-million behemoth Project Mercury—a groundbreaking undertaking spurred on by the prospects of transporting Americans into space (NASA 1961; Garber and Launius 2005). In selecting the USA's first voyagers into space, Eisenhower simplified the process considerably by narrowing the search to members of U.S. military branches. At the start of 1959, NASA's Stanley C. White, Robert B. Voas, and William S. Augerson whittled down 508 candidates to 110 based on their screening of service records at the military personnel bureaus located in Washington, D.C. Those who met the minimum requirements included 58 air force pilots, 47 navy men, and 5 Marines. Because a high percentage of candidates interviewed were willing to be part of the program, NASA administrator George Low recommended to decrease the desired number of finalists from 12 down to just six pilots (NASA 2017).

The procedures for selecting the Mercury pilots were led by NASA's committee consisting of senior management engineer Charles J. Donlan, test pilot engineer Warren J. North, psychologists Allen O. Gamble and Voas, psychiatrists Edwin Z. Levy and George E. Ruff, and flight surgeons Augerson and White; these members represented all branches of the military during their involvement in the evaluation and selection of the candidates (Burgess 2011, 28). By mid-February 1959, two groups of candidates had come to Washington, and 56 pilots were processed in the first batch of written tests, technical and psychiatric interviews, and medical history reviews. At the start of March, 36 men remained in the pool of candidates, and 32 of them accepted the offer to face "extraordinary physical examinations" awaiting them at the Lovelace Clinic in Albuquerque, New Mexico (NASA 2017).

The selectees arrived one by one at Lovelace, prepared for roughly one week's worth of medical assessments. Upward of 30 distinct lab tests recorded cardiographic, chemical, and encephalographic data. Each man's body was mapped by thorough X-ray exams, and his eyes, ears, nose, and throat were all evaluated in great detail. "Special physiological examinations included bicycle ergometer tests, a total-body radiation count, total-body water determination, and the specific gravity of the whole body. Heart specialists made complete cartiological examinations, and other clinicians worked out more complete medical histories on these men than probably had ever before been attempted on human beings" (NASA 2017). By the end of these evaluations, 31 were found to be exceeding in health, and only one man was unable to proceed to the following stage. Mercury-hopeful Scott Carpenter reflected, "It was intense competition. They examined every body opening; they made some others in doing that! It was a fascinating thing, because it gave us a new appreciation for what a marvelous machine the human body is" (Burgess 2011, 220–221).

The next phase consisted of "an amazingly elaborate set of environmental studies, physical endurance tests, anthropometric measurements, and psychiatric studies" realized at the Wright Air Development Center's Aeromedical Laboratory in Dayton, Ohio (NASA 2017). Another week-long test began in March for the 31 would-be astronauts—this time with more intense stressors that anticipated their unprecedented expeditions into space. To prove psychological and physical aptitude, the responses to each strain encountered needed to be both appropriate and effective for the particular situation: "In addition to pressure suit tests, acceleration tests, vibration tests, heat tests, and loud noise tests, each candidate had to prove his physical endurance on treadmills, tilt tables, with his feet in ice water, and by blowing up balloons until exhausted. Continuous psychiatric interviews, the necessity of living with two psychologists throughout the week, and extensive self-examination through a battery of 13 psychological tests for personality and motivation, and another dozen different tests on intellectual functions and special aptitudes—these were all part of the week of truth at Dayton" (NASA 2017).

Nearing the end of March, the fifth phase was underway, as the Space Task Group headquarters at Langley in Hampton, Virginia, processed the statistical and clinical data gleaned from Albuquerque and Dayton. The quantitative information presented was too close between the finalists to make a final judgment accordingly, so the selectors included the candidates' personalities and temperaments as factors in their deliberation. The process of decision-making was so much of a challenge that they could not settle on only six candidates; therefore, Space Task Group director Robert Gilruth chose to go with seven (Burgess 2011, 303–306). Each individual received a telephone call from Donlan, who heard glad affirmations to the offer to become one of America's first astronauts. Thus the Mercury Seven were solidified (NASA 2017).

At 2:00 p.m. on April 9, 1959, the nation's capital was bustling with activity as NASA held a press conference in its temporary headquarters at the Dolley Madison House on Lafayette Square. The ballroom was bursting at the seams with "a thundering herd of reporters and photographers" eagerly awaiting NASA's history-making announcement of America's original crew of spacemen (Burgess 2016, 37). "As television cameras came to life and flashbulbs popped in a dazzling crescendo of light and sound, seven men dressed in civilian clothing were ushered in" (Burgess 2011, 276–277). After they sat in alphabetical order at a long table covered in felt, NASA's Administrator, T. Keith Glennan, gave the crowd what they were longing for: "It is my pleasure to introduce to you—and I consider it a very real honor, gentlemen—from your right: Malcolm S. Carpenter, Leroy G. Cooper [Jr.], John H. Glenn Jr., Virgil I. Grissom, Walter M. Schirra Jr., Alan B. Shepard Jr., and Donald K. Slayton . . . the nation's Mercury astronauts!" (Burgess 2011, 277).

Before Glennan's announcement, surges of cameramen were flocking the stage area, attempting to secure the perfect photograph—so much that Shepard said to Schirra sitting next to him, "I can't believe this. These people are nuts" (Thompson 2007, 201). An hour-and-a-half question-and-answer session followed, as the Select Seven told the world about their personal lives—Glenn distinguishing himself with a strong dose of charisma and the apparent embodiment of classic American values. Later that day, the band of astronauts signed a $500,000 deal with *Life* magazine, which secured exclusive coverage of their stories, evenly splitting the earnings seven ways. "Together, they were about to soar irretrievably away from their military peers to create their own seven-man fraternity—and a whole new brand of cold war celebrity" (Thompson 2007, 200).

The seven male specimens shared a few commonalities: ranging from 32 to 37 years old, weighing from 150 and 180 pounds, and measuring from 5 feet 7 inches to 5 feet 11 inches tall. All sons of military fathers, they also had mother figures who played key roles in their formative years. The Seven were seasoned test pilots, and six of them had experienced aerial combat against Korean or Japanese forces. All were married men, fathers of two or three children each. Additionally, as noted by the psychologists and psychiatrists scrutinizing over their data, the astronauts shared traits such as varying degrees of obsessive compulsiveness, a tendency toward proactivity rather than self-examination, and an extraordinary measure of self-sufficiency (Thompson 2007): "One writer would describe them as 'square-jawed trim halfbacks recruited from an All-American football team.'. . . Others hailed the 'virile' new 'space voyagers'—'daring and courageous.' Only a few quietly reminded readers that these were 'military pilots' and, so far, premature heroes. Even though the public affairs guy had warned the new astronauts about the deep probe of the press, not even Glenn, the savviest of them all, was prepared for what was to come. 'Not one of us knew what he was in for,' Glenn would recall" (p. 203).

During the second half of 1959, the seven committed themselves to a training regimen unlike anything the world had yet seen. Shepard depicted an overview of the training as "a mix of academics, meetings with engineers to discuss the mechanics of the rockets and capsules, and rigorous physical and stamina exercises designed to tone and prepare their bodies for the expected labors of space flight" (Thompson 2007, 217). For this purpose, NASA engineers constructed machines replicating the "excruciating tremors and pressures of sitting on the nose of a rocket traveling faster than any human had ever traveled," mimicking the anticipated weightless condition of being in space, and even simulating the feeling of hurtling through space in an out-of-control, disabled spacecraft (Thompson 2007, 220).

Constantly in the background of all of their endeavors was the realization that communism was spreading around the world and desperately needed to be confronted. "The astronauts' training regimen, therefore, was fueled by an almost combatlike mentality and a belief that gaining control of space might just save the world. The men threw themselves into their training exercises, spending extremely long and stressful days at various facilities around the country, strapped inside machines designed to punish their bodies and prove the cynics wrong. And in classrooms, they absorbed Ph.D.-level lessons on astrophysics, rocket propulsion, and mechanical engineering" (Thompson 2007, 218).

On September 12, 1959, the Soviets aimed their Luna 2 spacecraft skyward, and 33.5 hours later, the 860-pound probe made contact with the moon. Then on April 12, 1961, USSR air force pilot Yuri Alekseyevich Gagarin was launched from the Baikonur Cosmodrome into a 108-minute flight in the Vostok 1 spacecraft—securing fame as the first human in space and the first to orbit the planet. The Soviets' success with Gagarin's flight dealt a forceful blow to the United States and ended up sparking an even more intense drive to answer back. As a part of Project Mercury, NASA's engineers devised a cone-shaped capsule that was smaller and more lightweight compared to the Soviets' Vostok. The craft was tested with chimpanzees aboard first (to the amusement of the Mercury men in training), and NASA conducted a final test just a few weeks before Gagarin made history.

On May 5, 1961, the 37-year-old commander, Alan Bartlett Shepard Jr., became America's first voyager in space, lifted from Cape Canaveral by the Mercury-Redstone 3 rocket into a close-to-perfect suborbital flight. "It was one of the most thrilling of the flights; perhaps, in a sense, the most fearful for me," said broadcast journalist Walter Cronkite, who was present at Shepard's launch. "We had watched Redstone rockets blowing up on the pad and blowing up in test flights. I had a strong feeling that perhaps we were rushing the launching of man into space to compete with the Russians. I really had my fingers crossed" (Roberts 1991). "A lean, crew-cut former Navy test pilot . . . [Shepard] began the day lying on his back in a cramped Mercury capsule atop a seven-story Redstone rocket filled with explosive fuel. After four tense hours of weather and mechanical delays, he was shot into the sky on a 15-minute flight that grazed the fringes of space, at an altitude of 115 miles, and ended in a splashdown in the Atlantic Ocean 302 miles downrange from Cape Canaveral" (Wilford 1998).

"Boy—what a ride!" was the space traveler's first exclamation as a recovery helicopter whisked him away (Burgess 2011, 307). America at large was both ecstatic and relieved to witness Shepard's safe return. Three days later, President John Fitzgerald Kennedy honored Shepard at the White House with NASA's Distinguished Service Medal. Soon after, on May 25, with momentum now building for the U.S. space program, JFK had the confidence to proclaim his vision for the remainder of the 1960s: "I believe that this nation should commit itself to achieving the goal, before this decade is out, of landing a man on the moon and returning him safely to the earth. No single space project in this period will be more impressive to mankind, or more important for the long-range exploration of space; and none will be so difficult or expensive to accomplish" (JFK Library Foundation 1961).

In the wake of the president's visionary words, Virgil Ivan "Gus" Grissom, a 35-year-old air force captain, would reach for the stars in the second Mercury flight on July 21, 1961. Aboard the Liberty Bell 7, the stocky Grissom survived another successful 15-minute suborbital flight—although the only snag came after splashdown. With a recovery chopper overhead, the astronaut finished the necessary checks inside the capsule, arming the explosive bolts in preparation for opening the hatch. "Without warning, the hatch suddenly blew off, and water began to pour in" (Burgess 2011, 312). Grissom escaped the sinking metal chamber, but a leaking suit led to a great struggle for him to stay afloat, treading water for almost four minutes before being lifted to safety (Armstrong 2007). Meanwhile, the Liberty Bell 7 was lost to the ocean's depths following a passionate effort to save the costly spacecraft. Overshadowed by the embarrassing incident, Grissom avowed that he did nothing, whether intentionally or unintentionally, that caused the hatch to blow. And NASA accepted his statement as truth (Burgess 2011, 313).

The rocket-fueled race progressed, and the Soviet Union responded on August 6, propelling Gherman Stepanovich Titov in Vostok 2 through an impressive 17 orbits around the Earth and more than 24 hours of spaceflight. After being beaten to the punch of sending humans into orbital space, NASA was vigorously getting ready for Mercury's first orbital mission, to which Glenn would lay claim. Lieutenant colonel John Herschel Glenn Jr. was a man of many distinctions: This 38-year-old Marine was the most decorated of the Seven, boasted the most combat experience, and recently had clocked in a new record in flying a jet across the country at supersonic speeds. Plus, citizens across the country knew his personable qualities from a 1957 appearance on the game show *Name That Tune*. The months in anticipation of his flight would be particularly taxing on Glenn's (and the nation's) patience, as 11 different flights were postponed due to inclement weather or technical issues. On January 27, 1962, Glenn hopped aboard Friendship 7 and ended up enduring a five-hour wait, only to have the mission delayed once again because of the weather (Burgess 2011, 316–320).

Finally, on the morning of February 20, 1962, there were only agreeable skies above Cape Canaveral's Kennedy Space Center. Wearing a 20-pound pressurized spacesuit, Glenn boarded the 4,200-pound, 9.5-by-6-foot Mercury-Atlas 6 spacecraft at 6:03 a.m. (NASA 1961; Swenson et al. 1966, 422–23). After everything was checked and secured, at 9:47 a.m. the bell-shaped Friendship 7 was lifted skyward by a blazing Atlas rocket—all while 135 million Americans were transfixed by live radio and television broadcasts of the historic moment (Shetterly 2016, 223). After a flawless entry into orbit, Glenn enjoyed a smooth first go-around, as he marveled at the unequaled views of his home planet beneath and even ate a tube of applesauce while flying high over Australia (Bond 1987, 36–47). "From his height and speed, stars and planets disappeared over the horizon at 18 times the normal earthbound rate and 'that makes for a pretty speedy sunset.' He was disappointed by the stars, which seemed small and distant, but . . . [the] most amazing sight was a host of particles 'bright yellowish-green, about the size and intensity of fireflies' which swarmed all around his capsule at each of three sunrises" (Mandel 1962, 36). At the end of his first orbit, one of the yaw attitude control jets clogged, forcing Glenn to switch to manual control of the flight, which did not pose any problems for the seasoned airman (Dunbar 2017).

As Friendship 7 was nearing the close of its second orbit, a warning light illuminated that was connected to the heat shield. In order to compensate for the possibility that the critical shield had come loose, Mission Control improvised and ordered Glenn to retain the retropack during reentry as an added measure of security. "Glenn recognized this was a radical and untried departure from plan," yet when he reached the end of orbit three, he engaged the retrorockets and prepared for reentry (Mandel 1962, 39). Leaving zero gravity, the astronaut felt a bump from behind and noticed an orange glow surrounding the spacecraft. "Now," Glenn described in an interview with *Life* published just days later, "it became apparent that something was tearing up on the heat shield end of the capsule . . . large pieces were coming back up past the window and flaming very brightly" (Mandel 1962). The tense spaceman held on for his life, not knowing for certain whether the heat shield or retropack was being dissolved in the intense heat (McCombs 1987).

After several minutes of silence between radio contact due to the ionization barrier, the astronaut's voice reappeared with the exclamation "Boy, that was a real fireball!" (Mandel 1962, 39). NASA eventually found that a malfunction had triggered the warning light and the heat shield had remained secure for the flight's full duration. After traveling 75,679 miles and circling the Earth three times in just under five hours, Friendship 7 hit the waters of the Atlantic about 800 miles to the southeast of Bermuda (Dunbar 2017). America's "Ace of Space" was retrieved safely and enjoyed much fanfare as the nation celebrated in the days to follow: "He was showered with ticker-tape during a parade in New York City that was attended by some four million people, had presidential meetings, and gave an address to a rare joint meeting of Congress" (Burgess 2011, 321).

After serving as Glenn's backup, Malcolm Scott Carpenter, a 37-year-old navy lieutenant, would follow in his own mission three months later. Air force captain Donald Kent Slayton had been next in line, but three weeks after Friendship 7's mission, he received the unexpected diagnosis of idiopathic atrial fibrillation after doctors noticed an irregular heartbeat. NASA's decision-makers erred on the side of caution, and Slayton reluctantly would not venture into space for another 13 years (though, in the meantime, acting with "extraordinary influence" at the helm of the Astronaut Office) (Burgess 2011, 343). On May 24, 1962, Carpenter lifted into space aboard Aurora 7 and conducted a large assortment of tasks during the orbital flight. In his three loops around the planet, the astronaut basked in a trio of sunrises and sunsets, ingested solid food, and identified Glenn's "fireflies" as particles of ice dislodging from the craft's frigid exterior. A few technical malfunctions led to Carpenter upholding the necessity of human pilots in spaceflight, as he had to manually control Aurora 7 in reentry and partially correct a significant misalignment. In the end, his trajectory overshot the landing zone in the Atlantic by roughly 250 miles, but he was located 40 minutes after splashdown and recovered not long after (Burgess 2011, 327–328).

On July 4, 1962, the Mercury Seven received a roaring welcome to Houston, along with their families and around 7,000 personnel of NASA's Manned Spacecraft Center. Awaiting them in the Sam Houston Coliseum was "an old-fashioned Texas barbecue" comprised of over 6,000 pounds of meat, 500 pounds of onions, and 150 gallons of beans. The festive welcome to the astronauts and NASA employees was, in the words of Vice President Lyndon Baines Johnson, a "proud day for Houston, Texas, and the nation" (Porterfield 1962). Then on October 3, Walter Marty Schirra Jr., the 39-year-old navy lieutenant commander, took his Sigma 7 spacecraft through six orbits, covering 153,900 miles. This 9-hour-13-minute mission was successful, although not distinguished much in the media. Schirra characteristically understated the mission as "a routine, textbook flight. I was able to accomplish everything I wanted during the flight. It was a honey of a machine" (Furniss 1983, 23).

The youngest member of the Select Seven, 36-year-old air force captain Leroy Gordon Cooper Jr., piloted the final Mercury mission on May 15, 1963. Faith 7 left the earth at 8:04 a.m. in a spot-on trajectory. Transporting the spacecraft and voyager well beyond all previous U.S. missions, the flight took Cooper through 22 orbits, lasting 34 hours and 20 minutes from start to finish. Seven of those hours he slept through—the first astronaut to doze in space. Yet Cooper had his share of issues to deal with: He experienced excessive overheating in the capsule (ending the flight seven pounds lighter) along with high readings in carbon dioxide and a slow leak in oxygen. To top things off, the electronics linked to the automatic control system went out just prior to reentry. This malfunction forced him to take the reins of Faith 7, align it with the horizon, engage the retro-rockets, and steer the spacecraft manually. The reentry, riddled with hazards, was realized without flaw, landing Cooper's capsule within four miles of the recovery ship awaiting him in the Pacific Ocean. Although dizzy, soaked in sweat, and a bit pale, Cooper acted with great accuracy and poise during an intense reentry process (Burgess 2011, 339).

Still in the stark California setting of Edwards, Yeager ever possessed the drive to break another record—this time trying to surpass the altitude of 113,890 feet that the Russians had reached in 1961. On the morning of December 10, 1963, the veteran pilot took the Lockheed NF-104A supersonic jet up to 108,000 feet in a smooth run. Later that day, Yeager attempted a second flight, but at the peak of his 104,000-foot arc, the plane's nose pitched up and proved unyielding to all attempts to be lowered. The craft then whirled helplessly out of control, and Yeager ejected after falling 90,000 feet through 13 flat spins—just in time, for the plane collided with the ground after the 14th spin (Yeager and Janos 1986, 355–356). He sustained significant injuries due to a collision between his facemask and the burning seat, but a month of recovery in the hospital would heal his charred face. While Yeager resumed his life of flying, that day's events were his last crack at setting a record in the skies (Wolfe 2008, 348).

DEPICTION AND CULTURAL CONTEXT

While tracking the historical lives of daring test pilots and the first U.S. astronauts, *The Right Stuff* presents an insider's view of Cold War America's high-flying heroes before, during, and after their significant achievements leading into the early 1960s. The movie shows the Mercury Seven as national celebrities amid the glamour and spectacle of the media, contrasted with their gritty and unceremonious personal lives. *The Right Stuff* reflects how America overcame Cold War preoccupations with a unified if not frenzied love of its space explorers. Basing the screenplay on Wolfe's edgy book, director Kaufman said, "I really wanted to go back to Tom Wolfe's attitude, atmosphere, and humor. I really wanted to find that Tom Wolfe quality, the craziness of the American circus—how the astronauts would be defined publicly by a *Life* magazine story while the truth was far more interesting, important, and heroic" (French and Kahn 2014).

Like Wolfe's book, the film attempts to draw audiences behind the curtains of the hype and theatrics created in the public narrative about America's astronauts. "What we had done in the Air Force was being overshadowed by NASA," said Chuck Yeager in a 2017 interview. "That's where Tom Wolfe really shined. In doing a book on the seven Mercury astronauts, he began to see that they got professional PR guys to blow them out of shape. He looked back and saw the guys at Edwards were killing themselves doing research for NASA, but no one knew about it. That's what made his book so very, very good" (Clash 2017). While not a documentary, the movie attempted to depict the historical pilots as authentic, down-to-earth men. Kaufman commented on the preparation involved in making the film: "Research went on in every area, all through the movie. When the actors showed up, each of them got a book that we had prepared with 30 to 40 pages on each character—every damn thing we could find" (French and Kahn 2014).

As is common in Hollywood, theatrics can sometimes get the best of historicity, but on a large scale, *The Right Stuff* does not stray too far from fact. Yeager opined, "[The movie] was interesting. I did a lot of flying in it, and Sam Shepard did a good job portraying me. Barbara Hershey looked exactly like [my wife] Glennis, too—wonderful. Though it's sort of 'Hollywoodized,' the whole story is accurate. I did get burned badly in an F-104 crash. All in all, the movie is educational, and it's very well made" (Clash 2017). To represent such a wide variety of flying machines, the production made use of numerous model aircraft and mockups as well as authentic period jets. The cinematographers meshed footage of the life-size and miniature aircraft in their masterful orchestration of high-speed flight. The crew added historical newsreel footage in a few instances to bolster a sense of realism. "We combined the great NASA footage with pieces that were built on the set," noted Kaufman. "We were pioneering in that kind of insertion of actors into historical events. For example, we combined footage of the real Alan Shepard being loaded into the capsule with Scott Glenn doing it on the stage. We had Scott Glenn shaking hands with Kennedy; they did the same thing in *Forrest Gump* and made a big thing out of spending a million dollars to do it. We did that in one afternoon" (French and Kahn 2014).

In its lengthy and detailed storytelling, the movie sometimes seems to prefer drama to strict history. Yeager commented on the apparently erratic decisions that his character makes in the film when taking on substantial, record-breaking flights: "Hollywood is in the business of make-believe. I didn't just walk out and fly the X-1 supersonic. It took unpowered flights and then nine powered flights" (French and Kahn 2014). Two days before his ninth flight, Yeager broke two ribs during a twilit horseback ride on Pancho's dude ranch. Unlike in the film, Yeager actually crashed into a closed gate that had been previously open but that he noticed too late. Subsequently, his close companion Jack Ridley sawed off a 10-inch portion of a broomstick, which Yeager used to close the cockpit door handle once inside the cockpit; this trick was accurately portrayed in the movie, although they performed it during the gap day between the accident and the historic flight, not on the day of the event (Yeager and Janos 1986, 163).

Although the six remaining Mercury astronauts commented that *The Right Stuff* "in most scenarios . . . was close to reality," they nevertheless "had big problems" with the movie's portrayal of Grissom, who died in a tragic fire within Apollo 1 spacecraft in 1967 (Buckbee and Schirra 2005, 85). Both the book and movie iterations of *The Right Stuff* incited renewed attention to the controversial ending of Grissom's Mercury mission. In his written account, Wolfe blatantly portrays the astronaut as panic-stricken and ultimately guilty of messing up (Wolfe 2008, 226–232); the film suggests the same conclusion, albeit with less firmness. Lowell Grissom, the late astronaut's youngest brother, strongly opined that *The Right Stuff* did not, in fact, get the story right. "He was actually there getting his readings," said Lowell in a 1999 interview, making note of Gus's handling of the post-flight checklist. "That, to me, doesn't lend itself to be panicky if you're doing something like that" (Dunn 1999).

Gordon Cooper went on record in the same spirit: "I believed him. I knew that if he had screwed up, Gus would have been the first to admit it" (Cooper and Henderson 2018). Wally Schirra labeled the film a "travesty" because it painted Grissom as cowardly and insecure. After sustaining a hand injury linked to detonating the hatch explosives on his own Sigma 7, Schirra asserted that Grissom "would've had a real welt" if he had accidentally hit the button: "I think that should be quick to put to rest, once and for all, that ridiculous story. Gus did not do that and a movie that would portray Gus as that kind of man should be banned" (Buckbee and Schirra 2005, 72). Despite Grissom's insistency that he was not at fault, *The Right Stuff* exaggerated the alleged disgraces that the Grissoms experienced after Liberty Bell 7 was lost to the sea. Grissom "admitted to being scared during lift-off, but the Hollywood film gave the impression of a panicky astronaut who completely lost control after splashdown, which is simply not true. Grissom, completely exonerated, was still one of NASA's and his country's favourite sons" (Burgess 2011, 313).

With a slightly more buoyant story to tell, the movie depicts Cooper as a swaggering, self-assured pilot with his off-the-cuff catchphrase, "Who's the best pilot you ever saw? You're lookin' at him!" In real life, Cooper has been described as "a mild-mannered but accomplished test pilot with a soft Oklahoma drawl" (Burgess 2011, 336). While the astronaut rejected the notion that he ever used the disposable line that Wolfe attributed to him, Cooper said, "It was something he picked up that I hinted to him I kind of said" (Burgess 2011). Tom Wolfe, on his part of the equation, gave his stamp of approval for the theatrical version of Cooper: "Having Dennis Quaid play Gordon Cooper was a good stroke. Cooper, as a pilot, didn't have much of a background. He was an OK military pilot. They chose him because he was so cool. He fell asleep on the launchpad. These holds would go on for hours. He also fell asleep during a spaceflight. He was an absolutely cool human being" (French and Kahn 2014).

Perhaps the most well-known Mercury personage, John Glenn figures prominently in the movie, which ended up overlapping with the real-life astronaut's presidential campaign in anticipation of the 1984 elections. Actor Ed Harris recalls how the American media threw the film a curveball right as it was about to be released: "There was a big picture of me on the cover of *Newsweek*: 'Can a Movie Help Make a President?' It gave a much different impression of what the movie was about" (French and Kahn 2014). For a film that highlights the circus-like mentality of the American media, the real influence of the press, ironically, may be partially to blame for the film's lackluster performance in the box office. Rather than focusing on the gritty behind-the-scenes story of the Mercury pilots, the media may have misrepresented the movie by focusing on celebrity, coloring it with political overtones affiliated with the Ohio senator's presidential bid. "The movie suffered from that approach," director Philip Kaufman affirmed. "I really wanted the film to be sold as about 'the right stuff': men in leather jackets, their connection to the cowboy thing. But somebody somewhere at the studio wanted to go back to that magazine-story approach. The movie should have been marketed as tougher and more mysterious than that magazine cover" (French and Kahn 2014).

Just as the contents of *The Right Stuff* were more substantial than the simple facade of a magazine, the lives of the Mercury Seven had more depth than the glossy "magazine-story approach" that chronicled their lives during the early 1960s. "As time went on, NASA made its program damned attractive to recruits," Yeager reflects. "They were in a tough spot, needing outstanding pilots who were little more than Spam in the can. . . . For signing up, a guy got a free expensive house, donated by a local realtor in Houston, and a cut of a lucrative contract with Time-Life. The glamor, splash, and money made it attractive to some pilots" (Yeager and Janos 1986, 341). When the Select Seven struck their initial deal with *Life*, the men were told that "this was the best way to ensure they would not be constantly hounded for information and personal stories by reporters while engaged in their training schedule. It would also shield their families from the media circus" (Burgess 2011, 281). Schirra recollected, "We were seven veteran test pilots but unsophisticated in many ways, not very well prepared for the sudden fame of being America's first astronauts" (Burgess 2016, 37). And their families were likewise unequipped for the journey into stardom (Thompson 2007, 204).

The movie attempts to depict such a "media circus," with paparazzi flooding the backyard of Annie Glenn and the other wives during their husbands' epic flights. Just as the male astronauts became a tight-knit group, these seven women banded together and formed what was known as the Astronaut Wives Club. "To be an astronaut wife meant tea with Jackie Kennedy, high-society galas, and instant celebrity. . . . To help with the astronomical pressures of publicity, the wives couldn't turn to their husbands, who were too busy training, or to NASA, which was too busy figuring out how to get their husbands to the Moon. So the wives turned to each other" (Koppel 2013). One of their shared tactics was to shield the house with drawn curtains, to prevent zealous photographers from nabbing candid shots of the interior. Only then could they endure the nationwide launch report, which was cheekily dubbed the "Death Watch" by one of the Astrowives. The seven ladies wielded influence in American culture, as citizens far and wide were faithfully observing how the wives dressed and carried themselves, conversed and parented, and especially how they expressed their patriotism (Koppel 2013).

In a similar vein, the movie shows the astronauts leveraging their newfound status to get what they wanted behind the scenes, such as retaining active control as pilots of the spacecraft (not just passive passengers). In a confrontation with NASA engineers, the Seven highlight the necessity of a positive message in the media, which the government was watching as it confidently funded the space program. The astronauts emphatically proclaim, "No bucks, no Buck Rogers!" America's spacemen often were depicted as "military men, death-defying test pilots, cowboys of the sky extending manifest destiny to the moon" (Tewksbury 2019). Slayton would later reflect, "It happened without us doing a damn thing. . . . We show up for a news conference . . . and now we're the bravest men in the country. Talk about crazy!" (Shepard et al. 1995, 70).

> At the time, all they had done was volunteer for some creepy tests and pose for some embarrassing pictures. But in the weeks and months to come, the seven would be praised as heroic cold warriors, the men who would help battle the evil Soviet empire and then claim the sky above for democracy. The aviators must have realized at some point that the instant fame had nothing to do with them directly. A nation of frightened citizens wanted desperately to latch on to some tangible evidence of America's technical determination and superiority. They wanted the astronauts to be supermen. (Thompson 2007, 203)

Astromania ensued. Novels, television shows, rock songs, dolls, and more solidified the galactic significance of America's space voyagers. Yet, "there was more than just a cold war need for personified symbols of America's superiority. The nation also sought a new type of male role model . . . who knew how to 'follow the rebellious imperative of the self'" (Thompson 2007, 204). The Mercury Seven were emblematic of the age in which they lived—on the cusp of historical transition, leading Americans into the great unknown of space travel, carrying on their shoulders much more than the weight of their personal vocations. "[T]he power of commercial competition for publicity and the pressure for political prestige in the space race also whetted an insatiable public appetite for this new kind of celebrity" (NASA 2017).

NASA's first group of space explorers carved out a place in U.S. history as remarkable pilots, prominent personalities, and admirable countrymen. *The Right Stuff* closes with a poignant image of the classic American pilot, summed up in the figure of Chuck Yeager, fading away into the pages of history with his own under-recognized glory—as the new national heroes soar into space, carried on by the vast promise of future glories. "In volunteering to entrust their lives to Mercury's spirit and Atlas's strength to blaze a trail for man into the empyrean, they chose to lead by following the opportunity that chance, circumstance, technology, and history had prepared for them. . . . All men must balance their hubris with their humility, but, as one of those aspiring astronauts said, 'How could anyone turn down a chance to be a part of something like this?'" (NASA 2017).

FURTHER READING

Armstrong, Dennis. 2007. "Mercury-Redstone 4 (19)." NASA. November 16, 2007. https://www.nasa.gov/mission_pages/mercury/missions/libertybell7.html

Benson, Sheila. 1983. "Our Original Film Review of 'The Right Stuff' Holds Clues for John Glenn's Path to Senator." *Los Angeles Times*, October 21, 1983. Republished December 8, 2016. https://www.latimes.com/entertainment/movies/la-et-mn-archives-the-right-stuff-review-john-glenn-20161208-story.html

Bond, Peter R. 1987. *Heroes in Space: From Gagarin to Challenger*. New York: Basil Blackwell.

Buckbee, Ed, and Wally Schirra. 2005. *The Real Space Cowboys*. Burlington, Canada: Apogee Books.

Burgess, Colin. 2011. *Selecting the Mercury Seven: The Search for America's First Astronauts*. New York: Springer.

Burgess, Colin. 2016. *Sigma 7: The Six Mercury Orbits of Walter M. Schirra, Jr*. New York: Springer.

Canby, Vincent. 1983. "Film: 'Right Stuff,' on Astronauts." *The New York Times*, October 21, 1983. https://www.nytimes.com/1983/10/21/movies/film-right-stuff-on-astronauts.html

Carney, Emily. 2016. "Space Myths Busted: Gus Grissom Didn't Blow the Hatch on Liberty Bell 7." January 10, 2016. https://space.nss.org/space-myths-busted-gus-grissom-didnt-blow-the-hatch-on-liberty-bell-7/

Clash, Jim. 2017. "Chuck Yeager, Who Tweets, Says Sam Shepard's 'Right Stuff' Character Was Right-On." *Forbes*, January 23, 2017. https://www.forbes.com/sites/jimclash/2017/01/23/chuck-yeager-who-tweets-says-sam-shepards-right-stuff-character-was-right-on/#5fdc83ff2874

Cooper, Gordon, and Bruce Henderson. 2018. *Leap of Faith: An Astronaut's Journey Into the Unknown*. New York: Open Road Media.

Dunbar, Brian. 2017. "Friendship 7." NASA, August 7, 2017. https://www.nasa.gov/mission_pages/mercury/missions/friendship7.html

Dunn, Marcia. 1999. "Liberty Bell 7 Yields Clues to Its Sinking." *Los Angeles Times*, December 12, 1999. articles.latimes.com/1999/dec/12/news/mn-43115

Ebert, Roger. 1983. "The Right Stuff." RogerEbert.com, October 21, 1983. https://www.rogerebert.com/reviews/the-right-stuff-1983

Ebert, Roger. 2002. "The Right Stuff." RogerEbert.com, March 16, 2002. https://www.rogerebert.com/reviews/great-movie-the-right-stuff-1983

French, Alex, and Howie Kahn. 2014. "An Oral History of 'The Right Stuff'." *Wired*, November 19, 2014. https://www.wired.com/2014/11/oral-history-of-right-stuff/

Furniss, Tim. 1983. *Manned Spaceflight Log*. London: Jane's Publishing Company, Ltd.

Garber, Steve, and Roger Launius. 2005. "A Brief History of NASA." NASA. July 25, 2005. https://history.nasa.gov/factsheet.htm

Hanser, Kathleen. 2015. "Mercury Primate Capsule and Ham the Astrochimp." Smithsonian National Air and Space Museum, November 10, 2015. https://airandspace.si.edu/stories/editorial/mercury-primate-capsule-and-ham-astrochimp

"A Happy End for Ham's First Flight." 1961. *Life*, February 10, 1961.

Harbaugh, Jennifer. 2017. "Biography of Wernher Von Braun." NASA, August 3, 2017. https://www.nasa.gov/centers/marshall/history/vonbraun/bio.html

JFK Library Foundation. 1961. "Address to Joint Session of Congress." May 25, 1961. https://www.jfklibrary.org/learn/about-jfk/historic-speeches/address-to-joint-session-of-congress-may-25-1961

Kaplan, Sarah. 2016. "John Glenn and the Courage of the Mercury Seven." *The Washington Post*, December 8, 2016. https://www.washingtonpost.com/news/speaking-of-science/wp/2016/12/08/john-glenn-and-the-courage-of-the-mercury-seven

Kauderer, Amiko. 2010. "Baikonur Cosmodrome." NASA, October 23, 2010. https://www.nasa.gov/mission_pages/station/structure/elements/baikonur.html

Koppel, Lily. 2013. *The Astronaut Wives Club*. New York: Grand Central Publishing. https://books.google.com/books/about/The_Astronaut_Wives_Club.html?id=Sj_M2jWuXvYC&

Loff, Sarah. 2017. "Explorer 1 Overview." NASA, August 3, 2017. https://www.nasa.gov/mission_pages/explorer/explorer-overview.html

Mandel, Paul. 1962. "'First Off It Was Quite a Day'." *Life*, March 2, 1962.

McCombs, Phil. 1987. "John Glenn at Liftoff Plus 25 Years." *The Washington Post*, February 20, 1987. https://www.washingtonpost.com/archive/lifestyle/1987/02/20/john-glenn-at-liftoff-plus-25-years/e201be00-f395-429b-b09b-e92b471806e6

NASA. 1961. "Mercury-Atlas 6 at a Glance." January 21, 1961. Archived from the original (PDF) May 25, 2009. https://web.archive.org/web/20090525123504/https://mira.hq.nasa.gov/history/ws/hdmshrc/all/main/DDD/16286.PDF

NASA. 1962. "Transcript of Presidential Meeting in the Cabinet Room of the White House—Topic: Supplemental appropriations for the National Aeronautics and Space Administration (NASA)." November 21, 1962. https://history.nasa.gov/JFK-Webbconv/pages/transcript.pdf

NASA. 2017. "Project Mercury Overview—Astronaut Selection." August 7, 2017. https://www.nasa.gov/mission_pages/mercury/missions/astronaut.html

Phillips, Stephen. 2019. "On the Front Lines of Space, Conservation." *Los Angeles Times*, February 17, 2019.

Porterfield, Bill. 1962. "7 Astronauts Honored in Texas-Size Parade." *Houston Chronicle*, July 4, 1962. Reprinted December 19, 2018. https://www.chron.com/local/history/medical-science/article/7-Astronauts-Honored-In-Texas-Size-Parade-11013097.php

Roberts, Roxanne. 1991. "Blastoff to the Past." *The Washington Post*, May 4, 1991. https://www.washingtonpost.com/archive/lifestyle/1991/05/04/blastoff-to-the-past/a361e495-61f0-4a34-8fbe-4d00d3bb961c/?noredirect=on&utm_term=.d0294b60a971

Sagdeev, Roald, and Susan Eisenhower. 2008. "United States-Soviet Space Cooperation during the Cold War." NASA, May 28, 2008. https://www.nasa.gov/50th/50th_magazine/coldWarCoOp.html

Shepard, Alan, Deke Slayton, Jay Barbree, and Howard Benedict. 1995. *Moon Shot: The Inside Story of America's Race to the Moon*. Atlanta, GA: Turner Publishing.

Shetterly, Margot Lee. 2016. *Hidden Figures: The American Dream and the Untold Story of the Black Women Who Helped Win the Space Race*. New York: William Morrow and Company.

Swenson, Loyd S., James M. Grimwood, and Charles C. Alexander. 1966. *This New Ocean: A History of Project Mercury*. Washington, DC: National Aeronautics and Space Administration.

Tewksbury, Drew. 2019. "In Sublime Orbit with 'NASA'." *Los Angeles Times*, February 17, 2019.

Thompson, Neal. 2007. *Light This Candle: The Life and Times of Alan Shepard*. Ebook. New York: Crown/Archetype.

Weber, Bruce. 2017. "Bill Dana, Comic Best Known for José Jiménez Character, Dies at 92." June 19, 2017. https://www.nytimes.com/2017/06/19/arts/television/bill-dana-comic-best-known-for-jose-jimenez-character-dies-at-92.html

Wilford, John Noble. 1983. "'The Right Stuff': From Space to the Screen." *The New York Times*, October 16, 1983. https://www.nytimes.com/1983/10/16/movies/the-right-stuff-from-space-to-the-screen.html

Wilford, John Noble. 1998. "Alan B. Shepard Jr. Is Dead at 74; First American to Travel in Space." *The New York Times*, July 23, 1998. https://archive.nytimes.com/www.nytimes.com/learning/general/onthisday/bday/1118.html

Wolfe, Tom. 2008. *The Right Stuff*. New York: Picador.

Yeager, Chuck, and Leo Janos. 1986. *Yeager: An Autobiography*. New York: Bantam Books.

Chapter 5

Mississippi Burning (1988)

Mississippi Burning is a 1988 film that tells the story of what happened to three young college men when they went south in the summer of 1964 as part of a civil rights movement to help African Americans register to vote. The story then doubles back to show how and why they met with their tragic end, and then it delivers the impact of all of that. The film was directed by Alan Parker (*Midnight Express*, *The Commitments*, *Bugsy Malone*) and distributed by MGM's Orion Pictures. Producers were Frederick Zollo and Robert F. Colesberry, and the film premiered on December 11, 1988. The film is based on a true June 1964 incident in Neshoba County, Mississippi. To add authenticity to the movie, most of it was actually shot in Mississippi near the towns of Jackson and Vicksburg, although a few scenes were shot in Alabama. Chris Gerolmo (*Over There*, *Citizen X*) wrote the screenplay, and his story followed the general outline of what actually happened, while adding in some dramatic elements and characters that formed the fictionalized parts of the film.

The film was shot on a budget of about $15 million and returned a domestic total gross of $34,603,943, finishing 34th in revenue rankings of 1988 films. Not only did the movie do well at the box office, but it also received strongly positive critical reviews, was nominated for seven Academy Awards, including Best Picture, and won the Oscar for Best Cinematography.

The story begins with the killing of the three young civil rights workers: James Chaney, Andrew Goodman, and Michael Schwerner (the real names of the actual slain trio). When word gets out they are missing and nothing is being done by local law enforcement to find them, the FBI sends two agents, Anderson (Gene Hackman) and Ward (Willem Dafoe), to find out what happened. The pair are not greeted with enthusiasm by the area's residents, nor by the local sheriff's department. Most of the whites in town do not seem to care what happened to three northern "agitators," and some say they are just off hiding somewhere and having a good laugh. The Blacks in the county are leery of helping the federal agents for fear of reprisal from the whites in town. Ward and Anderson can tell a cover-up is underway, but they cannot get anyone to talk or help them, with the lone exception of Mrs. Pell (Frances McDormand). She is a local beautician in Jessup County (the alias for the real Neshoba County), and she also happens to be married to the local deputy sheriff, Clayton Pell (Brad Dourif).

While they are both federal agents, Ward and Anderson come from different parts of the country and from different backgrounds. Ward is from the north and is a well-educated man who is liberal in politics and social issues. He is a proponent of the civil rights movement. Anderson, on the other hand, is a Southerner and former sheriff in a rural country like Jessup County. He believes in the law and sees the need for the FBI and its more sophisticated methods of crime detection. Even though he understands the mentality of these Southerners and knows how to get along with them, he is not a racist and does not believe in racist behavior and its violence. So on that issue, the two agents agree. But they disagree on how to solve the crime, and Anderson sees Ward's methods of bringing in additional agents as only inflaming the situation and creating more walls between people in town who might otherwise confide one on one with the agents.

Ward does not understand where the South's racism comes from. Anderson does, having grown up amid it and having a father who was racist. That dichotomy between the two is represented by this exchange when Anderson wonders why these three young civil rights workers risked their lives. "Some things are worth dying for," says Ward. "People down here think some things are worth killing for," Anderson replies.

Anderson also comes to believe that the would-be informers, who knew what happened that night to the missing men and who are helping cover it up, need to be pressured in ways that go outside of normal constitutional bounds. Ward disagrees strongly, but after brutal reprisals occur in town against a Black family and against Mrs. Pell, he gives in to Anderson's methods and looks the other way. Mrs. Pell and Anderson develop a relationship that leads her to do what she has wanted to do all along: tell them what happened, that her husband was involved, and even tell them where the bodies of the three young men are buried. The pressure Anderson and his handpicked agents apply to a few suspects pays off, and the culprits in the murder are brought to some semblance of justice in a federal court for civil rights violations where they receive sentences from 3 to 10 years.

Reflecting on the film and its stars, director Parker said he wanted to bring an engaging story of the horrific triple murder of Chaney, Goodman, and Schwerner to the big screen because he felt it needed to be told to a new generation of young people. As for casting its two main stars, Parker said, "Gene Hackman had been set and one meeting with Willem Dafoe in Los Angeles was enough for me to know that he would be the excellent buttoned-down 'Ward' to Hackman's renegade 'Anderson.' Their chemistry together was all important, and the forward energy of our narrative was firmly placed on their shoulders" (Parker n.d.).

Critical reaction to the film was good. Typical of the reviews it received was this one from *The Washington Post*: "*Mississippi Burning* speeds down the complicated, painful path of civil rights in search of a good thriller. Surprisingly, it finds it—right there among the shacks and chicken coops, on Main Street, Mississippi, and in those dark backwaters where the Klan takes care of its own and the bodies of three slain civil rights workers lie buried. But also submerged with those workers are complexity, subtlety, and artistic light-handedness" (Howe 1988). Having placed the entertainment value of the film against its historic value, Howe finds it's not a bad result; nevertheless, as he said, it is "the sort of Hollywood movie triumph that blacks could have used more of during—and since—that era" (Howe 1988).

HISTORICAL BACKGROUND

In June of 1964, three young civil rights workers, who joined the Freedom Summer movement in Mississippi to register African Americans to vote, disappeared. The men, two from New York and one from Mississippi, had been angered and deeply saddened by news of the burning of an African American church in Mississippi by members of the Ku Klux Klan, and they felt it was time to help. Upon arriving, the men eagerly turned their attention to their task, and one of them, New Yorker Andrew Goodman, seemed to enjoy his new surroundings. Arriving in the city of Meridian, he wrote to his parents the following: "This is a wonderful town and the weather is fine. I wish you were here. The people in this city are wonderful and our reception was very good. All my love, Andy" (Smith 2014).

Goodman, 20, dropped his postcard into the mail on June 21, 1964. He died later that day, along with his two coworkers James Chaney, 21, and Michael Schwerner, 24, on a country road outside the small town of Philadelphia, Mississippi.

When the three men were reported missing, President Lyndon Baines Johnson ordered the FBI to help local law enforcement agencies in finding out what happened. The bodies of Goodman, Chaney, and Schwerner were found some six weeks later. They had been buried in an earthen dam. Autopsies showed they had all been shot at close range and that Chaney, the Black man among them, had first been severely beaten. These so-called Freedom Summer murders formed the focus of *Mississippi Burning*. The three victims were part of the voter registration drive organized by the Congress of Racial Equality (CORE) that was launched to combat a seven-decades-old policy in several Southern states. The policy was intended to disenfranchise potential voters among the African American population. It was carried out at a time when Southern states were fighting for states' rights over federal laws concerning how they governed themselves regarding segregation of the races. So when FBI Director J. Edgar Hoover sent some 150 agents into the state to probe the sudden disappearance of the three civil rights workers, those federal lawmen were not welcomed by most local residents. The Freedom Summer events ignited several flashpoints in Mississippi, and the murders of Chaney, Goodman, and Schwerner in Neshoba County were the most violent and outrageous of all.

The year 1964 was a century removed from the bloody Civil War that had engulfed America, and one would think that this war's racial issues would have been settled by then. It was not so, and that was especially not so in the South that had been home to the institution of slavery. Although whites no longer could own Blacks and require forced labor, and although attitudes had changed among many enlightened Southerners, strong resistance to change was still the norm in much of the rural South. The mindset of many Southerners was that Blacks were inferior to whites and needed to know their place in society, which included being segregated in schools, restaurants, and movie theaters and literally relegated to the back of the bus. Those Blacks who dared to challenge this system could face grave danger from whites.

It is appropriate to note—since this book looks at history through the lens of film—that Blacks were not only relegated to the balconies in movie theaters, but they also had to enter those theaters via their own entrances. And in many theaters across much of the United States, those entrances were in the back in alleyways. In many theaters, they had to use Blacks-only bathrooms and buy their snacks from Blacks-only concession stands.

Dr. Mayme Agnew Clayton, founder of the Black American Cinema Society, recalls her own moviegoing experiences growing up: "When I was a child living in Van Buren, Arkansas, the only theatre that we could attend we could have changed. We had to go up a real steep stairs. And then you open up a little door for the black people, and you go into the theatre. I do remember one occasion when my sister put her foot over the balcony and her shoe fell down on the white people down the stairs, and she was scared to go get it. She went home crying" (Gordon 2006).

Not only were Blacks and whites segregated within movie theaters, but the films also had all-white casts, with the exception of some stereotyped, minor roles played by Black actors. Usually, they were housekeepers or servants or those whom white actors would treat in a subjugated manner or poke fun at.

In reflecting on this on-screen segregation—especially in films made for mixed audiences—writer and filmmaker Saundra Pearl Sharp, herself an African American—noted: "Raised in Ohio, the only brown skin star I saw on the big screen was Bambi; yes, the deer. Then in high school in the late

1950s, the problem was not segregation, but integration. The school ran feature films in segments during lunchtime everyday. But they weren't showing films that featured a suave and handsome Lorenzo Tucker, known as the black Valentino. So I thought that swooning over Rock Hudson and cheering on white cowboys was all there was" (Gordon 2006).

Sharp said it wasn't until she saw a film series presented by Dr. Clayton in 1977 that she became aware of movies that had been made for Black audiences by Black directors and starring Black actors. Two such directors were Oscar Micheaux and Spencer Williams. Micheaux was the first African American to produce a feature-length film, which was *The Homesteader* that was released in 1919. Williams wrote and directed *The Blood of Jesus*, an African American movie (known at the time as a "race film") that did very well at the box office among its targeted audience of Blacks. But Williams found greater fame in playing the role of Andy in the Black comedy duo of radio and television's *The Amos 'n' Andy Show* that first appeared in 1951. Clayton presented the film series, *Black Talkies on Parade*, that featured films made between 1910 and the early 1950s. Updated versions of the series are still being presented today by the Mayme A. Clayton Library and Museum in Culver City, California.

"I was transported into a whole other world," Sharp said. "There was one of my heroes, the esteemed, dignified Paul Robeson (best known among general audiences for his role in the film *Showboat*, in which he sang *Ol Man River*), playing a shady hustler. It was sort of the original *Hustle and Flow* film made by a black director, Oscar Micheaux 80 years ago. And was that a black cowboy on the screen?" (Gordon 2006).

Segregation was made possible by the so-called "Jim Crow" laws prevalent before the passage of the 1964 Civil Rights Act and subsequent Voting Rights Act. They appear to be named after a fictional Black song-and-dance man satirized by Thomas D. Rice, a white performer who appeared before in blackface in the early nineteenth century. The name Jim Crow took on a meaning of its own, used as a derisive term for African Americans.

The Jim Crow laws were a series of enactments by state and local governments that mandated and enforced segregation of the races across the South. They had been pushed into law by white state legislatures in the late nineteenth century and were ruled constitutional in 1896 by the U.S. Supreme Court in the landmark case known as *Plessy v. Ferguson*. That ruling established the Court's "separate but equal" doctrine. The acts were still being enforced as late as 1965, following a series of states-rights battles between Southern state governments and the federal government.

For most Blacks in America, what they had experienced and witnessed during the prior decade of the 1950s left them angry, frustrated, and wanting more for themselves, their families, friends, and loved ones. Those experiences and memories would light the fire of civil rights protests that spread throughout the South in the 1960s. And the successes of those marches and demonstrations—championed by the eloquence, charisma, and courage of Dr. Martin Luther King Jr.—would propel President Johnson into successfully pressing Congress for passage of the National Civil Rights Act of 1964 and then the Voting Rights Act of 1965. It is ironic and tragic that the very year that the Civil Rights Act was passed was the same year that James Chaney, Andrew Goodman, and Michael Schwerner would lose their lives on the back roads of Neshoba County, Mississippi. A reality in American history, especially regarding laws relating to civil rights, is that passing them is one thing; enforcing them and seeing the norms of behavior changed among resisters were something else. And the latter has taken a lot longer than it should have.

Just a few years prior to this triple murder, the political power in the South had maintained a "separate but equal" mantra for schools and public facilities as well as restaurants and public transportation. And, in many areas, those "whites only" and "Blacks only" signs and local laws were still present after the Civil Rights Act. The problem with the separate-but-equal mantra was these schools and facilities were more separate than equal, and what was needed was integration of Blacks and whites and equal access to all facilities. The civil rights movement was focused on achieving that, and this was what consumed much of Black America in the 1960s. The movement had its successes, such as the election of the first modern-era African American to the U.S. Senate (Republican Edward Brook from Massachusetts in 1966) and the first African American woman to Congress (Shirley Chisholm from New York in 1968), but it would also have its failures, such as the murder of three young civil rights workers in Mississippi in 1964 and the assassination of Rev. Martin Luther King in 1968.

One African American, Otis Sanford, would grow up in racist Mississippi, and as an adult, he went on to become the managing editor of one of the South's largest daily newspapers, the *Memphis Commercial Appeal*. He recalls what life was like for him and other Blacks in the 1960s and early 1970s: "The civil rights workers killed in the 60s. That kind of stuff was more of an issue for us," Sanford said. "It culminated in the death of Martin Luther King. That's when things began to change. The eyes of the world were trained on what was going on in the South. Finally, in 1969 and 1970 where I lived, they said we can no longer sustain this kind of separate-but-equal mentality. Let's not divide our public amenities any more. People started, slowly but surely, to come to their senses. There were injustices we all had to overcome to get somewhere; especially the ambitious ones, and I was ambitious" (Sanford 2017).

Dr. Marti Watson Garlett, a white educator and former television host on a children's show, recalled her coming-of-age experience over the issue of racial equality. Her family moved from Illinois to South Carolina in 1952 when she was in elementary school and when segregation was the law of the land in the South—white water fountains, Black water fountains; white restrooms, Black restrooms, the works. "I was an aware little girl, and I'd never seen anything like it," she said. "The impact of witnessing what I did in Greenville, while Jesse Jackson was growing up in the same city, during the height of Jim Crow, has lasted me all of my life. I became a civil rights activist at age 8 but had no idea of that yet" (Garlett 2018). In college, Garlett and a friend signed up to become one of the Mississippi Freedom Riders in the summer of 1964, the same summer that witnessed the murder of Goodman, Schwerner, and Chaney. Garlett's parents refused to let her participate, however, so her friend went and she stayed home. Reflecting on that, she said, "I still morally wrestle with that lost opportunity" (Garlett 2018).

An important incident happened in October, 1962, that would emerge as a landmark event in the fight for civil rights in the South and in Mississippi itself. That was the time that James Howard Meredith became the first African American to enroll at the University of Mississippi (Ole Miss). This move touched off a violent clash where two people died. The result was that President Kennedy ordered 31,000 National Guard troops to Ole Miss to quell the violence and restore order. Meredith would, in fact, enroll, and he became the first Black graduate of Ole Miss. He remained an icon in the civil rights movement to this day.

DEPICTION AND CULTURAL CONTEXT

Director Alan Parker has acknowledged that *Mississippi Burning* had to fit commercial Hollywood criteria for box-office drama and therefore contained fictionalized characters and elements of the events that took place in and around Philadelphia, Mississippi, in June, 1964. But the core story was a true one. "Our film cannot be the definitive film of the black civil rights struggle," Parker said. "Our heroes were still white and, in truth, the film would probably have never been made if they weren't. This is, perhaps, as much a sad reflection on present-day society as it is on the film industry. But with all its possible flaws and shortcomings, I hope that our film can provoke thought and kindle the debate allowing other films to be made, because the struggle against racism continues" (Parker n.d.).

Parker added that in the 1980s, there were not many film projects that offered insight into important events and eras of American history while offering terrific dramatic possibilities. When he received a copy of the script written by Gerolmo, he felt instantly that *Mississippi Burning* could be one of these few good films. Together with producer Colesberry, Parker traveled to Neshoba County to experience firsthand the places represented in the story. They stood on the exact spot where the three young men were shot down to gain a deeper understanding of what that night was like for them. He said they stood on that murder spot "for a few minutes in silence, realizing that true life and death are so much more important than the movies" (Parker n.d.).

By 1964, the time of the Mississippi Freedom Summer and the murders of civil rights workers Chaney, Goodman, and Schwerner, the Jim Crow laws and their attitudes still prevailed in places like Neshoba County, Mississippi. Lynchings and violence against Blacks were still occurring in the American South, especially targeted at those Blacks who dared to rebel against what was seen as their place in society. *Mississippi Burning* depicts that kind of hatred, humiliation, and racism not only in the killings of the three young men, who are never named, but also those who are clearly meant to represent Chaney, Goodman, and Schwerner. But the film also depicts the complicit—or at least uncaring—attitude among most white inhabitants of Neshoba County. That attitude was portrayed in the general lack of cooperation with the FBI agents—who were perceived as the real threat to established order—sent to find out what happened to the trio. As for the Black residents, most were too afraid of the whites to reveal what—if anything—they knew of the missing men.

In the film, the danger faced by whites and Blacks who did cooperate was portrayed in individual scenes. Even though some of the characters were fictionalized, they represented those who did face grave risks. In one scene, a young Black boy was chased from his home at night by angry white extremists who wanted to beat him for talking with the FBI. And in another scene, a woman with knowledge of the crimes is severely beaten.

The film depicts the plight of the three slain civil rights workers who are first arrested, allegedly for speeding, by sheriff's deputies in the fictionally named Jessup County. The men are jailed and then released, only to have their car forced off a country road by a band of hooded men as they were leaving the county. The men drag them from the car and shoot them. The gunshots are heard off-screen as the following text appears: *Mississippi, 1964*. The film then shifts to the arrival of two FBI agents, Anderson and Ward, who could not be from more different backgrounds yet who nevertheless share the same hatred of racism and unequal justice. Ward learned his ideals through his northern middle-class upbringing and his college education. He is a liberal and a devotee of President John F. Kennedy. But he is also a lawman who works strictly by the book in going after lawbreakers. Anderson, on the other hand, is from a Mississippi county similar to Jessup County where he served as the sheriff before joining the FBI. As noted by the director Parker earlier in this chapter, the real-life agent who headed the Neshoba County murder investigation was from Mississippi, so that is one of the factual parts of the film.

Anderson understands the people of this county and knows firsthand the history that made many the racists they are. He is not sympathetic with that racism, but he is aware of it from his own experience, and that knowledge makes him a good counterpart to Ward, who learns the context of the crime from Anderson. It is not always an easy partnership, however, as the two clash on how to pry information out of those who have it but will not share it. Eventually, Ward gives in to Anderson's rougher and more physical ways of getting people to talk.

In one telling exchange between the two agents after a young Black man is maimed by the Ku Klux Klan, Ward asks Anderson where all this racial hatred comes from. He then tells Ward a story.

> You know, when I was a little boy, there was an old Negro farmer who lived down the road from us by the name of Monroe. He bought himself a mule. Now my daddy hated that mule because his friends kept saying they saw Monroe out plowing with his new mule and Monroe was renting a new field. One morning that mule just showed up dead. They'd poisoned the water. . . . And one morning we were passing Monroe's place and it was empty. He'd just left, packed up and gone up north, I guess. And I looked over at my daddy's face, and I knew he'd done it ... And he knew I knew. He was ashamed, I guess. He looked at me and said, "If you ain't any better than a nigger, Son, then who are you better than?" (*Mississippi Burning* 1988)

That scene, and several others like it, suggests that what was driving racial bigotry in Southern counties like the fictional Jessup (a stand-in for the real Neshoba County) was not rational decision-making, nor an educated assessment of white-Black relations. As communication scholars often point out, facts do not always undergird the beliefs for many people. In place of facts are things like tradition, emotion, peer pressure, tenacity or stubbornness, the need to belong, and the need to believe. All of these motivators were at work in the Jessup counties of America during the time of the three murders that these FBI agents were trying to solve. Many who wanted to belong to the community realized that that meant buying into its history; its conventions; and its ways of believing, thinking, and acting. In other aspects of their lives, these people were honest, compassionate churchgoers who would help a neighbor without giving it a second thought. Some would carry that attitude over to Blacks, but most seemed to feel race relations were best handled by keeping Blacks separate and in their own place in the town's society.

That is what makes one character in the film particularly interesting, because although she wanted to fit into the town as much as anyone else, she could not sacrifice truth, nor sanction murder. So she went against the grain. That character is Mrs. Pell, the wife of Deputy Clinton Pell who was involved in the murders of the three young men. When she was called upon by Agent Anderson who sensed she knew more than she was saying and also felt she was ready to talk, she showed her courage. This was a woman who had led a modest and muted life in the town, one who evoked the persona of a bully's victim. In this case, the bully was her husband, who kept her in line with implicit and explicit threats. Mrs. Pell had spent much of her adult life biting her tongue.

As writer Jason Bailey observes about the actress playing Mrs. Pell, "[Frances] McDormand puts across the strength that's burning inside this woman. She shares most of her scenes with Gene Hackman, and reveals herself to be very much his equal, gifted at playing characters of quiet dignity and unexpected complexity" (Bailey 2017).

One can imagine there were many women and men like Mrs. Pell who lived in the South during these turbulent decades and who believed racial hatred, discrimination, and violence were wrong. They were just too scared to speak up. In cases like Mrs. Pell's, when they did, they were beaten down as she was when Deputy Pell used his fists on her. Yet she stood her ground and ultimately helped lead FBI agents to the truth about the deaths of the civil rights workers.

Along the way, members of the Klan firebomb the home of a Black family whose son has been talking to Anderson and Ward, and KKK members beat parishioners exiting a Black church service, in an effort to silence other possible witnesses from the Black community. At one point, Klansmen take a young Black witness into the woods and castrate him. Even Ward and Anderson are attacked in their motel room by Klan gunmen, and the two agents narrowly escape the shotgun blast.

It quickly becomes apparent that two agents are not enough to investigate this town that refuses to talk, so Ward puts out the call for help. Anderson tells him it is absolutely the wrong thing to do and that it would do more harm than good and likely "start a war." Nevertheless, the FBI sends a large company of agents to probe for answers about what happened to the three missing men. This adds to the tension in Jessup County, a place that does not welcome federal agents coming to press federal law on a region that believes in traditional states' rights and solving their own problems. Even the town's Mayor Tillman (played by R. Lee Ermey) insists this is a peaceful town. He tells the agents they are wasting their time and that the missing boys will turn up somewhere and have a good laugh about the problems they have caused. As it turns out, Tillman is representing those Southern lawmakers in sympathy with the Ku Klux Klan who have not taken part in the crimes themselves, but who do nothing to prevent them and look the other way when it comes to solving them.

Eventually, after the arrival of 100 Naval Reservists who were summoned to help find the bodies of the three young men, those bodies are found (in real life, it took 44 days for the bodies to be found). That answers the question of what happened to them, but still leaves the question of who actually killed them. Anderson and Ward are convinced that the sheriff's department is involved, but they disagree on how to proceed. Anderson wants to use physical force—or at least threats of it—to coax people out, but Ward objects strenuously, even to the point of pulling a gun on his partner. Still, after they receive word that Mrs. Pell is in the hospital suffering from the beating her husband gave her, Ward gives in to his partner's plan and methods. Anderson finds Deputy Pell in a barber's chair getting a shave. He steps in and takes over for the barber and, with a straight razor in hand, threatens

Pell. His purpose is to get Pell and his cohorts to make a mistake, which they do. Anderson recruits a few of the other agents to help him issue similar threats to other principal suspects. In one of the most elaborate schemes, a Black FBI agent (Badja Djola) kidnaps Mayor Tillman, takes him to an isolated cabin, tells him the story of a young Black man who was kidnapped by the Klan and castrated, and then threatens to do the same to him if he doesn't tell them what he knows. In another, Anderson and Ward pick up a local Klansman, Lester Cowens, question him to no avail, and then let him go. But before they do, they drive him around town for the locals to see and then drop him off in the Black section of town. That night, he is chased from his home by men he believes are Klansmen. They take him to the woods, tie him to a tree, and demand he tells them what he told the FBI. Out of nowhere, FBI agents arrive to "rescue" Lester, who doesn't realize until too late that it was agents in disguise who were posing as the Klansmen who attacked him. Both Mayor Tillman and Lester confess what they know about the murders, and the roof collapses for the killers. Six men are arrested, including Pell, Lester, and the sheriff. Five of them are convicted, but the sheriff is acquitted, and the mayor, although not charged, is found hanging in the basement of his home, overcome with guilt for standing by and letting the murders happen.

In the final scenes, Agent Anderson goes to see Mrs. Pell a final time. She is sweeping up a mess made in her home by angry townspeople. Anderson thanks her for her bravery and apologizes for endangering her. When asked what her plans are, she tells Anderson she is staying because there are still some good people left in town. Then, before departing Jessup County for good, Anderson and Ward attend a memorial service at the local cemetery where a Black female gospel singer is leading an interracial group in a promise to try and come together. But a later scene shows that the real Chaney's grave has been vandalized.

Star Gene Hackman said he became a voracious reader about the civil rights era as he went about preparing for *Mississippi Burning*, as well as the murderous incident itself. One of the books that he found helpful was *Three Lives for Mississippi* by William Bradford Hule, published in 1965. But Hackman said he found added insight from another book, one focused on a boy born in Philadelphia, Mississippi, which was the town near where the murders occurred. Further, Dupree was born in the summer of 1964 within a few days after the civil rights workers were killed. That book was *The Courting of Marcus Dupree*, and its eponymous figure would go on to become a major college football player. Hackman felt his story showed that new life had arisen from the ashes of the three slayings (Walker n.d.).

Costar Willem Dafoe, who played FBI agent Alan Ward, looked back on the film in 2018 and recalled that there was some controversy surrounding some of the aspects of the story that were fictionalized for dramatic effect. Still, he said most of the film was accurate and that it also conveyed other relevant points about the era. "One of the things I really loved about the movie is it showed that sometimes political decisions are made in the name of morality and they aren't truly about morality or justice. They're made for very personal, political reasons. For example, one of the reasons J. Edgar Hoover went after the Klan is that he was more scared of them than the civil rights workers. So that's really why he finally decided to enforce some of the laws" (Dafoe 2018). On a lighter note, Dafoe confided, "One of the things that is interesting is I did that movie basically to work with Gene Hackman. And it was a beautiful script, although I had what I thought was basically a flat role. But that was okay because Alan Parker was a great director and I just wanted to be around Hackman to do scenes with him. But as I started doing the movie, the role became very interesting and, in retrospect, it was a beautiful role" (Dafoe 2018). In the film, Ward is an idealistic northern liberal who finds himself marching with Blacks in the fictionally named Jessup County in protest of the three murders there, even though he is one of the chief agents investigating those killings.

The movie was generally greeted with enthusiasm by those promoting civil rights when it appeared in 1988, but several critics pointed out that—despite its good intentions—it got barely passing grades in historicity. It was also faulted for being a film in which white saviors ride into the South to free Blacks who seem unable to do it for themselves. Here is how the British newspaper *The Guardian* framed it:

> Though Mississippi Burning depicts many appalling (and broadly accurate) incidents of racist violence, its narrative focus is on what race politics meant to white people. Most of the black characters in the film are passive, with two notable exceptions. First, the screenplay puts a few aspirations to freedom in the mouth of an angelic young boy, perhaps hoping that the fact he is a child will render anything that sounds like a demand less threatening to any jittery white people in the audience. Second, it creates a flip side to the innocent black child: the scary black monster. Badass FBI Agent Monk (Badja Djola) kidnaps the town's racist mayor and threatens to chop his privates off with a razor blade if he doesn't give up the guilty men. (Von Tunzelmann 2013)

For its part, *The New York Times* wrote that, yes, the film did mix fact with fiction, but added this is common in historical films made in Hollywood. And, it concluded, the result was still beneficial. Writer Wayne King said in 1988, "Much of the power of 'Mississippi Burning' derives from the audience's knowledge that the essential horror it is witnessing onscreen really happened. Even the title of the movie is the actual F.B.I. code name for the investigation. Many details are drawn from life." An example is the following line from the film: "You didn't leave me nothin' but a n—," says James Chaney's killer in the film. "But at least I killed me a n—." That piece of dialogue comes directly from FBI files, the confession of one of the participants (King 1988).

In real life, 18 men were arrested for complicity in the murders of Goodman, Chaney, and Schwerner. U.S. Attorney General Robert F. Kennedy knew local white juries in Mississippi would not convict any of them for murder, so they were all tried for violations of a federal civil rights law from the post-reconstruction era in 1870. None of the seven convicted men drew sentences longer than six years. However, 41 years after the murder, one of the 18 arrested was at last indicted for overseeing the three murders of Goodman, Chaney, and Schwerner. That man was Edgar Ray Killen, who was 89 when he was arrested for murder in 2005. He was convicted of manslaughter and sentenced to 60 years in prison. The arrest came about as a result of intrepid research and reporting by Jerry Mitchell, an investigative reporter for Jackson's *The Clarion-Ledger* newspaper. Mitchell was honored with a Pulitzer Prize nomination for his intrepid reporting that brought Killen and other civil rights offenders to justice over the years.

Mitchell said he had been inspired in his reporting on Killen after seeing the movie *Mississippi Burning* in 1988. That may well be the most important real-life impact of this film.

Any company of screenwriters, director, and actors has a special and serious responsibility when depicting a story based on true events, especially when those events and that era were so divisive, violent, and important as the 1964 murders of Andrew Goodman, James Chaney, and Michael Schwerner. If the film were in the genre of a documentary, it would be somewhat easier to present a story that coincided exactly with the details of the real-life event. But when the film is meant to be an entertaining box-office success, the challenge becomes harder. Now the filmmakers must devise a way of staying close to the real events, real people, and real sequencing and provide a story that follows an engaging dramatic arc that entertains as well as informs. To a lot of filmgoers and critics alike, *Mississippi Burning* did that job and did it well. If fictional characters were introduced, if the sequencing of events was off, and even if a side plot was introduced (such as the tension between a northern and Southern FBI agent and the implied romantic feelings of Agent Anderson and Mrs. Pell), most will understand those were needed to keep the audience in their seats. Some filmgoers felt the charades pulled by Anderson's FBI cohorts toward the end of the movie bespoke more of Hollywood screenwriters than history, but it was a way to pump some action into an otherwise long and tedious investigation.

In sum, *Mississippi Burning* did an admirable job of what it was intended to do: depict the context and horror of the Freedom Summer killings. It did not do what it didn't intend to do: show the relative weight of contributions by Black and white Americans in overcoming violence and racial injustices in the American South of the 1960s. It gave Americans a narrative that helped shine a spotlight on an episode they either never heard of or perhaps had crammed into a dark corner of their memory.

One postscript on the depiction of these murders, and it says something about what resonates with much of white America: As the real-life search for Goodman, Chaney, and Schwerner was underway in Neshoba County, searchers actually pulled nine murdered bodies of African Americans out of the swamps. Yet the attention of the nation—as well as the film *Mississippi Burning*—was fixated only on the three slain civil rights workers, two of whom were white. Said Andrew Goodman's younger brother David, "It took two white kids to legitimize the tragedy of being murdered if you wanted to vote" (Smith 2014).

FURTHER READING

Bailey, Jason. n.d. "Yearly Box Office 1988." Box Office Mojo. Accessed August 20, 2018. https://www.boxofficemojo.com/yearly/chart/?yr=1988&p=.htm

Bailey, Jason. 2017. "Mississippi Burning: Watching." *The New York Times*, November 9, 2017. https://www.nytimes.com/watching/titles/mississippi-burning

Dafoe, Willem. 2018. "Discusses Mississippi Burning and the FBI." YTW Films Video, posted on YouTube on February 2, 2018. https://www.youtube.com/watch?v=DHAs6XoG2dU

Garlett, Marti Watson. 2018. Personal interview, January 12, 2018.

Gordon, Ed. 2006. "Memories of the Movies in Segregated America." NPR, March 1, 2006. https://www.npr.org/templates/story/story.php?storyId=5239254

Howe, Desson. 1988. "Mississippi Burning." *The Washington Post*, December 9, 1988. https://www.washingtonpost.com/wp-srv/style/longterm/movies/videos/mississippiburningrhowe_a0b1d2.htm

King, Wayne. 1988. "Film: Fact vs. Fiction in Mississippi." *The New York Times* Archives, December 4, 1988. https://www.nytimes.com/1988/12/04/movies/film-fact-vs-fiction-in-mississippi.html

Mississippi Burning. Alan Parker, director, Orion Pictures, 1988.

Parker, Alan. n.d. "The Making of Mississippi Burning." n.d. Accessed August 14, 2018. http://alanparker.com/film/mississippi-burning/making

Sanford, Otis. 2017. Personal interview, August 27, 2017.

Smith, Stephen. 2014. "'Mississippi Burning' Murders Resonate 50 Years Later." CBS News, June 20, 2014. https://www.cbsnews.com/news/mississippi-burning-murders-resonate-50-years-later/

Von Tunzelmann, Alex. 2013. "Reel History: Mississippi Burning: A Civil Rights Story of Good Intentions and Suspect Politics." *The Guardian*, April 10, 2013. https://www.theguardian.com/film/2013/apr/10/reel-history-mississippi-burning

Walker, Beverly. n.d. "Interview: Gene Hackman." *Film Comment*. Accessed April 12, 2021. https://www.filmcomment.com/article/interview-gene-hackman/

Chapter 6

JFK (1991)

As filmmaking goes, the 1991 film *JFK* hits the target with an excellent cast, script, photography, and editing. As history, the 189-minute movie is problematic and controversial. The film lays out a massive, alternative theory of how President John F. Kennedy was assassinated on November 22, 1963. It presents a multipronged conspiracy that differs from the official Warren Report version in which Lee Harvey Oswald was the lone assassin who gunned down the president from the sixth floor of the Texas School Book Depository overlooking Dealey Plaza in downtown Dallas. Actually, the film presents an amalgam of conspiracy theories that come to a head in a New Orleans courtroom. It is there that District Attorney Jim Garrison, played by Kevin Costner, prosecutes local businessman Clay Laverne Shaw (Tommy Lee Jones) for his alleged role in the assassination conspiracy. Garrison presents a very detailed hypothesis of the conspiracy plot but has very little to say about the defendant's personal involvement. In reality, the jury appeared to sense that, too, and returned a verdict of not guilty within the space of an hour.

JFK opened to generally good, albeit controversial, critical reviews. The positive reviews praised the filmmaking skills of Stone; the negative reviews said the film stretched the truth of history to a snapping point, presenting a complex theory that—albeit plausible—rested on fiction on too many points. One noted *New York Times* national security correspondent, George Lardner, wrote a scathing article on the film that was headlined "On the Set: Dallas in Wonderland" (Lardner 1991).

Despite the controversies, *JFK* was nominated for eight Academy Awards, including Best Picture and Best Director, but won only two for cinematography and editing. More importantly from a box office standpoint, it was one of those films that created a lot of buzz around America and got people talking, energizing many to go and see the film who might not otherwise have done so. The film cost an estimated $40 million to make, and it took a while for it to fill enough seats, but it eventually wound up grossing $70 million domestically and $205 million worldwide. Worldwide, it became the sixth highest-grossing film of 1991, finishing behind such movies as *Beauty and the Beast*, *Silence of the Lambs*, and *Terminator 2: Judgment Day*.

The film was directed by Oliver Stone, who was also coproducer and who had tackled another controversial American episode—the Vietnam War—in his critically acclaimed films *Platoon* (1986) and *Born on the Fourth of July* (1989). Written by Stone and Zachary Sklar, *JFK* was shot in both color and black and white to enhance its realism. Warner Brothers was the production company. The film was a partial adaptation of Jim Garrison's 1988 book, *On the Trail of the Assassins*, and Jim Marrs's 1989 book, *Crossfire*. Marrs, who died in 2017, was a newspaper reporter and author who wrote articles and books about the various conspiracy theories swirling around Kennedy's assassination and was a prominent figure in conspiracy belief circles.

The conspiracy that the film lays out was somewhat easier to follow for those moviegoers who had lived through the time of Kennedy's assassination and who were aware of the events and theories surrounding them. It begins with narrated, original film footage of President Dwight D. Eisenhower's farewell speech to the nation in 1961 as he was leaving the office. In that speech, Eisenhower warned about the danger of escalating the "military-industrial establishment" in America and making the industry too dependent on contracts for the production of weapons of war. That danger served as the underlying theme in Stone's interpretation of JFK's assassination. The Eisenhower footage is followed by clips summarizing Kennedy's short time in the White House that seem to focus on events Stone sees as significant building blocks to the president's assassination in Dallas. Key among those scenes are of the failed U.S.-directed Bay of Pigs invasion of Cuba in which many Cuban exiles, hoping to overthrow Fidel Castro, lost their lives and blamed a lack of air cover from the United States. The opening sequence concludes with shots heard on a blacked-out screen just as Kennedy's motorcade turns into Dealey Plaza in Dallas. Lyndon Johnson is then sworn in as president on the Love Field runway shortly after Kennedy was pronounced dead.

Jim Garrison, operating as district attorney in neighboring Louisiana, was a longtime Kennedy admirer; he plunges into sadness at the news of his death and becomes obsessed with the killing. That obsession is ratcheted up when he begins hearing differing accounts of the assassination and learns about potential New Orleans ties to a plausible plot behind the assassination. Various roadblocks force Garrison to shut down his investigation, but he reopens it in 1966 after the official Warren Commission Report on Kennedy's death is published. In that report, Garrison perceives a number of mistakes and other things that don't make sense to him. He and his staff begin a series of interviews with witnesses and associates (both real and alleged) of Lee Harvey Oswald (played by Gary Oldman) and Oswald's own killer, Jack Ruby (played by Brian Doyle Murray). Garrison is told it is impossible that Oswald or anyone else could have fired three accurate shots in under 6 seconds from a bolt-action rifle from the distance that Oswald allegedly did.

Garrison's team begins uncovering other facts involving stolen files from a former FBI agent's office in New Orleans. The ex-agent turned private detective was Guy Banister (played by Ed Asner) and had apparently met with Oswald a few times, and Garrison was told that the two had a common associate in a pilot, David Ferrie (played by Joe Pesci), who had worked with Oswald on a former anti-communist project in Cuba. Another interview produces an allegation that Oswald and Ferrie had discussed the Kennedy assassination together and with some Cubans. This witness, Willie O'Keefe (played by Kevin Bacon), was a male prostitute serving time in prison for soliciting. He told Garrison he had a romantic relationship with wealthy New Orleans businessman Clay Bertrand, later found to be local luminary Clay Shaw and whose name had surfaced in previous interviews as a person of interest in the alleged assassination plot. O'Keefe (who was a fictional composite character for the story) also said he had met Oswald and that Shaw knew Oswald too. When Shaw was interviewed by Garrison, however, he denied any knowledge of meeting Ferrie, O'Keefe, or Oswald. Nevertheless, Garrison charges Shaw with conspiring to murder President Kennedy.

Meanwhile, in Dallas, other statements are being made by witnesses in Dealey Plaza to Kennedy's shooting. One woman, Jean Hill, tells investigators something different from her official statements that had appeared in the Warren Report. She had heard more than three shots fired, four to six in fact, and that at least some of those shots came from the grassy knoll along the plaza. However, she claimed that Secret Service agents told her to say there were only three shots and that they came from the school book depository. Garrison believed her that the Warren Commission had changed her testimony for the report.

All this and other witness statements led Garrison to believe others were involved in the shooting, but that the Warren Commission had ignored statements and facts that would have cast doubts on its conclusion that Oswald was the single assassin. He finds himself believing Oswald when he said on television, "I'm a patsy just because I lived in the Soviet Union!"

His belief in a conspiracy is only strengthened when Garrison finds his office has been bugged and a high-level Washington operative identified only as "X" tells him the assassination was a product of a multifaceted, high-level government conspiracy that involved the CIA, FBI, Secret Service, the Mafia, Cuban-American exiles, and the military-industrial complex. He even implicates now-president Lyndon Johnson in the plot. This source, who was a retired top air force special operations colonel, tells Garrison the motive behind killing Kennedy was the fear his foreign policy was endangering the production of war weaponry, and that was threatening the profits of the companies relying on those government contracts. He says Kennedy was also seen as weak by top military officials, and they blamed him for the failed Bay of Pigs Invasion, which cost anti-Castro rebels their lives and cemented Fidel Castro as dictator of the island nation. The Mafia was also furious over that failed invasion because it cost them the huge revenues they had lost when their casinos were taken over by Castro's government. "X" then spins a detailed and complex account of how operatives from these conspirator forces constructed a way to have security minimized for Kennedy's trip to Dallas and to have himself sent to the South Pole so he couldn't help with that security and then to frame an unwitting Oswald to take the sole blame for the assassination.

As the film moves along, viewers can see Garrison becoming more and more obsessed with the conspiracy theory and bringing the guilty parties to justice, even though he has only one living New Orleans suspect to charge. At least one member of his prosecuting team leaves because he doubts Garrison's far-reaching conclusions about President Johnson being involved and as Garrison's wife (played by Sissy Spacek) finds him so obsessed with the conspiracy probe that he isn't leaving any time for her, their children, or home life.

Finally, the trial of Clay Shaw begins in January, 1969, more than five years after Kennedy's assassination. In the courtroom, Garrison plays the silent 8 mm home movie film shot by Abraham Zapruder of Kennedy passing through Dealey Plaza and being shot. Garrison has acquired the film, never before shown to the public (although still frames had been), from Time-Life Publishing Co. that owns it. Slowing the film down, Garrison tells the jury it shows up to six shots were fired by three different assassins in three different locations. He then lays out the massive conspiracy he believes to be true that involved both the federal government and large corporations dependent upon government contracts. He even ropes in President Johnson as a co-conspirator. Moreover, although Shaw is sitting at the defendant's table charged with conspiring to murder the president, Garrison seems more interested in charging everyone else other than Shaw, who he only mentions a couple times in his remarks to the jury.

In the end, the jury votes to acquit Shaw on all charges. Later the film shows one jury member saying the jury believed there was a conspiracy, but that Garrison had not made a case connecting Shaw to it. Garrison and his wife are shown leaving the courthouse as he vows to reporters that he will continue to bring the true assassins to justice. Then the end credits reveal that the House Select Committee on Assassinations did find, in 1987, that there was a fourth shot fired and that this meant others were involved in the assassination. It also notes that government's secret files on the assassination are still classified and will not be opened to the public until the year 2029. Since *JFK* was made seven years before Congress voted in 1998 to declassify those files in 2017 instead, no mention could be made of that development.

HISTORICAL BACKGROUND

No other event in American history has been scrutinized more than the assassination of President John F. Kennedy on November 23, 1963, and that debate over whether Oswald acted alone—or even if he was a shooter at all—continues to the present day. On the 50th anniversary of that assassination in 2013, the whole assassination was brought to the public consciousness yet again in numerous depictions, debates, and dramatizations across the media platforms. As journalist Michael Miller wrote in 2017, "Long before there was 'fake news,' there was the assassination of President John F. Kennedy and the scores of conspiracy theories it ignited. One author estimated that conspiracy theorists have accused '42 groups, 82 assassins, and 214 people by name of being involved in the assassination.' According to a 2013 poll, no less than 62 percent of Americans believe there was a broader plot beyond just Lee Harvey Oswald on the sixth floor overlooking Dealey Plaza in Dallas" (Miller 2017).

Part of the reason for the long-running, intense interest in this event was the great popularity of this young, charismatic President Kennedy and the heartfelt loss so many Americans felt when he was struck down so suddenly and so violently. Much of the reason for the debate over who did it and how it was done comes from the fact that it's not easy to believe the official account of a lone, crazed gunman shooting three bullets from a bolt-action rifle in 8.3 seconds (ostensibly 5.6 seconds between the two that struck Kennedy). And this was supposedly done from the sixth floor of a building, 80 yards away, as the motorcade was moving away from him below in the street. One bullet struck Kennedy in the back—and then zigzagged and hit front-seat passenger Texas Gov. John Connally twice. The fatal second bullet hit Kennedy in the head. In a country that has become used to the official story being the wrong one (as the exposure of Sen. Joseph McCarthy's lies showed in the 1950s and documents such as the Pentagon Papers and investigations such as Watergate showed in the 1970s), it is not hard for Americans to disbelieve the official account, especially if it seems far-fetched. According to the History Channel, "These criticisms took their toll. By the early 1970s, many Americans were skeptical of the [Warren] commission and its conclusions. The most serious threat . . . came from a new government investigation. In December 1978, the House Select Committee on Assassinations, after two years of work, concluded that Oswald was the assassin, but there was a conspiracy involving a second gunman. . . . Two acoustics experts said there was a 95 percent certainty that the [police radio] recording revealed that four shots had been fired. As a result, the House Select Committee came to the bizarre conclusion that there was a second shooter on the grassy knoll, and that shooter fired at the president but missed" (Gillon 2019).

During the first two years of his presidency, Kennedy's approval rating hovered around the 75 percent mark and dipped toward the second half of 1963 to about 60 percent, which was the time the United States began ordering more military advisers to Vietnam. Historian David Coleman put Kennedy's numbers into historical context this way: "President John F. Kennedy enjoyed very high public approval ratings compared with most modern presidents. His presidency was, of course, abbreviated, so his numbers weren't dragged down by the usual dip into the second term. Over the whole of his presidency, Kennedy averaged a 70.1 percent approval rating, comfortably the highest of any post-World War II president. By comparison, the average for all presidents between 1938 and 2012 is 54 percent" (Coleman n.d.).

This is not to say Kennedy was uniformly loved by all Americans, however. For all the tears and sadness exhibited on November 22, 1963, over his assassination, there were also the voices of those who disliked and distrusted this Massachusetts liberal—especially in the South—who found him weak on foreign policies and who blamed him for the failed Bay of Pigs invasion to oust Castro from Cuba. The film *JFK* portrays some of this in a scene with a lunchtime crowd in a bar and grill in New Orleans when the television news announces Kennedy's shooting. One man is heard yelling, "Die you b—!" And, in a flashback, the Ed Asner detective Guy Banister calls Kennedy a "b— president." Such comments were part of the national reaction to the assassination, although they were drowned out by the grief expressed by the majority of Americans.

Kennedy, the youngest president America had up to that time (Obama was two years younger when elected in 2008), embodied the charm, charisma, confidence, and idealism that resonated with many Americans and especially younger voters. He was also the first Catholic president, which didn't hurt him with most protestants and which undoubtedly helped him among Catholic voters. Many Americans seemed to envision Kennedy and his family as a kind of American royalty, and his White House was dubbed as Camelot. For the most part, however, he was not seen as elitist but instead as a genuine, caring person who cared about America and its ideals. Contributing to this was his personal history as a naval officer in World War II who heroically helped save his crew from his torpedo boat, *PT109*, that sank in the Pacific during a fight, and that he sustained an injury to his back that would last throughout his life. But a great deal of his appeal came from his good looks and his on-camera persona that seemed very real to those watching.

His inaugural address in January, 1961, has gone down as one of the most poignant and moving presidential speeches in history. The classic and most-often quoted line from that speech was, "And so, my fellow Americans, ask not what your country can do for you; ask what you can do for your country" (Kennedy 1961).

The speech reached out and included all Americans and challenged all citizens to aim for the highest standards. Historian Stacey Bredhoff wrote this about it: "The inaugural ceremony is a defining moment in a president's career, and no one knew this better than John F. Kennedy. . . . He wanted his address to be short and clear, devoid of any partisan rhetoric and focused on foreign policy" (Bredhoff 2001). Kennedy started putting the speech together about two months prior to the inauguration. Although he sought input from advisers and friends, the actual speech and its wording were his. Bredhoff said, "Aides recount that every sentence was worked, reworked and reduced. It was a meticulously crafted piece of oratory that dramatically announced a generational change in the White House and called on the nation to combat 'tyranny, poverty, disease, and war itself.' Kennedy wrote his thoughts in his nearly indecipherable longhand on a yellow legal pad. The climax of the speech and its most memorable phrase, 'Ask not what your country can do for you; ask what you can do for your country,' was honed down from a thought about sacrifice that Kennedy had long held in his mind and had expressed in various ways in campaign speeches" (Bredhoff 2001).

Kennedy had also pushed hard for civil rights, an impetus that culminated in the passage of the country's Civil Rights Act of 1964, not long after his death, and the Voting Rights Act of 1965. His growing commitment to equal rights boosted his popularity with those Americans who had suffered discrimination most of their lives.

Kennedy's popularity and admiration among Americans is important to understanding the depth of sadness that gripped the country when he was assassinated. Many also felt robbed of a chance to find out what happened, via the trial of Lee Harvey Oswald that never took place because of Oswald's own murder by Dallas strip club owner Jack Ruby, who died of cancer on January 3, 1967. Ruby had been convicted and sentenced to death for killing Oswald, but the Texas Court of Appeals had recently overturned that sentence, and Ruby was awaiting the second trial when he passed away.

Therefore, there was nothing but an official investigation by a government committee to tell the American people what had happened. That investigative group was established by President Lyndon Johnson a week following Kennedy's death, and Supreme Court Chief Justice Earl Warren was named to lead what came to be known as the Warren Commission. After a year's work, the commission concluded that there had been no conspiracy, neither domestic nor international, and that Oswald had acted alone in shooting and killing the president. Despite what seemed to be firm conclusions, later probes by investigators like Jim Garrison and his team as well as the House of Representatives Select Committee discussed earlier, the Warren

Commission report proved incapable of silencing critics and those believing the assassination was the work of conspiratorial partners.

The commission had focused on persons and events leading up to and including Kennedy's shooting and its immediate aftermath. Even what had happened after the shooting was in dispute. It is known that Dallas police arrested Oswald about an hour after the shooting. The suspect was an ex-Marine who had recently gotten a job working at the Texas School Book Depository Building. That much police had ascertained from those inside the building immediately after the shooting. Forty-five minutes later, when a veteran police officer, J.D. Tippit, questioned Oswald on the street near his Oak Cliff boarding house, police said the suspect pulled a pistol and shot and killed Tippit. Some witnesses were unable to identify Oswald as that shooter, however. Oswald was arrested a half hour later in a local theater. His arraignment came on November 23 when he was formally charged with murdering Kennedy and Tippit. On November 24, police took Oswald to the police headquarters basement to move him to a more secure jail cell. A throng of police, reporters, and cameramen had gathered there to see the transfer, but they weren't prepared for what happened net. Live television cameras rolled as Oswald was brought handcuffed into the room. It was then that Jack Ruby, who owned night clubs and had minor connections with organized crime figures, jumped out of the crowd, aimed his .38 caliber pistol at the helpless suspect, and fired once. That was enough, as Oswald fell to the floor. He was pronounced dead shortly thereafter. The murder was witnessed live by millions of Americans on television, and it was the first time that had ever happened. There was no doubt the killer was Ruby.

A few days after all this, the Warren Commission began trying to reconstruct how the assassination happened and who was involved and responsible. In addition to the chief justice, the commission included two U.S. senators (one of whom, Gerald Ford, would become president later), two members of the House of Representatives, a former president of the World Bank, and a former director of the CIA. For nearly a year, the commission conducted hundreds of interviews, read law enforcement and other judicial reports, and conducted a deep examination of the background and political affiliations of Lee Harvey Oswald. The group also conducted on-site observations in Dallas so they could get a visual of what happened and how. Finally, on September 24, 1964, the Warren Commission submitted its 888-page report to President Johnson. It concluded that Oswald was the sole assassin, that he fired three shots, two of which struck Kennedy and one of which wounded Texas Gov. John Connally, and that he fired them from a window overlooking Dealey Plaza on the sixth floor of the depository building. The report did not speculate on Oswald's reasons for killing Kennedy, although it did thoroughly describe his life, the time he spent in Russia, and his political affiliation as a Marxist-Leninist. The Warren report further chided the Secret Service for failing to provide adequate safety and security for President Kennedy in Dallas and also found that Jack Ruby had acted alone in murdering Oswald.

Rather than providing closure to the national debate over who killed Kennedy, the Warren report seemed to fuel the theories circulating over the assassination. If anything, it made many Americans even more convinced that the government had been involved and was trying hard to cover it up and provide a revision of history to the American public. Critics wondered how the report could square with the Zapruder film and how the first bullet that hit Kennedy could have zigzagged to strike Governor Connally twice, one in the wrist and in the leg. That was dubbed by disbelievers as the "magic bullet" that stopped in midair and then changed directions to lodge in the governor's knee. They also wondered how a former Marine, who had been graded medium in his marksmanship, could have fired two accurate shots from 80 yards at a target moving away from him within the span of under 6 seconds. There had to be more than three shots, they insisted, and there had to be a second shooter.

In 1998, the House Select Committee on Assassinations found credence to the fourth bullet theory. But if there was a fourth fired, where did it come from and who fired it? Nevertheless, the Warren Commission report remains the official report on the Kennedy assassination, and its reams of sources and documents are housed in the National Archives where much of it is public record. However, the autopsy report on President Kennedy is accessible only via permission from the Kennedy family or by future members of congressional or White House commissions who may be assigned to probe the shooting further.

Such sustained disagreement over such an emotional event for so many Americans provided good reasons for producers to ponder the making of *JFK*, especially with the then-recent publications of the books by Garrison and Marrs. And when the books and film came out, it was like an old wound was reopened and needed to be healed again in the American consciousness. Instead, *JFK* provoked more of the prolonged debate over who killed the most popular American president in history.

DEPICTION AND CULTURAL CONTEXT

In a *Chicago Tribune* article on *JFK*, writer Jon Margolis took director Oliver Stone to task for rewriting history concerning the Kennedy assassination. Among film critics and news commentators, Margolis was not alone, although his article was written in May 1991, seven months before the film opened in theaters. So his attack is focused more on the Jim Garrison book, *On the Trail of the Assassins*, on which the movie's script is partially based. To be fair, Margolis did interview at least one person who had read the script of the film, however. The Tribune article begins, "Whether or not it's a gift, artistic talent conveys a responsibility. Those who can sway emotions ought to know what they are talking about, less emotions be swayed toward foolishness" (Margolis 1991).

The polling group Gallup noted that between two-thirds and three-quarters of Americans believe there was a conspiracy behind John F. Kennedy's murder, a belief that is sustained by this movie. Gallup notes, "Support of the conspiracy theory remained high in 1992 (77 percent), and 1993 (75 percent) following the release of the popular Oliver Stone film *JFK* in 1991, which presented a variety of assassination conspiracy theories" (Carlson 2001a).

What *JFK* seems to present are connections, associations, and plausible conclusions arising from them. As for verified facts that lead to such conclusions, however, the ground is shaky in places. The film is more entertainment than confirmed history.

As one of several examples of inaccuracy in the Garrison book, Margolis points out the belief that Lyndon Johnson was also in on the conspiracy plot. To this suggestion, Margolis writes, "The suggestion that Johnson would stoop to murder, stupidly plotting with men he knew enough to distrust, is even less credible than Johnson at his worst. Then there is the matter of evidence. Not a scintilla of it links Johnson to Kennedy's assassination. Not that there's much to link anyone at all to it other than Lee Harvey Oswald" (Margolis 1991).

This and other critiques of director Stone are at least partially based on published interviews that Stone had given prior to the film's release. In these interviews, Stone disclosed his cynicism with the federal government. For example, the director had told a *Los Angeles Times* reporter in 1989, "The vandals are at the gate. We have a fascist security state running this country. [George] Orwell did happen. But it's so subtle that no one noticed" (Dutka 1989).

The characterization of Stone that has often been presented by various professional film critics shows that he is a master of filmmaking, but that he has views of history that are not corroborated enough by facts and that this is problematic because he likes to make films about historical people, issues, and events.

The late longtime *Washington Post* reporter George Lardner, who won a Pulitzer Prize for the investigation of his 21-year-old daughter's murder, wrote a lot about assassinations and national security issues. After the Garrison book and Stone's *JFK* came out, he researched and wrote several articles citing problems with the allegations and speculations within both the book and the film script. In an obituary on Lardner, who died in 2019, *The New York Times* wrote the following: "For many years he followed the threads emanating from President John F. Kennedy's assassination, from conspiracy theories to investigations. His expertise was clear in a 1991 article critical of the director Oliver Stone for 'chasing fiction,' as Mr. Lardner put it, in his film *JFK*. Based on his reading of the original script, Mr. Lardner wrote that 'there isn't space to list all the errors and absurdities, large and small'" (Sandomir 2019).

Lardner found two hollow building blocks for Garrison's conspiracy case in the book and script. First, one of the targeted suspects for Garrison was the New Orleans–based flight instructor and pilot David Ferrie, who is reported to have known Oswald and Clay Shaw. There were reports made to the FBI that Ferrie had hypnotized Oswald, that Oswald had been a member of Ferrie's Civil Air Patrol unit, and that Ferrie flew to Dallas to be the getaway pilot for Oswald after he killed Kennedy. However, Ferrie told investigators that he never met Oswald and that he was sitting in a federal courthouse in New Orleans during the time of Kennedy's assassination and for several hours afterward. Afterward, he did drive to Texas, but he didn't go to Dallas; he went to Houston and Galveston. Ferrie was questioned by the FBI, but agents released him, finding nothing linking him to an assassination conspiracy. He died on February 22, 1967, less than a week after a New Orleans newspaper announced Ferrie was a target of Garrison's probe. Although Garrison pronounced the cause of death as suicide, the New Orleans coroner pronounced it natural causes: a cerebral hemorrhage. He said Ferrie could only have killed himself by "worrying himself to death." Still, the original script and the film depicted Ferrie being attacked by two Cubans in his apartment the night before he was found dead, and the scene shows the attackers jerking his head back by the hair and shoving pills down his throat. But Lardner, who believes he was the last person to see Ferrie alive and who had interviewed him, said he was at Ferrie's apartment until 4 a.m. the day of his death and that Ferrie said he was fine and told him he thought Garrison's probe would be seen as a witch hunt. And finally, the coroner's report showed Ferrie's body had no marks of violence.

Second, the *JFK* script shows that, on February 24, 1963, Garrison found another man, Perry Russo (who was part of the composite character Willie O'Keefe in the film), who he felt was a star witness because he had known Ferrie. Russo revealed a damning incident involving Shaw. In Garrison's book, Russo agreed to be interviewed by Garrison, under sodium pentothol ("truth serum"), which produced hypnosis. This was not shown in the film, however. Under the effects of the drug, Russo recalled attending a September 1963 party in which a plot to kill Kennedy was discussed in hushed tones by Oswald, Ferrie, and Shaw, although the first name of "Clay" was first suggested to Russo by the hypnotist. Based on that interview, Garrison ordered Shaw to be arrested for conspiring to murder the president.

The trial that didn't begin for another 22 months didn't go as planned for Garrison's team as they were victims of damaging surprises. One of them was an accountant from New York named Charles I. Spiesel, who Garrison presented as a witness for the prosecution. Spiesel testified about a party he had attended in June 1963 in New Orleans at which he, along with Shaw and Ferrie, discussed how Kennedy might be killed. However, Shaw's defense team undercut Spiesel's testimony by showing that the witness had filed multimillion-dollar lawsuits against the New York City Police Department and others for hypnotizing and torturing him until he divulged information they were seeking. Overall, Russo claimed he had been tortured up to 60 different times over a period of years and that his captors had implanted crazy thoughts and ideas in his brain. Based on testimony and shaky evidence like that, the jury returned a verdict of acquittal in under an hour. However, neither the Spiesel character nor his testimony made it into the film *JFK*. Apparently, O'Keefe's testimony was a stand-in for that, although the information about the lawsuits and torturing was not used.

Lardner's research revealed other substantial errors of fact in the book and film script, and they all led him to conclude that "what that means is that Oliver Stone is chasing fiction. Garrison's investigation was a fraud" (Lardner 1991). Lardner adds that, when he tried to obtain an interview with Stone about *JFK*, Stone declined.

Once again, however, Lardner was working off his reading of the *JFK* script and not the film itself. There were, however, other researchers who found gaps between evidence and the film's portrayal of events. One was author Jeremy Bojczuk who found several problems, most notably the reliance on the testimony of three witnesses (Julia Ann Mercer, Beverly Oliver, and Jean Hill) to the assassination. Here is what he said about each:

Julia Ann Mercer (played by Jo Anderson): This woman described seeing a man who looked like Jack Ruby deliver a rifle to the grassy knoll area just before the assassination. However, in earlier statements, Mercer was not able to identify this delivery man. But she insisted in a later interview that the man was Ruby and that her earlier statement was wrong (Bojczuk 2014).

Beverly Oliver (played by Lolita Davidovich): This was a woman who was a singer at Jack Ruby's club who said Ruby had introduced her one night to Oswald. Bojczuk explains, however, there was no corroborating evidence of this implausible story of Ruby introducing Oswald as a CIA agent to a then-17-year-old Oliver. Further, Oliver told Garrison she was the same woman who was seen in several photos of Dealey Plaza who was filming Kennedy as he was shot. However, as Bojczuk states, "Unfortunately, the camera that Beverly Oliver claimed to have used did not become available until more than three years after the assassination" (Bojczuk 2014).

Jean Hill (played by Ellen McElduff): She was another witness to the assassination and was even closer to the motorcade than the woman Oliver claimed to be. In Stone's movie, she says she heard at least four, and as many as six, shots. She also claims she saw a man running away from the grassy knoll. She also told the Warren Commission this. But in her statement on November 22, 1963, she said she witnessed a man running toward the monument; not away from the fence. The problem, Bojczuk writes, is that "photographs show that the unidentified man who ran up the steps was merely a spectator. In the film [*JFK*], Jean Hill identifies the man as Jack Ruby, for which there is no credible corroboration." Further, there is no independent corroboration that Hill was, as she told Garrison, threatened by investigators to support the single-shooter hypothesis (Bojczuk 2014).

Bojczuk concludes, "She was not the only witness who claimed that the official investigators were unsympathetic to evidence that contradicted the lone-nut hypothesis. Perhaps Jean Hill's account was utilized to represent such experiences. The specific incidents she described do provide entertaining cinema, but they have no independent corroboration" (Bojczuk 2014).

Another question raised in a scene between Garrison and one of his team is whether Oswald even fired the rifle alleged to have been the murder weapon. The claim is that nitrate tests confirmed that Oswald hadn't fired it. It is true that the paraffin tests did show the presence of nitrates on Oswald's hands—just not his right cheek that he would have rested the weapon against. Nitrates exist in gunpowder residue, but they are also present in printer's ink, and Oswald had been handling a lot of printed material—mostly books—that morning. It is also true that, if the nitrate tests were accurate, the absence of that chemical on his cheek would have indicated he had not fired the rifle. But critics of that thinking explain that the spectrographic tests done by Dallas police were not too reliable then. As Bojczuk writes, "Not only does a positive result not necessarily indicate the presence of gunpowder residues, but a negative result may simply mean that the test is insufficiently incisive to detect the presence of such residues" (Bojczuk 2014).

The degree to which any of these specific critiques might detract from the believability or accuracy of *JFK* is a matter of debate itself, just like the debate over who killed John F. Kennedy. Some say what's the point in having eyewitnesses at all if—even though more than one report the same thing—you still need independent corroboration before believing their testimony. Others might say that changing one's statements is a red flag and a cause for disbelief.

One thing that does stand out in the film, however, is the amount of screen time—7 minutes—given to just one informant (played by Donald Sutherland) and to the massive government and industrial conspiracy theory he reeled off in detail to Garrison on a park bench, without naming anyone in the story. This is the man who called Garrison and asked him to fly to Washington to hear his story. In the film, he refuses to identify himself by name to Garrison ("You can call me X," he says), although Stone modeled him after the real-life L. Fletcher Prouty, a former air force colonel who led special operations for the Joint Chiefs of Staff under President Kennedy, resigned after Kennedy's death, and believed the president's assassination was a coup d'état perpetrated by the military and intelligence community. In the film, he identified himself to Garrison by his former occupation, a colonel who was in charge of special operations for the military, who had decades of experience in running covert operations for the government, and who knew the actors in the real-life saga he was describing. The conspiracy laid out by "X" boggles the mind, while still appealing to the skepticism that everyone has—at one time or another—that their government is lying to them. He believed the final straw was when Kennedy decided to back all troops out of Vietnam by 1965 and that the military-industrial complex would not allow that. So X concluded, "Like Caesar, he's surrounded by enemies, and something's underway. . . . It's a story as old as the crucifixion."

If one is going to use lack of independent corroboration as an argument against believability, "X's" story is unbelievable. Further, it is also highly unclear as to how this story helped Garrison in his prosecution of Clay Shaw. Nevertheless, judging just by the time Stone allotted to this scene—dramatic as it was—the director obviously thought that "X's" theory was important.

Looking back on *JFK* in 2016 on the 25th anniversary of its release, Stone seemed freer to discuss his feelings on it than when it initially premiered. "It was a hot potato from the get-go, much hotter than I thought," he said. "I didn't realize it would hit the central nerve core of the establishment . . . and it did take its toll. I think it's changed the perception of me forever. Many now dismiss me as a filmmaker who is political and only into conspiracy theories. It labeled me and I was staggered. I wish, in a way, it had just died off" (Tapley 2016). He told *Variety* magazine that he wanted to do a film where "you look at a crime, you accept the first version of it—the official version—then you look at it again" (Tapley 2016). An admirer of the Greek-French filmmaker Costas Garvas, Stone said *JFK* was meant to be in the same vein as Garvas's classic political thriller, *Z*, made in 1969, which presented the twisting trauma of an oppressive Greek government. Contrary to belief by some critics, Stone did pay a lot of attention to research and was often flipping from pages of script to the research supporting those depictions.

Stone said the film was closely adapted from the Garrison and Marr books on the assassination, but that he also had advice from L. Fletcher Prouty. As noted earlier, Prouty was former U.S. chief of special operations and the basis for the character "X." *The Guardian* newspaper is one of the media voices critiquing Stone for placing so much value on the character of "X." Yes, that character was based on Air Force Colonel Prouty, but Prouty was not part of Garrison's actual investigation, although he was used as a technical advisor for *JFK*. That was ill advised, wrote *The Guardian*, because "Prouty's credibility was demolished in a critique of *JFK* by investigative journalist Edward Jay Epstein. The mega-conspiracy to which X alludes is drawn from a famous spoof, 'The Report from Iron Mountain,' published in 1967 and revealed in 1972 by its author to have been a hoax" (Von Tunzelmann 2011).

When Stone was asked why he chose to keep Prouty's identity secret in *JFK*, he said: "Because the man does not want to be known, he doesn't want to be traced." Yet, as Michael Carlson pointed out in his obituary of Prouty in 2001, "his identity was common knowledge. It seemed that the shadowy image of the figure Sutherland portrayed, instructing the naive New Orleans attorney Jim Garrison (Kevin Costner), was one Prouty was proud to fit" (Carlson 2001b).

Stone said he knew he had a highly complex and detailed script, but that he decided to hold back on some of the details in the script given to Warner Brothers in hopes that that would prevent them from trying to simplify the story for viewers (Tapley 2016). Looking back on his interviews at the time of the film, he said he "may have been in defensive mode. I had never made a movie where I had to defend it six months later in the press. The media was very nasty and they'd set me up on shows. At some point I had quite a bit of research on my side, but I'd have to recall it all [on the spot] and I couldn't do that" (Tapley 2016).

Interviewed in 2016, Stone noted that Garrison's prosecution of Clay Shaw was the only "public record" of the Kennedy assassination. That, of course, would not count the Warren Commission report from the 1960s and—a year after Stone's interview with *Variety*—the public release of the assassination files held in the National Archives. "He (Garrison) rolled the ball into a public arena for the first time and allowed the Zapruder film to come out" (Tapley 2016).

Many believe Stone's film caused Congress to vote to release the sealed records early in 2017. Originally not scheduled for declassification until 2029, Congress passed the JFK Assassination Records Collection Act in 1992, ordering the National Archives to release the files by October 26, 2017. "Why?" asks writer Alissa Wilkinson. "One big reason: America saw a movie. Oliver Stone kicked up a huge furor in 1991 with the release of *JFK*" (Wilkinson 2017). Acknowledging that the film was based largely on some shaky facts and speculations, she said the film still did a masterful job in making the statement that the official account of the Kennedy assassination left a lot to be desired: there was obviously more to the story. She said Stone cemented those questions in viewers' minds. "Images and well-crafted stories are more powerful shapers of public imagination than official government accounts and documents, though," Wilkinson wrote. "And in the face of Stone's film, the assertions that Lee Harvey Oswald acted alone—and that there was no conspiracy—paled. The JFK Assassination Records Collection Act was passed partly in response" (Wilkinson 2017).

Cinematographer Robert Richardson, who won an Academy Award for the film, praised Stone, his filmmaking skill, and his research. "In my opinion," he said, "*JFK* retains its relevancy regarding political corruption, as well as corporate and personal corruption, which is sadly inherent in this narcissistic world" (Tapley 2016).

As for Costner, who was at the peak of his career with *Field of Dreams* and *Dances with Wolves*, he enjoyed heading up an all-star cast. "Everybody that came was ready to work, because Oliver is really on point," he said. "We needed to go and we had to be sharp all the way through. Every day was going to be a workload. There was nothing casual about that movie. . . . A movie like *JFK* has a chance for generations to visit it when they come of an age where that interests them, and the questions posed are really important. There was a shift in the country. We used to think . . . that people in power told you the truth, and it's not always the case. We've seen that for the last 60 years" (Tapley 2016).

FURTHER READING

Bojczuk, Jeremy. 2014. *22 November, 1963: A Brief Guide to the JFK Assassination.* London: Boxgrove Publishing.

Bredhoff, Stacey. 2001. *American Originals.* Seattle: The University of Washington Press.

Carlson, Darren K. 2001a. "Most Americans Believe Oswald Conspired with Others to Kill JFK." Gallup, April 11, 2001. https://news.gallup.com/poll/1813/most-americans-believe-oswald-conspired-others-kill-jfk.aspx

Carlson, Michael. 2001b. "L. Fletcher Prouty: US Officer Obsessed by the Conspiracy Theory of President Kennedy's Assassination." *The Guardian*, June 21, 2001. https://www.theguardian.com/news/2001/jun/22/guardianobituaries

Coleman, David. n.d. "JFK's Presidential Approval Ratings." https://historyinpieces.com/research/jfks-presidential-approval-ratings

Dutka, Elaine. 1989. "The Latest Exorcism of Oliver Stone." *Los Angeles Times*, December 17, 1989. https://www.latimes.com/archives/la-xpm-1989-12-17-ca-1635-story.html

Gillon, Steven M. 2019. "Why the Public Stopped Believing the Government about JFK's Murder." History.com, November 21, 2019. https://www.history.com/news/why-the-public-stopped-believing-the-government-about-jfks-murder

Kennedy, John F. 1961. "Inaugural Address." John F. Kennedy Presidential Library, January 20, 1961. https://www.jfklibrary.org/asset-viewer/archives/JFKPOF/034/JFKPOF-034-002

Lardner, George, Jr. 1991. "Dallas in Wonderland." *The Washington Post*, May 1991. https://www.washingtonpost.com/archive/opinions/1991/05/19/on-the-set-dallas-in-wonderland/0c958035-3fc2-48a7-a108-da0855c92a94/

Margolis, Jon. 1991. "JFK: Movie and Book Attempt to Rewrite History." *Chicago Tribune*, May 14, 1991. https://www.chicagotribune.com/news/ct-xpm-1991-05-14-9102120591-story.html

Miller, Michael E. 2017. "JFK Assassination Conspiracy Theories: The Grassy Knoll, Umbrella Man, LBJ, and Ted Cruz's Dad." *The Washington Post*, October 27, 2017. https://www.washingtonpost.com/news/retropolis/wp/2017/10/24/jfk-assassination-conspiracy-theories-the-grassy-knoll-umbrella-man-lbj-and-ted-cruzs-dad/

Sandomir, Richard. 2019. "George Lardner, 85, Dies." *The New York Times*, September 26, 2019. https://www.nytimes.com/2019/09/26/business/media/george-lardner-dead.html

Tapley, Kristopher. 2016. "Oliver Stone and Kevin Costner Look Back at the Legacy of 'JFK,' 25 Years Later." *Variety*, December 20, 2016. https://variety.com/2016/film/in-contention/jfk-25th-anniversary-oliver-stone-kevin-costner-1201945702/

Von Tunzelmann, Alex. 2011. "Reel History: Oliver Stone's JFK: A Basket Case for Conspiracy." *The Guardian*, April 28, 2011. https://www.theguardian.com/film/series/reelhistory

Wilkinson, Alissa. 2017. "How a 1991 Movie Resulted in JFK's Assassination Files Being Released in 2017." *VOX*, October 28, 2017. https://www.vox.com/culture/2017/10/26/16536122/oliver-stone-jfk-assassination-trump

Chapter 7

Thirteen Days (2000)

The 2000 film *Thirteen Days* shows how the real-life drama of the 1962 Cuban missile crisis played out and how close the whole episode took the world to the brink of nuclear war. The film follows the unfolding of the crisis, from the moment that an American spy plane captures photos of missiles being installed at various sites in Cuba. The news is brought to the attention of President John F. Kennedy (Bruce Greenwood) and his two most trusted assistants, Ken O'Donnell (Kevin Costner) and Attorney General Robert F. Kennedy (Stephen Culp), who is also the president's younger brother. Further study shows these are Russian missiles, and the threat of having them located 90 miles off the Florida Coast, at a time when Cold War tensions are at their highest between Russia and the United States, is deemed too great a risk to let stand.

President Kennedy calls in a larger team of advisers for their counsel on how to force Russia to dismantle these missiles without starting World War III in the process. Among the members of this Executive Team on National Security (EXCOMM) are Secretary of Defense Robert McNamara (Dylan Baker), Secretary of State Dean Rusk (Henry Stozier), National Security Adviser McGeorge Bundy (Frank Wood), Army General Maxwell Taylor (Bill Smitrovich), Air Force General Curtis LeMay (Kevin Conway), and former Secretary of Defense Dean Acheson (Len Cariou). A naval blockade is ordered to prevent Soviet ships from transporting any more missile parts into Cuba, a tense standoff at sea ensues while the EXCOMM team tries to decipher the real meaning of Russian communiques to the White House, and the action builds to a climactic one-on-one, make-or-break negotiating session between Robert F. Kennedy and Soviet Premier Anatoly Dobrinyn (Elya Baskin).

The film *Thirteen Days* was largely a detailed exhibition of how the analysis of communication discourse—as conveyed by both word and deed—is carried out by a nation's leaders when their relationship with another country teeters on the edge of nuclear war.

Roger Donaldson directed the film and David Self wrote the screenplay. Further writing credit was given to Ernest R. May and Philip D. Zelikow who wrote the book *The Kennedy Tapes: Inside the White House during the Cuban Missile Crisis* (1997), on which the film was based. Released by New Line Cinema, the film opened in the United States on Christmas Day to a disappointing weekend box office of $46,668. Shot on a budget estimated at $80 million, the film returned a U.S. gross of about $34.6 million and a cumulative worldwide gross of $66.6 million. Critical response to the film was generally favorable, and it was felt that the docudrama generally stayed within the dramatic parameters allowed for the genre. The film did not receive any award nominations.

The film's box office problem may have had something to do with the fact that the best-known actor in it did not play the lead character of John F. Kennedy but instead one of Kennedy's advisers. While Bruce Greenwood is an excellent actor, he is known by moviegoers more on sight as a character actor, while his name isn't that well known. Or it may have had to do with varying concerns over the accuracy of the story it was telling. *Entertainment Weekly* writer Bruce Fretts warned of that three days before the film's limited release: "The inevitable controversy over the film's accuracy, however, may be what really sinks 'Thirteen Days.' Rumblings have already begun about how O'Donnell's role has been overstated. He's portrayed as the Kennedys' closest confidant, while veep Lyndon Johnson, for one, is nowhere to be seen during the crisis. I don't know if this is true, and frankly, I don't give a damn. If I wanted a factual account, I'd read one of the many history books written about the incident. Still, such fact versus fiction quibbling damaged a number of recent docudramas" (Fretts 2000).

Nevertheless, the late famed film critic Roger Ebert said, "The movie's taut, flat style is appropriate for a story that is more about facts and speculation than about action. Kennedy and his advisers study high-altitude photos and intelligence reports and wonder if Khrushchev's word can be trusted. Everything depends on what they decide. The movie shows men in unknotted ties and shirt-sleeves, grasping coffee cups or whiskey glasses and trying to sound rational while they are at some level terrified. . . . Things might not have happened exactly like this, but it sure did feel like they did" (Ebert 2001).

As is depicted in the film, American spy planes flying over Cuba in October 1962 spotted the construction of what looked like missile sites belonging to the Soviet Union. As a Communist nation, Cuba had strong connections with the Soviet Union, and the threat of Russian missiles being installed just 90 miles from Florida during the height of the Cold War between America and the Soviet Union was too much for the United States to allow. President Kennedy was briefed on the situation on October 16, when the reconnaissance photos were validated. However, even though everyone at the White House agreed that the Russian missile installations could not be allowed to be completed, there was disagreement on how to prevent that. The generals believed the only sure way to shut down the construction was to attack them from the sky and then to have ground troops invade Cuba. However, the two Kennedys and O'Donnell foresaw negative consequences with that approach. They believed that, if Cuba were invaded, it would spur the Soviet Union into a relatively easy invasion of West Berlin (the entire city of Berlin was in the GDR-controlled East Germany). That, then, would likely lead to an all-out war between America and the Soviet Union, both countries having nuclear weaponry.

In the face of this dilemma, the president relies upon his younger brother Robert and close friend O'Donnell to develop a third option that will prevent the missiles from being finalized and still prevent a nuclear war with the Soviet Union. It is at this point that Kennedy's secretary of defense, Robert McNamara, comes up with the idea of a naval blockade of Cuba that would prevent any Soviet ships from bringing the supplies needed in Cuba to complete the missile installations. This blockade quickly becomes a reality and is also approved by the Organization of American States. Over the next two-week period, until October 28, the White House holds its breath and maneuvers very carefully to see whether the Russians would try to run the blockade.

The tag line of the film *Thirteen Days* summed up the severity of the situation and what might have happened if Kennedy's approach was wrong: "You'll never believe how close we came."

HISTORICAL BACKGROUND

Although Russia was an important ally to America in helping defeat the Germans in World War II, the country and the Soviet Union it headed became a communist threat to the United States from the time that war ended. So much so that some American military generals—most notably Gen. George S. Patton—wanted to take on Russia militarily right after the war against the Nazis ended and as America still had its troops in Europe.

The 1950s was a decade of saber rattling between Russia and the United States as fears arose in America that the Soviet Union would "bury" America. Since both countries possessed nuclear weapons, those fears of destruction intensified. Americans were taught, in schools and through various public service announcements on radio and television, how to "duck and cover" should a Russian nuclear attack occur. Fallout shelters were built and sold to families across the United States in the mistaken belief one could survive an all-out nuclear war. Schools held special programs for students on how to identify and report supposed communists in their midst.

In Congress, the House Un-American Activities Committee (HUAC) held hearings to identify communists who might have infiltrated American institutions and even the Hollywood movie industry. Politicians like Sen. Joseph McCarthy, the Republican junior senator from Wisconsin, were using these fears of communism to boost their own careers. All of these forces created a "Red Scare" throughout the United States, and it intensified as the 1960s began when Russia decided to "protect" the Soviet Union from Western democratic influences by erecting what came to be known as the "Iron Curtain." The most visible stretch of that border was the Berlin Wall, which went up in 1961, separating the Russian-controlled German Democratic Republic (GDR) from the rest of Berlin, Germany, and the rest of Western Europe. The Russians and their state of East Germany called the wall the "Anti-Fascist Protection Barrier." West Berliners came to call it "the monster."

One year after the Soviets constructed the Berlin Wall, conditions between Russia and the United States reached a boiling point. From October 16 to 28, 1962, the world teetered on the edge of World War III as America and Russia faced off over the issue of Russian missiles placed in Cuba, 90 miles from U.S. soil. This Caribbean island nation, a short boat ride from Florida, aligned with the Soviet Union when a young revolutionary named Fidel Castro took control in a 1959 coup and installed his leftist government. Prior to this, Cuba aligned more with the United States and, as depicted in films like *The Godfather Part II* (1974), welcomed American investments and tourists who flocked to its sunny capital of Havana. Many U.S. tourists compared the trip to a Las Vegas vacation, and it had been that way for some time. As the *Smithsonian* magazine wrote,

> Cuba's reputation as an exotic and permissive playground came to light in the 1920s when the country became a favorite destination for robber barons and bohemians. Scions like the Whitneys and the Biltmores, along with luminaries such as New York City Mayor Jimmy "Beau James" Walker, flocked to Cuba for winter bouts of gambling, horse racing, golfing and country clubbing. Sugar was Cuba's economic lifeline, but its tropical beauty—and tropical beauties—made American tourism a natural and flowing source of revenue. A 1956 issue of *Cabaret Quarterly*, a now-defunct tourism magazine, describes Havana as "a mistress of pleasure, the lush and opulent goddess of delights." By the 1950s, Cuba was playing host to celebrities like Ava Gardner, Frank Sinatra, and Ernest Hemingway. (Gelling 2007)

Although to tourists Cuba seemed like a hedonistic island paradise, the picture of daily life was much different for middle and lower classes among the native Cuban population. The benefits of a good economy were going to those at the top of the socioeconomic and political food chain, while most of the people below them were struggling just to get by. Therefore, in 1957, leftist revolutionary sentiment reached a boiling point and armed resistance to the right-wing government began filling the streets. Castro led the revolution and took over the reins of government in 1959. Castro's government severed ties with American investment and tourists, and Cuba instead turned to the Soviet Union for economic and military assistance. Thus began a long-term dependency on the Soviet Union. All this took place amid the Cold War between the United States and Russia that lasted until 1991 when European communism fell apart.

Among the many confrontations that took place between Russia and the United States (many along the infamous Berlin Wall that divided oppression from freedom), none was more serious than the Cuban Missile Crisis of 1962. That episode started when the pilot of an American U-2 spy plane, flying a routine high-altitude run over Cuba on October 14, photographed a Soviet SS-4 medium-range ballistic missile as it underwent ground installation. When that mission ended and the film was processed two days later, President Kennedy was told about it, and he immediately gathered his cadre of close advisors known as EXCOMM. Key among these advisors was Kennedy's brother, Robert, and Ken O'Donnell. They all realized the United States faced an unparalleled threat from the Soviet Union that would give the Russians the upper hand in the nuclear arms race, which was at the center of the Cold War. They read it correctly as a move by Soviet Premier Nikita Khrushchev to boost Russia's capability to strike America with nuclear missiles. To the hard-liners in the Russian government, it was a way of balancing the playing field after they felt threatened by the presence of U.S. nuclear missiles in nearby Turkey and Western Europe.

The advisors in EXCOMM also realized how hostile the relationship was between Cuba and America. The Castro revolution had made an enemy of the American government after Kennedy had supported a failed attempt by Cuban exiles to invade Cuba in 1961 (the failed Bay of Pigs invasion) to overthrow the dictator. To Castro and Khrushchev, the missile installations would help prevent any other such hostile efforts by the United States.

Faced with a problem that Kennedy and EXCOMM found totally unacceptable, they knew it was an extremely dangerous one. If they did not approach the removal of the missiles in the right way, they could create an even bigger problem and possibly push the two superpowers into a nuclear war. One option, favored by some in the team, was an all-out military invasion of Cuba to destroy the missiles. While such an invasion would undoubtedly prove successful, it would probably draw Russia into a larger war. A similar option—with similar consequences—was a bombing raid on the missile sites themselves. Kennedy, however, was reluctant to pursue those two options and decided to send naval ships to blockade Cuban ports of entry from receiving any more missiles or supplies from the Soviet Union. Concurrently, he demanded that the Soviets remove the missiles already there or else, and the "or else" translated to war with Russia.

President Kennedy went on national television on October 22 to tell the American people what was happening. In an address from the White House, he explained that American naval ships would be blockading Cuba and that, should any Soviet ships attempt to run the blockade, they would be fired upon and prevented from delivering additional military supplies. He framed the situation as an imminent threat to the national security of the United States. His announcement caused great concern and tension among Americans, already weary from the threat of the nuclear arms race between the United States and Russia.

Many Americans had already either constructed their own "fallout shelters" or seriously considered doing so. Although President Dwight D. Eisenhower did not encourage Americans to build these shelters, trying to assure them the United States could successfully negotiate its troubles with Russia without going to war, President Kennedy announced that shelters were a good idea. Even while Eisenhower was still in office, a 1957 report known as the *Gaither Report* supported the building of shelters that could help people survive a nuclear attack. Then Kennedy delivered a speech on October 6, 1961, promoting the shelters. He said, "We owe that kind of insurance to our families and to our country. . . . The time to start is now. In the coming months, I hope to let every citizen know what steps he can take without delay to protect his family in case of attack. I know you would not want to do less" ("A Look Back at America's Fallout Shelter Fatuation" 2010). The president then lobbied Congress to fund the construction of more than $100 million worth of public fallout shelters, and Congress allocated $169 million. Major media championed the need for fallout shelters, and the largest-circulating magazine of the time, *Life*, featured a cover story about fallout shelters with the headline, "The Drive for Mass Shelters: New Facts You Must Know About Fallout."

Kennedy's October 22, 1962, announcement of the Cuban missile crisis ratcheted up the worry, and word quickly spread through the population that nuclear war could be imminent. People began hoarding food and gas and thinking about where to go in case of an attack. Two days later, on October 24, a key moment in the unfolding blockade drama occurred when Russian ships approached the line of blockading U.S. ships off the coast of Cuba. This was a turning-point moment, as top naval officers debated whether to fire on the Soviet ships. They were finally ordered not to, and at the last minute, the supply ships began to reverse course, averting disaster.

However, the larger crisis remained. As far as Kennedy and EXCOMM knew, the missiles that had already been installed in Cuba were still there. To assess that situation further, another American reconnaissance airplane flew over Cuba to photograph what was happening at those missile sites. On October 27, that plane was shot down over Cuba, and the American pilot, Major Rudolf Anderson, was killed. He became the only American casualty of the entire Cuban missile crisis. Some EXCOMM members saw the downed reconnaissance plane as an act of war, and Kennedy ordered that an invasion force be readied and put on standby in Florida. The tension caused by Major Anderson's death and the downing of an American aircraft by a Russian missile was felt to be the last straw by top U.S. government officials. "I thought it was the last Saturday I would ever see," recalled Secretary of Defense Robert McNamara ("A Look Back at America's Fallout Shelter Fatuation" 2010). Top Russian leaders felt the same way, as similar memoirs showed.

President Kennedy's inner circle worked for nearly two weeks to divine the meaning of various forms of discourse from Russian Premier Nikita Khrushchev and then formulate and implement a negotiating strategy built upon those interpretations. It was not an academic exercise. The Oval Office discussions of messages received from the Russian Kremlin became a high-stakes, subjective exercise of trying to discern the meaning of words written, and actions taken, by Russian leaders. It was important to discern those meanings correctly, because an imminent nuclear war hung in the balance. In terms of communication that scholars use, Kennedy and his advisers were engaging in the process of "critical discourse analysis." They were trying to find the meaning behind the words and actions from the Russians, and it is often a subjective exercise and open to debate. In the hands of trained diplomats, however, it can prevent war. Such was the case when President Kennedy and his team were trying to divine the meaning behind communications and related actions coming from Soviet Premier Nikita Khrushchev and his team during the thirteen fateful days of October, 1962.

In doing so, Team Kennedy and Team Khrushchev found their way in a difficult situation to avoid an escalation that would lead to war. A key dilemma had presented itself when, on October 26, Kennedy received a message from Khrushchev offering to remove the missiles if the United States would promise not to invade Cuba. Then the president received a second message on the following day, which was troubling and clouded the situation. That message offered a different ultimatum: The United States must remove its missiles in Turkey in order for Russia to dismantle its missiles in Cuba. Kennedy's team wondered if the second message had actually been sent by Khrushchev or the hard-liners in his government who may have been attempting a coup.

The decision—and it proved an important one—was made to ignore the second message and agree to the first one: no invasion if the missiles were removed. Kennedy had no idea whether his strategy would work, and he was risking a lot when he dispatched Robert Kennedy to deliver his response to that first message to the Russian ambassador, Anatoly Dobrynin. However, there was to be another part to that response that his brother was to deliver, if necessary. If Russia would not agree to the no-invasion promise, then the United States would secretly promise Khrushchev that it would dismantle its Russian missiles in six months. That would only happen, however, if Russia kept that part of the deal confidential; any leak of it would negate that offer. In addition, Kennedy demanded a response within 24 hours or he would order military action against the Cuban missiles. To say it was a sleepless night for U.S. and Russian leaders would be an understatement. By the end of the next day, October 28, however, the deal was in place.

Following this crisis—indeed because of it—the U.S. and Russian governments established a direct hotline communication link between Moscow and Washington to help avert and defuse any such future episodes. Additionally, the two governments signed two treaties concerning the use of nuclear weapons. The Cold War continued until 1991, but the thaw that took place in October 1962 served as a guide to future negotiators that options other than war could work. On the downside, however, Russia simply turned its attention to developing and building long-range intercontinental ballistic missiles that could reach the United States from Russian-controlled launch sites.

DEPICTION AND CULTURAL CONTEXT

In a 2005 interview with the Associated Press, the man who piloted the American U-2 spy plane, and who took pictures of curious ground installations in Cuba on October 14, 1962, reflected on how that felt. Experts analyzed the photos the next day, and the photographs clearly showed the installations were new ballistic missile launch sites, aimed in the direction of the United States 90 miles away. It was the threat of a nuclear war the Kennedy administration could not ignore. However, to Major Richard Heyser, the U-2 pilot, it meant something even more personal that he dreaded. "I kind of felt like I was going to be looked at as the guy who started the whole thing," he said. "I wasn't anxious to have that reputation" (Kaczor 2005).

Eight days after Heyser took his pictures, President Kennedy announced to the nation that Russia had installed nuclear-tipped missiles in Cuba and that he was ordering a naval blockade of Cuban harbors to prevent additional supplies from entering and was demanding that the launch sites be dismantled. The tens of millions of Americans hearing that message understood the gravity of the crisis because they had been living with the fear of a nuclear missile attack by the Soviet Union for years. In recalling his own situation at the time—just one of many such vignettes occurring around America then—famed film critic Roger Ebert noted, "At the University of Illinois, I remember classes being suspended or ignored as we crowded around TV sets and the ships drew closer in the Atlantic. There was a real possibility that nuclear bombs might fall in the next hour. And then Walter Cronkite [CBS news anchor] had the good news: The Soviets had turned back. Secretary of State Dean Rusk famously said to McGeorge Bundy, 'We're eyeball to eyeball, and I think the other fellow just blinked'" (Lindsay 2012).

Turning to the film *Thirteen Days*, Ebert said it was an "intelligent new political thriller," but he added that the most argued question about the movie's depiction is who actually did blink first in the tense standoff between American and Russia. The film portrays leaders of both countries blinking and suggests that American military commanders, who were itching for a fight with Russia, backed off from hawkish stance. According to the film, when confronted by Kennedy, Defense Secretary Robert McNamara, and presidential advisor Ken O'Donnell, these commanders blinked. "This is a setup," O'Donnell warned Kennedy about what he perceived as Russian baiting in shooting down Major Rudolph Anderson's U-2 spy plane on October 27. "If fighting breaks out at a low level, say with Castro shooting at an American spy plane, the chiefs [joint chiefs of staff] will force us to start shooting."

In his review of the film, Ebert wondered if this interpretation might have had more to do with the requirements of screenwriting than actual historical fact. The essence of drama is conflict, and since the Russian antagonists are never actually seen on screen, perhaps the top American military commanders had to become the villains pushing America toward war. Ebert is one of the critics who wondered whether or not the film overstated O'Donnell's role in the crisis. Much of the movie is told through his eyes, yet actual tapes of White House conversations during this crisis period do not feature O'Donnell's voice much. Ebert theorized that O'Donnell's character was used as a fly on the wall in the Oval Office, an observer who could relay to the audience what was happening behind these closed doors. Certainly, he was—in real life—close friends with both John and Robert Kennedy, but the question remains as to how pivotal his role was in defusing the Cuban missile crisis (Ebert 2001).

As for the portrayal of President Kennedy himself, veteran character actor Bruce Greenwood drew uniform praise for his interpretation of the man. *San Francisco Chronicle* writer Mick LaSalle noted, "Greenwood is smaller than our historical image of the president, and he looks a bit older, but that seems appropriate. Kennedy, in fact, looked much older up close, and also more frail, according to people who knew him. Greenwood's appearance, as well as his quiet, sober demeanor, gives us the sense of seeing the private Kennedy. His performance is the best thing in the movie" (LaSalle 2001).

About the film itself, LaSalle was one of the many critics heaping praise on it. "*Thirteen Days* is fascinating in its depiction of presidential leadership in action. . . . [It] gives the lie to the notion that it's okay to have a knucklehead as president as long as he has intelligent advisors. The movie makes it clear that only Kennedy's intelligence—and his brave willingness to appear indecisive while he settled on a course of action—kept the world from disaster" (LaSalle 2001).

The film kept audiences glued to their seats despite knowing how the crisis ended. The film built suspense by showing viewers what they did not perhaps know, which was how close the world came to World War III and how a few leaders in the White House skillfully avoided such a disaster. *Thirteen Days* managed to turn a procedural story into a thriller, much as the film *Spotlight* would do years later in 2015 in showing how a dedicated team of reporters uncovered a huge child molestation scandal among priests in the Catholic Church. Both films did it by showing viewers what made these principal characters tick and how their own skill and dedication to doing the right thing led to successful outcomes. When it comes to presidential portrayals, *Thirteen Days* can be seen as a timeless classic that resonates today as the nation continues to debate whether a president's character or policies is more important. What this film shows is that policies do not develop in a vacuum, apart from the values, skill, and commitment of the nation's leader himself or herself. If *Thirteen Days* delivered only that lesson, it would be enough.

The discernable meaning, earlier referred to as critical discourse analysis, was clearly on display in this film. Such discourse comes in both word and action, and the latter is featured in the film when a top navy admiral ordered the commander of a U.S. naval vessel to fire a warning shot of phosphorous across the bow of a Russian ship nearing the blockade point in waters off Cuba. To the admiral, it was just an action designed to get the Russian captain's attention, but to the secretary of defense it was something else. "This is not a blockade. This is language. A new vocabulary, the likes of which the world has never seen. This is President Kennedy communicating with Secretary Khrushchev," McNamara says in the film. And the worry was that this action could be misinterpreted by the Russian leader and his team who were also engaged in critical discourse analysis as they judged the meaning of Kennedy's talk and actions.

It was not the first film to display this type of discourse analysis, however. An earlier film, the 1990 adaptation of Tom Clancy's *The Hunt for Red October*, featured a Hollywood portrayal of discourse analysis. When a White House task force was trying to understand why a state-of-the-art Russian submarine (*Red October*) seemed missing from the Russian fleet, Central Intelligence Agency advisor Jack Ryan was brought in for advice. Ryan was a voracious reader and historian who knew a great deal about the man commanding *Red October*, Marko Ramius. Based on that knowledge, he believed Ramius was defecting and offering his submarine up to the United States. Without that expert knowledge, Captain Ramius's tactics with his sub might have been inferred as a threat. As the story goes, Ryan was correct in his assessment. The same kind of critical discourse analysis runs through *Thirteen Days* and the only thing different is that this is a discussion of foreign policy and actions by leaders of an antagonistic country.

Oliver Daddow, a senior lecturer of international relations at Nottingham Trent University in England, is an expert in the roles that leaders and teams like Kennedy's EXCOMM, together with their ability to analyze discourse involving foreign leaders, play in diplomacy. Fifty years later, assessing the role of discourse analysis in diplomacy, Daddow wrote the following in an article for the London School of Economics and Political Science:

> Constructivist accounts ... rely on an implicit or sometimes explicit judgment about the kind of national identity elites [government leaders] want to express through foreign policy activity. Second, elites possess assumptions about the character of the international environment in which they operate. Third, elites tend to merge values and interests in foreign policy decisions, often in complex ways. The crux is that methods such as discourse analysis can tap directly into the identity-policy nexus that lies at the heart of a constructivist-interpretivist appreciation of foreign policy decision-making. ... In a discourse account, the agents are central to the analysis, with the agents' views on the relative importance of different inputs and influences on policy being the guide to what features in the final analysis. (Daddow 2015)

Looking back on the Cuban missile crisis four decades later, McNamara himself said, "I don't believe that today we as a nation, or we as a world, understand how close the world came to nuclear disaster ... and I don't believe we've learned the lessons from that. We wouldn't have survived the 13 days had JFK not shaped and directed the way in which his senior advisors confronted the crisis" ("13 Days: An Insider's Perspective" 2002).

What *Thirteen Days* shows more than anything else is what a false reading of Russian meaning and intentions might well have cost in October 1962. Instead of the peaceful result that Kennedy's team produced through their analysis of Russia's interrelated texts, the planet might have been looking at World War III. If the United States had invaded Cuba to forcibly remove the Russian nuclear missiles—and possibly even taken out Fidel Castro while they were there—Khrushchev and the Soviet Union would not have stood idly by. Their own dire warnings about what they would do if Kennedy were to authorize such an invasion were plain enough and left no ambiguity.

It is interesting to read how the film was perceived by a film critic for the newspaper that uncovered Watergate and whose reporting helped lead to the forced resignation of a later president, Richard M. Nixon. *The Washington Post*'s Desson Howe wrote in 2001, "For a drama that's obliged to turn on ideas, memos, nuances and situation room chatter (rather than the more visceral, visual fare of most Hollywood thrillers), *Thirteen Days* is tremendously effective" (Howe 2001). Howe notes that the film's screenplay is built upon an array of primary documents and tape recordings from the days of the crisis, coupled with interviews that key players gave and personal memoirs they wrote about the experience. "It feels like classic television theater at its best," Howe writes. "It's easy to accept these performers as the very real people they portray. What emerges in *Thirteen Days* isn't the menace of the Russians; it's the political pressure that informs every decision. Of course, the future of America is at stake. But so is the integrity of Kennedy's decision-making power" (Howe 2001).

The film explores how Kennedy and his EXCOMM team managed to find the elusive path between military overreaction and pacifism. That path is made even more difficult to discover given the political climate surrounding—and threatening to overgrow—it. The liberal John F. Kennedy must find a way to square his own beliefs with the differing leanings of his top military advisors like Air Force General Curtis LeMay and Army General Maxwell Taylor, as well as Secretary of State Dean Acheson. To them, a military strike to remove the missiles makes more sense. As LeMay tells Kennedy, "The big red dog is digging in our back yard, and we are justified in shooting him" (Howe 2001).

Eventually, Kennedy alone must make the decision. It was a classic depiction of what President Harry S. Truman had said during his term in office, "The buck stops here." Howe is another critic who felt the film exaggerated O'Donnell's role in the crisis, but called it justifiable in order to convey the larger story. As the critic concludes, "The Filmmakers retain the emotional truth of those terrifying days and the idea that the Cuban missile crisis was a war of public relations, which craftily worded communiques, stern exchanges before the United Nations and other public signals became the weapons of choice. This was about who would blink first" (Howe 2001).

The film does give a great deal of credit to O'Donnell, who was a close friend and special assistant to John and Robert Kennedy and one of the Kennedy inner circle dubbed the "Irish Mafia." According to the description of O'Donnell given by Kennedy press secretary Pierre Salinger in his 1966 biography, *With Kennedy*, the film's depiction of O'Donnell was right on target. Salinger wrote:

> It was my impression that O'Donnell had the greatest influence in shaping the President's most important decisions. He was able to set aside his own prejudices against individuals and his own ideological commitments (I would rate him a moderate Democrat) and appraise the alternatives with total objectivity. It was impossible to categorize O'Donnell, as White House observers did with other staff members, as either a "hawk" or a "dove" on foreign policy, or a Stevenson liberal or Truman conservative on civil rights. JFK gave extra weight to O'Donnell's opinions because he knew he had no personal cause to argue. Ken had only one criterion: Will this action help or hurt the President? And that, for O'Donnell, was another way of asking: Will it help or hurt the country? (Salinger 1966)

Salinger's comment notwithstanding, some other advisors, interviewed after President Kennedy's death, felt the importance the film attached to O'Donnell's role in the Cuban missile crisis was somewhat overstated.

Costner was one of a dozen producers listed on the film and, because of his star power, was largely responsible for getting a green light for the film from distributor New Line Cinema. It was Costner's second film about John F. Kennedy, as he had starred as New Orleans District Attorney Jim

Garrison in the 1991 Oliver Stone docudrama, *JFK*, about Kennedy's assassination and conspiracy theory swirling around it. When interviewed about bringing *Thirteen Days* to the screen after that attempt had stalled for two years, Costner said, "The studios look at what's out there and ask themselves if a film is commercially viable, what they think it'll do on paper. And this movie is practically an art film. An expensive art film. And that's a bad combination, at least from their point of view. But it's really a very easy movie to watch. It should be very popular" (Svetkey 2000).

Part of that statement proved true. The film is very easy to watch because it is so engaging. However, its popularity failed to match producers' expectations, as noted earlier in this chapter. The film grossed $66.6 million worldwide against an $80 million cost to make it.

Asked the obvious question of why he himself did not play the central figure of President Kennedy, given the magnitude of his stardom, he said he thought that would get in the way of verisimilitude of the film. "I just felt there were too many minefields for me to play John Kennedy," Costner said. "I mean, he's such an icon that you needed someone—I'm trying to think of the words here—someone with less flesh impact. Somebody that isn't as well known as I am. Because otherwise the question becomes, How well is Costner doing as Kennedy? It would become all about everything that I was doing wrong. You'd never get into Kennedy" (Svetkey 2000).

However, Costner was not able to avoid those minefields totally in playing what some see as a Kenny O'Donnell who was interpreted as having more influence in the crisis than he actually did. Costner talked about that too. "Well, the Kennedys are getting their due," he said. "They're the ones who are really golden in this story. And we checked in with Kevin O'Donnell [Kenny's son] to find out when he was getting uncomfortable with the script. He was really good about it. He told us when he thought we were going too far. But we had to create some dramatic leaps, and Kenny was the only character we had that could do that. This could turn out to be a hotbed over who's done what in history. But Kenny was our window into the story, and he has to bridge some scenes, bridge some conversations that maybe did or didn't happen. People may take issue with it, but, you know, this is a good movie. So I'm not concerned" (Svetkey 2000).

Given the worldwide cataclysmic disaster that could well have occurred over the Cuban missile crisis, one would think it would have been the focus of several Hollywood films since 1962. However, with the exception of *Thirteen Days*, no big-screen Hollywood film ever focused on this event. On television, there was a 1974 movie called *The Missiles of October*, but that was all. The only other TV movies made about the event were documentaries.

Costner described *Thirteen Days* as more of an "art film," because it is an astute psychological thriller rather than a blood-and-guts action picture. To be sure, there is action in the film, but that intensity comes from smart government leaders trying to think their way out of a nuclear war.

An interesting article appeared in *The New York Times*, 30 years after the missile crisis, but eight years before *Thirteen Days* hit the theaters. The story, by Robert Pear, revealed something about Kennedy's negotiations with Khrushchev that had not been publicly known before because the records had been kept classified until January 1992. As the movie pointed out, the secret part of the deal that sealed the agreement with Russia was that the United States would remove its missiles from Turkey six months later in exchange for Russia dismantling its missiles in Cuba. Kennedy did in fact promise not to invade Cuba if that was done, but apparently, that promise was not a 100 percent guarantee. Up until the declassification of these records in 1992, however, most historians assumed the no-invasion promise was ironclad. Pear wrote, "Records of the 1962 Cuban missile crisis, made publicly available today for the first time, suggest that the United States did not give Moscow any ironclad assurance that it would refrain from invading Cuba. The disclosure comes as a surprise to some historians of the crisis, who believed that the Soviet leader, Nikita S. Khrushchev, had agreed to remove Soviet intermediate-range ballistic missiles from Cuba after giving such an assurance" (Pear 1992).

Since *Thirteen Days* was written a few years after this disclosure, the film correctly pointed out that the turning point of the negotiations came with the private assurance over dismantling the U.S. missiles in Turkey, and not with the promise to refrain from invading Cuba. That was an important element, but not the deciding factor. Philip Brenner, a political science professor at American University, whose Freedom of Information request produced the series of declassified letters between Kennedy and Khrushchev, said, "Over the last 29 years, American presidents have lived up to what we thought was a commitment. In fact, these newly released letters show that the United States did not give Cuba an ironclad assurance that the U.S. would not invade" (Pear 1992).

Brenner also discovered the declassified letters showed that the Cuban missile crisis actually went on at least three weeks longer than the October 28 date that people think it ended. The professor said, "We tend to think the missile crisis ended on Oct. 28, 1962. In fact, the missile crisis went on, because the United States kept its forces at the highest state of alert until November 20, 1962. The source of that U.S. concern was IL-28 bombers given to Cuba by the Soviet Union. Until November 20, Fidel Castro refused to return the bombers to the Soviet Union because he asserted they were needed for the defense of Cuba. On that date, he announced that he would return them" (Pear 1992). What Kennedy had actually told Khrushchev was that his no-invasion pledge would be dependent upon the "good behavior" exhibited by Castro, thereby giving the United States what Brenner described as a "loophole" to determine what behavior was deemed as bad or too aggressive by the Cuban dictator (Pear 1992).

It is not unusual for docudramas to feature some original footage of events or surroundings of those events depicted in the film. *Thirteen Days* kept that to a minimum, but one of the original bits of film used was of the most famous television newsman of the day, Walter Cronkite, delivering the news of the naval blockade of Cuba and of the high stakes involved in the U.S.-Russia standoff taking place 90 miles from Key West, Florida. The Cronkite clip was significant not only because of his fame at the time but also because of the singular importance of one television network, CBS, in the 1960s.

This was the era before cable television, 24-hour news channels, and streaming, and it was a time when all of America got their television news from CBS, NBC, or ABC. Of those three networks, CBS had the most respected and watched news programs, and Cronkite was the "most trusted man in America," in survey after survey. Therefore, in times of crisis and national ambiguity, the nation usually turned to Cronkite. It was as if the large, often-dysfunctional family of America would gather in the living room and watch the man dubbed "Uncle Walter." It would be that way the year after the missile crisis when, on November 22, 1963, this same President Kennedy would be assassinated on the streets of Dallas. There was Cronkite, in midday shirt sleeves, a catch in his voice, and a latent tear in his eye, announcing to the nation they had just lost this charismatic president who also happened to call Cronkite his friend.

One misconception about the origin of *Thirteen Days* is that it came from Robert F. Kennedy's book of the same name. But the former attorney general's book, *Thirteen Days: A Memoir of the Cuban Missile Crisis*, was not the source of the film although it was probably used in the research for the film. The movie was instead based on *The Kennedy Tapes: Inside the White House during the Cuban Missile Crisis*, by Ernest R. May and Philip D. Zelikow. This book was published in 1997, some three decades after Robert Kennedy's book had appeared in 1969, a year after Robert Kennedy's assassination. May was a well-respected historian who specialized in international relations and who taught at Harvard for 55 years. He researched and wrote 14 books that focused on events such as the U.S. involvement in World War I and the reasons for France's fall during World War II.

A decade after *The Kennedy Tapes* was made into *Thirteen Days* for the screen, May would be called to serve on the 9/11 Commission. He died in 2009. His coauthor, Zelikow, is a famed historian who teaches at the University of Virginia and who was the executive director of the 9/11 Commission and counselor of the State Department under President George W. Bush. He has coauthored several other books including *Germany Unified and Europe Transformed*, with former Secretary of State Condoleezza Rice. Clearly both May and Zelikow knew the territory they wrote about in *The Kennedy Tapes*.

May concluded about the film, "There are two ways to look at this movie: as a thriller and as history. In my opinion, Thirteen Days succeeds as a thriller. Donaldson also directed Costner in *No Way Out*, which was a hard movie to walk out on. *Thirteen Days* is many times more gripping" (May 2001).

Writer Kevin Dennehy of the *Cape Cod Times* notes that one aspect of verisimilitude in the film: Some scenes from the film were shot in one of the destroyers actually used in the blockade: the destroyer *Joseph P. Kennedy* (DD850). That very ship was on loan from the Battleship Massachusetts Foundation in Fall River, Massachusetts. The destroyer's engines were not operational, however, and a tugboat was used to bring it from Fall River to Narragansett Bay for the shoot. To add even more realism, the crew shown on that ship comprised actual active duty navy and reservist sailors whose uniforms were those of the era (Dennehy 2001).

FURTHER READING

Daddow, Oliver. 2015. "Interpreting Foreign Policy through Discourse Analysis." London School of Economics and Political Science (Blog), October 27, 2015. https://blogs.lse.ac.uk/politicsandpolicy/interpreting-foreign-policy-through-discourse-analysis/

Dennehy, Kevin. 2001. "A Moment's Fame in 'Thirteen Days." *The Cape Cod Times*, January 13, 2001. https://www.capecodtimes.com/article/20010115/news01/301159999

Ebert, Roger. 2001. "Thirteen Days." RogerEbert.com, January 12, 2001. https://www.rogerebert.com/reviews/thirteen-days-2001

Fretts, Bruce. 2000. "Why Thirteen Days May Struggle at the Box Office." EW, December 22, 2000. https://ew.com/article/2000/12/22/why-thirteen-days-may-struggle-box-office/

Gelling, Natasha. 2007. "Before the Revolution." *Smithsonian Magazine*, July 31, 2007. https://www.smithsonianmag.com/history/before-the-revolution-159682020/

Howe, Desson. 2001. "A Thrilling Thirteen Days." *The Washington Post*, January 12, 2001. https://www.washingtonpost.com/archive/lifestyle/2001/01/12/a-thrilling-thirteen-days/59341940-1c79-4058-ab36-475318e7f529/

Kaczor, Bill. 2005. "U-2 Pilot's Cuba Photos Made History." Associated Press, October 9, 2005. https://www.starnewsonline.com/news/20051009/u-2-pilotrsquos-cuba-photos-made-history

LaSalle, Mick. 2001. "On the Edge of War: Thirteen Days Explores Adrenaline and Angst of Cuban Missile Crisis." *San Francisco Chronicle*, January 12, 2001. https://www.sfgate.com/movies/article/ON-THE-EDGE-OF-WAR-Thirteen-Days-explores-2965412.php

Lindsay, James. 2012. "TWE Remembers: "Eyeball to Eyeball and the Other Fellow Just Blinked." Council on Foreign Relations, October 24, 2012. https://www.cfr.org/blog/twe-remembers-eyeball-eyeball-and-other-fellow-just-blinked-cuban-missile-crisis-day-nine

"A Look Back at America's Fallout Shelter Fatuation." CBS News, October 7, 2010. https://www.cbsnews.com/news/a-look-back-at-americas-fallout-shelter-fatuation/

May, Ernest. 2001. "Thirteen Days in 145 Minutes." The American Prospect, November 7, 2001. https://prospect.org/features/thirteen-days-145-minutes/

Nelson, Michael. 2001. "'Thirteen Days' Doesn't Add Up." *The Chronicle of Higher Education*, February 2, 2001: B15.

Pear, Robert. 1992. "The Cuba Missile Crisis: Kennedy Left a Loophole." *The New York Times*, January 7, 1992. https://www.nytimes.com/1992/01/07/world/the-cuba-missile-crisis-kennedy-left-a-loophole.html

Salinger, Pierre. 1966. *With Kennedy*. New York: Avon Books.

Svetkey, Kevin. 2000. "Kevin Costner Talks about *Thirteen Days*." *Entertainment Weekly*, November 17, 2000. https://ew.com/article/2000/11/17/kevin-costner-talks-about-thirteen-days/

"13 Days: An Insider's Perspective." JFK Library and Museum, October 1, 2002. https://www.jfklibrary.org/events-and-awards/forums/past-forums/transcripts/13-days-an-insiders-perspective

Chapter 8

Mad Men (2007–2015)

It would be hard to find a major issue or event of the 1960s that did not find itself in the storyline of the breakthrough television series *Mad Men* that aired for 92 episodes over a seven-year period from July 19, 2007, to May 17, 2015. In addition to the series' focus on the world of Madison Avenue advertising, the series weaved in such events as the Vietnam War, the civil rights struggle, the assassinations of President John F. Kennedy, Martin Luther King Jr. and Robert F. Kennedy, Neil Armstrong setting foot on the moon, and many other real-life events of the 1960s.

Mad Men is the kind of TV series known as an "episodic anthology," meaning it is a continuing story with a repertoire cast that changes over time with the exception of the main characters, and some subplots are wrapped up in individual episodes. The series aired on the AMC cable television channel on a weekly basis. The series is named for what New York City's Madison Avenue advertising executives have been known for decades, although the term has fallen out of favor because it no longer represents the equal role that women play in ad agencies.

The series was created by Matthew Weiner, who had been a writer on the situation comedy, *Becker* (starring Ted Danson), and who was more widely known for his work as writer and executive producer for the blockbuster series, *The Sopranos* (starring James Gandolfini). The series is not only set in the 1960s; it is *about* the 1960s and its Zeitgeist where so many things were either changing in American culture or were on the verge of change. It takes place in the fictional ad agency of Sterling Cooper (which morphs into Sterling Cooper Draper Pryce) on Madison Avenue near the Time-Life Building. Thus, the characters of *Mad Men* all operate in the core of the Big Apple.

Several of the issues and attitudes of the 1960s appeared by the end of the very first episode of *Mad Men*, including racism, free love, sexual harassment, anti-Semitism, gender inequality, male domination, smoking, alcoholism, and creative genius.

The series' main character, ad executive Don Draper (Jon Hamm), sits smoking at his restaurant table and casually asks the aged bus boy (Henry Afro-Bradley), who is Black, what he smokes and why. Observing the exchange, the manager comes up and apologizes to Draper for the gall the waiter showed in speaking with him, a white man, in the first place. Like issues of racism that are present throughout the series, the first episode also shows Draper's freedom to pursue extramarital sexual relations, as he chats with a woman named Midge Daniels (Rosemary DeWitt), who is apparently his go-to mistress. The conversation takes place just after the married Draper and Midge finish with their business in bed. Draper's sexual liaisons highlight not only the free love ideals of the 1960s but also the freedom his wealth and gender provide him.

On the same day, Draper's new secretary Peggy Olson (Elisabeth Moss) is on her way up to the advertising floor and is alone with an elevator full of men. Her appearance is the object of jokes that three of them make in her presence. Once at her desk, Peggy is visited by the head secretary, Joan Holloway (Christina Hendricks), who says the men are all "looking for something between a mother and the waitress. And the rest of the time . . . a girl like you with those darling little ankles, I'd make them sing for it!" Her final advice, for the moment? "Always be a supplicant." Later, the workplace sexual harassment goes further when Peggy meets junior ad exec Pete Campbell (Vincent Kartheiser) for the first time; her appearance comes up again as Campbell suggests she should dress more modern, so she looks more like a woman. Then he asks, "Are you Amish?"

The episode moves on to feelings about Judaism. Realizing that their advertising firm, Sterling-Cooper, has just landed a department store client owned by a Jewish family, Draper's boss, Roger Sterling (John Slattery) asks him, "Have we ever hired any Jewish guys?" Draper responds, "Most of the Jewish guys work for the Jewish firms. Want me to run down to the deli and hire somebody?"

A few minutes later, Draper meets the Jewish department store heiress Rachel Menken Katz (Maggie Siff), and the two disagree about the advertising approach for her store. Draper gets defensive and chides her, "Miss, you are way out of line! I'm not going to let a woman talk to me like this. Done. This meeting is over."

The issues of gender roles and inequality extend beyond the workplace, as Betty Draper (January Jones), Don's wife, is first shown at her doctor's office where she is asking hesitantly for a prescription for the new birth control pill, Enovid. The doctor, of course, is male and tells Betty—even though she did not ask for the advice—that there is nothing wrong with a woman wanting protection. However, his reason surprises her as he says, "Even in modern times, easy women don't find husbands." He winds up with an insulting warning: "Don't think you have to go out and become the town pump to make it worthwhile."

Even a casual viewer cannot help but also notice the love affair everyone has with smoking (in fact, the first episode was called "Smoke Gets in Your Eyes"). It is as if smoking was used as a visual metaphor for all the obfuscating smoke everyone was blowing at each other during the 1960s. After all, they all worked in or around the advertising industry. Moreover, it is hard to find any one scene in the entire series in which alcohol is not freely consumed, often to the extreme.

From his very first presentation to clients, creative director Draper shows how the 1960s was an innovative turning point for Madison Avenue advertising. This, after all, was the decade where Volkswagen began unveiling its counterintuitive ads, poking fun at its chief negative aspect, the small size, of its popular Beetle, or bug.

The show adds and confronts more issues regularly seen in the 1960s, as the series progresses, although those mentioned stay with the series through all 92 episodes of its run. Ever so slowly, attitudes start to change for the better over the course of the series, just as they did during the actual decade. For some attitudes, such as sexism, the change is incremental and not always forward-moving, but there is improvement. In other cases, change occurs fast. For example, by the end of the first season, Draper promotes young Peggy Olson to the job of junior copywriter, the first woman copywriter ever at Sterling Cooper. Throughout the series, people experiment with what they want out of life. They make good choices and bad choices for themselves and others. They sometimes turn introspective and question their thinking and behavior. Women become more confident. Men start showing their vulnerability.

In the early years of the series, the ad execs are all male, although a few of the female secretaries start to burst the glass bubble over time. The two showcased female characters are Peggy and Joan. While Peggy rises through the ranks of copywriting, Joan rides up the ladder of success using professional talents she did not even know she had, instead of her intentional sexual allure. As the series starts, Joan is the chief secretary at the agency, in charge of all the other secretaries, and she assigns them the bosses they are to work for. Although she does not carry the official title, she is also the de facto office manager who puts out the daily fires occurring in the workplace and sometimes beyond it. Her organizational and leadership abilities are too great for the male bosses at Sterling Cooper to overlook, and they ultimately set aside the fact she is a woman in favor of gaining the benefit of her talents and dedication. She rises to become an account executive and then a partner (albeit a minor one) before deciding to leave the agency and start her own company. Her journey toward self-fulfillment represents what many women were waking up to in this decade.

The *Mad Men* saga begins in 1960, while the story concludes in 1970, and each episode tracks the changing lives of the characters that mirror the evolution of the era. The show was one of the most watched and critically acclaimed television series ever produced. Altogether, *Mad Men* took home 16 Emmys and 5 Golden Globes. Additionally, it was the first time a basic cable television series had ever won the Emmy for Outstanding Drama Series. And it won it not just once, but each of its first four years from 2007 to 2011. Many critics have called it one of the best TV series of all time. Alex Witchel of *The New York Times* was one such critic. In June 2008, when the series was set to start its second season, Witchel wrote that HBO's and Showtime's loss (both rejected airing it) proved AMC's success story (along with *Breaking Bad*, which ran from 2008 to 2013). *Mad Men* was, as Witchel noted, AMC's first scripted drama series (Witchel 2008).

About Weiner, he writes, "He is both ultimate authority and divine messenger, some peculiar hybrid of God and Edith Head [the late famous Hollywood costume designer.] 'I do not feel any guilt about saying that the show comes from my mind, and that I'm a control freak,' he told me. 'I love being surrounded by perfectionists, and part of the problem of perfectionism is you are always failing'" (Witchel 2008).

Why did Weiner rate such all-encompassing attention? Because he not just created the series; he wrote the pilot also, and he worked with a team of four other writers in writing each episode. Not only that, but Weiner was also the series' executive producer, therefore the one who got the money to do those episodes, which averaged out to $2.3 million per episode (Witchel 2008). Weiner's control extended all the way to approving the hiring of each actor on the show and signing off on hairstyles, costumes, and props used in the episodes. Witchel also explained that Weiner directed some of the episodes, but usually held what he called a "tone meeting" when someone else of his choosing was directing. Says Witchel, "He essentially performs the entire show himself so it's perfectly clear how he wants it done" (Witchel 2008).

The kind of consistency in ratings that *Mad Men* enjoyed, over a period as long as seven years, is extremely difficult to achieve. Exciting audiences with something new and well done is one thing; continuing to do it for so long seems nearly impossible. The series also had strong appeal in England, although viewers there—and many in the United States as well—were new to the concept of the "episodic anthology." Said a critic for London's newspaper, *The Telegraph*: "If you miss what went unsaid in one episode, you won't understand what's being said in a later one. For fans, of course, this is part of the appeal. Equipped with these scattered and subtle clues, we're constantly trying to work out what's going on inside the characters' heads. Better still, just like real people, the characters are constantly trying to work that out, too. The overall result was as beautifully acted, written and filmed as ever—and as quietly enjoyable" (Walton 2009).

HISTORICAL BACKGROUND

Advertising in the decade of the 1960s grew out of changes produced by the 1950s, the immediate postwar decade for America when consumers began thinking again of shopping for things they wanted and not just what they needed. The war years had been a time of belt-tightening and rationing of many different kinds of consumer goods because the food and raw materials for everything for auto tires and women's hosiery were needed by the fighting forces in Europe and the Pacific. By 1950, however, all that was history, and America was looking to go on a buying spree. That opened the door for more advertising business and, as the money flowed to the ad agencies, so did the best talent the industry had to offer.

The 1950s and 1960s were also the years when the broadcast media—and particularly television—lured Americans into a nightly love affair with a greater variety of shows and celebrities. Ad agencies were needed by both clients wanting to showcase their goods and services on these shows, and they provided regular sponsors for the shows. The name of the sponsor was often featured as part of the show's name. For example, there was the Hallmark Hall of Fame, the Colgate Comedy Hour, the Texaco Star Theater, and the Kraft Television Theater. Sponsors' products were frequently featured in the shows. The popular animated show, *The Flintstones*, would sometimes feature Barney and Fred smoking a Winston. The FBI series would feature Ford cars being driven by the special agents. And Fibber McGee and Molly would feature in-story commercials for Johnson's Wax. The list was endless.

Newspapers and magazines were also in their heyday as advertising media, and ad agencies worked hard to impress both print and broadcast media—as well as advertising clients—with their abilities to produce ad campaigns that would draw in more readers and viewers for both the client and the media operation.

During the 1950s, advertising expenditures grew to the highest levels in history. J. Walter Thompson Co., one of the biggest of the New York agencies, increased its billings from $78 million in 1945 to $172 million in 1955 and to $250 million by the 1960s. Across the entire ad industry, the 1950s produced gross annual advertising billings of $6 billion in 1960, up from $1.3 billion just a decade earlier ("History: 1950s" 2003).

While the first few years of the 1950s were focused on manufacturers catching up with pent-up demand for household appliances, cars, and other consumer goods, the last six or seven years of the decade saw the surge of consumerism wherein Americans headed out to buy those new products. Helping convince consumers that they needed these goods, ad agencies touted the "new and improved" nature of these products and took advantage of new social science research in marketing them. Demographic targeting techniques were improved, and agencies hired motivational researchers and adopted generational marketing techniques to segment consumers into similar types or groups, each with a different advertising spin.

The 1950s and 1960s witnessed the growing up of the baby boomers (those born between 1945 and 1964), and that new influx of children and teenagers increased the demand for more housing, which was being built in the newly developed suburbs. By the 1960s, one out of every three families in America lived in suburbia, the epicenter of the new middle-class nation. The new homes fueled the need for new appliances, more cars to get to work in the cities, and more products like lawn mowers and snow blowers to take care of the property. All that meant the need for more advertising to showcase those products, differentiate them, and lure consumers into buying them.

Ground zero for much of the advertising ingenuity that created that felt need for more consumer goods was the advertising agency. And the biggest of those were headquartered in New York City. Agencies like J. Walter Thompson, Young & Rubicam, and McCann-Erickson led the way with their creative advertising genius, which would only grow more in the 1960s. Interestingly, McCann-Erickson was featured by name in the series, *Mad Men*, first as a respected competitor and then as the company that bought out and subsumed Sterling Cooper Draper Pryce.

Advertising pitches and campaigns were often built around the traditional family values of the 1950s. Print and broadcast advertising featured the ideal family life featuring a dad, hard at work at the office to support his family, a lovely and modern housewife taking care of the home and kids, and the eager youngsters awaiting the dad's arrival home for the family dinner. Generational marketing kicked in when, for the first time, children and teens became targets for advertisers luring the youngsters to buy everything from breakfast cereal to Cracker Jacks and records and phonographs to play them on.

By the middle of the 1950s, cars became the most heavily advertising products in America. To an ad agency, getting a car company was the sign it had entered the big leagues on Madison Avenue. Research shows that auto buyers saw the car as an extension of their own personality, and that was especially so with men. That was a huge reason the Chevrolet Corvette and the mid-1960s Ford Mustang became so immensely popular among male car buyers.

The main magazine of the advertising industry, *Ad Age*, noted that product demonstration became big in ads of the 1950s, and that would continue into the 1960s. "Demonstrations also helped differentiate similar packaged goods," the magazine noted. "Notable televised product demonstrations included Band-Aid brand's 'Super-Stick' bandages clinging to an egg in boiling water and Remington shaver's peach test in which a razor was used to shave peach fuzz" ("History: 1950s" 2003). The magazine continues, "Other memorable TV spots included the stop-motion antics of Speedy

Alka-Seltzer; Old Gold's dancing cigarette boxes; Dinah Shore singing 'See the USA in Your Chevrolet'; newsman John Cameron Swayze's matter-of-fact delivery of 'It takes a licking and keeps on ticking' for Timex watches; and animated depictions of the Ajax Pixies, Tony the Tiger, Hamm's beer bear and beer mavens Bert and Harry Piel. Picked as one of the best ads of the 20th century by *Advertising Age*, the TV spot for Anacin pain reliever showed how beneficial and intrusive TV advertising could be" ("History: 1950s" 2003). Ad agencies created slogans to summarize the theme of their products and used repetition of key points, conveyed in different ways, to position their product in the consumer's mind.

Advertising clients, working through their agencies, often exerted a great deal of control over programming and content within those programs. Single-sponsor shows were the norm in the 1950s, but all of this would diminish and dissolve in the fact of the infamous quiz show scandals of the 1950s. One of the most popular of the quiz shows was *The $64,000 Question*, sponsored by Revlon cosmetics. That sponsor kept tight control over the winners and losers on the show, and when that became known, the public felt betrayed. That would happen again in 1958 with an even more popular quiz show called *Twenty-One*, when the popular and charismatic contestant Charles VanDoren revealed he had been fed the questions and answers in advance of his many appearances on the show. That scandal produced congressional hearings into television, and by 1959, the networks had reasserted control over their programs and their content.

This was all a prelude to the America of the 1960s and to the advertising engine, which would react to those changes in ways meant to be profitable for their clients. For one thing, the changes allowed agencies to think beyond traditional family values and emboldened them to pitch ideas and frames that were more consistent with the questioning of those values in this new and very different decade.

Although the decade of the 1960s is most often remembered in America as the era of civil rights and the Vietnam War (1955–1975), those who lived it realized there were more day-to-day changes taking effect in American culture than these two overarching issues. Sometimes they were part of the introspection and fallout caused by those two issues. These were manifest in the many challenges to traditional values and the resistance by many in power to those challenges. The changes that occurred in society at large were presaged by changes occurring on its college campuses. Changes on college campuses indicated changing attitudes toward gender equality, the role of the state in controlling the lives of individual people, and the impact of the rebellion against traditional ideas on sex, which young people often perceived as prudery.

For example, at the start of the decade, many colleges restricted the movement of women on campus, locking those female students who lived on campus (as most were required to do) into their single-sex dorms at night;

meanwhile, male students were allowed to leave freely after nightly study halls. However, by the end of the decade, colleges equalized dorm rules for male and female students, and some colleges built the first coed dormitories. Attitudes toward public displays of affection (PDA) and sex changed through the decade as well, a change also evident on college campuses. Many state universities had PDA rules, and such behavior was to be kept at a minimum, especially around dorms. However, as the decade wore on, students openly held "love-ins" and "Gentle Thursdays" on campus, freely displaying love and affection in public.

These changes and others signaled different thinking in America that challenged the traditional ideas concerning gender equality, power, free expression, and individual choice. The Free Speech Movement (FSM) had begun on a college campus (the University of California at Berkeley), and it quickly spread throughout the land. Although much thinking did change, other ideas did not see much movement—at least not in heartland states.

Three recurring images seem to populate nearly every scene in every episode of this series: smoking, drinking, and sexual harassment of women. Historian Nancy Fraser wrote that white male supremacy in America had an economic foundation to it, ensuring that the moneymakers would be men. She wrote that the values challenged by young Americans and the new left included the inequality among genders and the disparate treatment of women in general. She said the 1960s "shattered" the "relative calm of the 'Golden Age'" of 1950s capitalism. "In an extraordinary international explosion, radical youth took to the streets, at first to oppose racial segregation in the U.S. and Vietnam War. Soon after, they therefore began to question core features of capitalist modernity that social democracy had heretofore naturalized: materialism, consumerism, and the 'achievement ethic'; bureaucracy, corporatism, and social control; sexual repression, sexism, and heteronormativity. Breaking through the normalized political routines of the previous era, new social actors formed new social movements, with second-wave feminism among the most visionary" (Fraser 2013).

It would take a while, however, for these radical youth protests to penetrate the bastions of capitalism like the huge advertising agencies on Manhattan's Madison Avenue, but it did start to happen during the sixties, and *Mad Men* does a nice job depicting its evolution from 1960 to 1970. The term "socialist feminism" has been used to describe what was taking place in the push for gender equality in business. It started gaining steam in the decades of the sixties and seventies, growing out of the feminist movement and the new left that zeroed in on the symbiotic relationship between capitalism and patriarchy (Lapovsky Kennedy 2008). "Socialist feminists argue that liberation can only be achieved by working to end both the economic and cultural sources of women's oppression. . . . Socialist feminists reject radical feminism's main claim that patriarchy is the only or primary source of oppression of women. Rather [they] assert that women are unable to be free due to their financial dependence on males. Women are subjects to the male rulers in capitalism due to an uneven balance in wealth. They see economic dependence as the driving force of women's subjugation to men" (Ehrenreich 1976).

As in other professions, however, women began charting a different course for themselves in the advertising industry. Contrary to the popular perception that Madison Avenue advertising was only a man's world in the 1960s, some talented women were successful in achieving professional positions in advertising agencies during that decade. That gender surge had actually begun in the late 1950s. Many of these women were copywriters, and some were responsible for developing slogans or entire campaigns that are still memorable today (Stampler 2012). Some of these women moved on to managerial positions. Their achievements include the following:

- Shirley Polykoff of the Foote, Cone, and Belding agency created the long-lasting advertising slogan "Does She . . . or Doesn't She?" for Clairol hair-coloring products on the eve of the 1960s.
- Jane Maas was a well-known copywriter at the Ogilvy agency in the 1960s. Among her later memorable slogans, after moving to the Wells Rich Greene agency, was the famous "I Love New York" slogan and logo.
- Paula Green was one of the first women to become lead copywriter for a national automotive account. She wrote the copy for the legendary and counterintuitive advertising campaign, "We Try Harder," for the Avis rental car company in 1962. That slogan continued on into the twenty-first century.
- Jane Trahey created the advertising campaign for Blackglama minks in 1968, with its slogan, "What becomes a legend most?" The campaign used the services of famed portrait photographer Richard Avedon and stars like Bette Davis modeling the minks.

Among the women who stood out from all the rest on Madison Avenue, however, was a young Norwegian-born woman named Mary Wells, who landed a copywriting job in the 1950s at the large and traditional McCann-Erickson agency. She would go on to work for the legendary Bill Bernbach, who revolutionized advertising that was, many believed, dishonest, boring, and disconnected from real consumers.

Bernbach injected new life into advertising with his agency, Doyle Dane Bernbach. Seeing that revolution in the making, Wells left McCann-Erickson and joined DDB for several years in the 1960s as a copywriter working for Ned Doyle on the Max Factor cosmetics account. It was standard business in the day to put women on accounts featuring feminine and household products, and that's where many of them stayed. Not Wells, however. She would go on to design an innovative advertising campaign ("The End of the Plain Plane") for Braniff Airlines, then one of the main airlines in the industry, and wound up marrying its chairman, Harding Lawrence. Thereafter she was known as Mary Wells Lawrence, and she would go on to found her own ad agency, Wells Rich Lawrence, and to become the first female CEO of a company that traded on the New York Stock Exchange. Among the notable ad campaigns of her agency were the following:

- "Plop, Plop Fizz, Fizz, Oh What a Relief It Is," for Alka-Seltzer.
- "I Can't Believe I Ate the Whole Thing," also for Alka-Seltzer.
- "At Ford, Quality is Job 1," for Ford.
- "Trust the Midas Touch," for Midas mufflers and automotive repair.
- "Flick Your Bic," for Bic cigarette lighters.
- "Raise Your Hand if You're Sure," for Sure deodorants.

By 1969, Mary Wells Lawrence was reported to be the highest-paid executive in the advertising industry. It is interesting to see how the idea of "The End of the Plain Plane" came to Wells as she thought about revolutionizing the image of Braniff Airlines, which was the campaign that helped send her career into a larger orbit. Reminiscing on that, Wells wrote:

> There was no color. I saw the opportunity in color the way Flo Ziegfeld must have seen an empty stage. I saw Braniff in a wash of color. I tore up a hundred magazines, collecting pictures of automobiles in color, colorful interiors, colorful clothes. [We] began exploring ways to make the planes colorful. Jo Hughes, the fashion expert at Bergdorf Goodman, set up a meeting for me with Emilio Pucci, who stood for color in women's clothing more than anyone else in the world. He and I met; he understood me before I opened my mouth. Emilio was phenomenally prescient and I got a clue to his energy at the meeting. He seemed to me to be on the ceiling most of the time. But then, we were doing everything possible to turn Braniff upside down. (Lawrence 2013)

Wells's campaign was a huge success for Braniff and wound up influencing Southwest Airlines' colorful look years later.

Women like Mary Wells Lawrence rebelled against the temptation to define themselves by anything other than their own professional abilities and ambition. They wanted more than to draw their identity and social class from their husbands and his social class. Whether they realized it or not, they were realizing the abstract notion of socialist feminist thinking, which was actually a part of Karl Marx's thinking as well. He believed that when class oppression disappeared, that gender oppression would go along with it. Therefore, when women like those noted above decided to challenge the male corner on the market of talent and creativity, they also challenged and won the battle of gender oppression.

Although the 1960s is often best remembered for the civil rights movement and Vietnam—as a time when protest and counterculture movements were the order of the day—it is often forgotten that most of mainstream

American business carried on as usual. Companies were primarily interested in making money and—in the case of the advertising world—in getting and keeping clients. In order for that to happen, ad agencies required the services of laser-focused, talented, and ambitious professionals. Management at these companies found that, in overlooking the professional value of women, they were actually denying themselves the services of some very talented people. Therefore, the door to promotion was opened to women. There was even some room for gays and lesbians if they were talented and kept their sexual orientation to themselves.

Thus, in many ways, the 1960s featured a divided America: two cultures coexisting within the same borders. There was the business-comes-first culture and there was the counterculture that came to question everything and set themselves apart from those who did not. In large measure, it was a generational split, but in other ways, it was not. Plenty of young people just wanted to be the young junior executives on Madison Avenue, make money, and get promotions. Sometimes young people tried to be a part of both worlds at the same time.

DEPICTION AND CULTURAL CONTEXT

Given the steady theme of male domination in the New York City advertising world depicted in *Mad Men*, it is valid to ask if the series overdid it in showing a significant lack of female agency professionally and inside the home. In most episodes of *Mad Men*, especially in the early seasons, women's dependence on men is front and center, both at the office and at home.

Things start to change noticeably in later episodes for a few key women at Sterling Cooper, but for most, it remains the same. While some women venture out into the workplace, it is understood those jobs are lower paying than those occupied by men. Therefore, the main breadwinner at home is the man. Many unhappy wives remain in their marriage more for economic reasons than for love. Moreover, should a divorce occur, the ex-wife is seen as an anomaly by other women in the suburban neighborhoods, where the working husbands commute each night. After all, the normal thing is to be married and to take care of the home and children and prepare for the arrival of the man in the evening. In *Mad Men*, there is a recently divorced woman on Don and Betty Draper's street, Helen Bishop (Darby Stanchfield), a single mother of two children who holds a job at a jewelry store. Although the other women of the neighborhood invite her into their informal gatherings, no one is ever quite sure what to say to her or what to talk about, since they do not know what a woman without a husband does. She winds up being treated in a second-class manner by the married women in the neighborhood.

For those women who did venture into the workplace, holding anything above switchboard, clerical, or secretarial positions at Sterling Cooper

Advertising Agency was seen as rare in the early years of the series, *Mad Men*. Indeed, Season 1 pays much attention to the new ingénue Peggy Olson who is able to produce even one clever thought that is used as the basis for an ad theme for a lipstick company. She is the talk of everyone at Sterling Cooper, and she winds up getting a promotion as a result. She is the only woman at the agency who is doing any copywriting.

In 2015, *Business Insider* asked if Madison Avenue truly was a male enclave when it came to creative and account executive positions. First, professional ad jobs for women did exist, although the numbers did not approach those for jobs for men. Still, large agencies like JWT (J. Walter Thompson) used women as copywriters and even put some in charge of accounts. JWT asserted it was the first ad agency to "recognize the importance of women's contribution to advertising" (Stampler 2015). Nevertheless, in most cases, female ad executives worked on accounts for products and services marketed to women. These were called "women-friendly" accounts and included products like shampoo, cosmetics, laundry and soaps, and kitchen housewares.

Even the brochures used to recruit talent to ad agencies delineated between the kinds of accounts women might service as opposed to men. Separate brochures were often created for male and female job candidates. Women were not guaranteed they would work diversified accounts, but they instead were told they "would deal with 'all kinds of people and an infinite variety of businesses'" (Stampler 2015). Agencies drew the line between accounts serviced by men and women, and it would be highly unusual for a female account executive to pitch a campaign to a car company or other "male-oriented" business. Still, some women did break the glass ceiling. One female ad executive, Jane Maas, worked at Ogilvy & Mather in the 1960s. In an interview, she said, "Working on the American Express account took longer than my becoming a vice president in 1970" (Stampler 2015). Note, however, that she did achieve that VP status as the decade came to a close.

Looking back on Madison Avenue in the 1960s, *The New York Daily News* interviewed former "Mad Men" and asked them to compare the real to the televised version of the life they lived. Larry McShane wrote, "The cigarette haze. The three-martini buzz. The interoffice intrigue. Alen York remembers it all, quite fondly: Madison Ave. in the '60s, where impeccably dressed, impressively paid, mostly white men convinced a nation to buy whatever they were selling. And yes, the ad agency ethos included plenty of nicotine, booze and dips in the steno pool. 'It was the Wild West,' recalls York, who ran a Manhattan ad agency through much of the decade. 'Yes, there were beautiful women around. And there was a certain glamour from the outside to the industry—maybe more than it deserved'" (McShane 2009). Another ad executive, Sandy Teller felt *Mad Men* was right on target, right down to the props in the offices and on the desks. "The look of the office, the IBM typewriters, even the coffee cups," he said. "I was there, and it's accurate" (McShane 2009).

His opinion is shared by a former female agency employee, Rose Mendicino, who took a job as secretary at age 21 at a Madison Avenue agency. She recalled, "Big, tall, suited, good-looking.... Definitely predators. Married or not." As for the women who worked there, Mendicino says they understood their second-class status and the need to be deferential to the men in the office. "All the account executives, all the art directors, all the copywriters—no matter how dumb—were men. I don't even know if the women even thought about it that much. A lot of them were looking for husbands" (McShane 2009).

One element of this "mad" lifestyle that both the men and women in the series exhibit is, ironically, an overriding sadness in their lives. The irony is twofold: first, they are lucky enough to have jobs at a successful ad agency on Madison Avenue in the heart of Manhattan, which is the career target that many might dream; second, they work in the field of advertising, which is all about promising people happiness and contentment. Amid all this superficial happiness are successful professionals who lead very unhappy personal lives. It is as if they have nothing left of their lives after giving so much of it to the Zeitgeist of their picturesque careers. Don Draper himself seems to be the saddest of all, despite the fact that his outward life appears idyllic, being a highly paid wunderkind of Sterling Cooper with a beautiful wife, two kids, and a lovely suburban home.

Writer Elisabeth K. Paefgen explores this in her essay, "Sadnesses of the Sixties": "Yet most of the *Mad Men* figures are above all imprisoned in sadnesses that have different grounds and assume varied configurations, and which stand in stark contrast to an advertising world subscribing to happiness and success. Incidentally, not only the men but also the women are sad, and not least of all the children are sad. In all of these cases, sadness has nothing to do with grief; it is not the discharge of something mourned but rather that the work conditions as well as the historical and sociopolitical conditions of the times incite a hidden, unfree, and burdened life which, even if it is economically secured, does not enable a carefree mode of existence" (Paefgen 2013).

Certainly, this kind of sad lifestyle was not unique to the 1960s and is often part of every generation who works so hard on the appearance of living that they box themselves out of the chance to actually live. But the ethos of the 1960s, where the ground was shaking beneath traditional values (and consequences of violating them), together with the false promises of a sexist-based lifestyle and economy, added greatly to the sadness so many experienced in the 1960s, as accurately depicted in *Mad Men*.

Not to be overlooked in a discussion of fact and fiction presented by Weiner is that *Mad Men* did present the 1960s as a time when advertising was undergoing a creative revolution in this country, and it started in Madison Avenue ad agencies like the fictional Sterling Cooper. As Draper and his creative team come up with slogans and pitches for their clients and prospective clients, the show presents a good inside look at what it takes, both in creativity and salesmanship, to succeed in this highest level of the advertising world. This decade began producing some successful counterintuitive ads like the ones that began appearing in newspapers and magazines for Volkswagen. In an era when automotive advertising was loudly proclaiming the spacious roominess and design of their flashy cars, VW ad campaigns featured simple ads, often one-liners, showing this small, minimalistic "Beetle" with no tail fins, dual headlights, barely room for a backseat, and with no engine at all under the hood. It was in a small rear area where other cars were sporting huge trunk space. Some of those counterintuitive ad slogans included the following:

- *Think Small.*
- *It makes your house look bigger.*
- *Live below your means.*
- *Don't laugh.*
- *You're missing a lot when you own a Volkswagen.*
- *Ever wonder how people who drive a snowplow get to the snowplow?*

Adding realism to the TV series, Draper and Sterling Cooper account executives discussed some of these VW ads in meetings as examples of the innovation coming from the fictional agency's competitors. The show also featured real-life slogans and ads for Pepsi Cola. In fact, most of Sterling Cooper's "clients" included real-life companies such as Lucky Strike cigarettes, Hilton Hotels, Admiral television, Clearasil, and (now-defunct) Mohawk Airlines, whom the agency decided to drop in favor of going after the much more lucrative American Airlines account.

The episode featuring this decision is important because it also shows how creator Matthew Weiner weaved real-life incidents (in this case a tragedy) into the plot to highlight another theme of the series. That theme could be described either as entrepreneurship or as amoral company activity in search of profit, or both. In the episode, junior account executive Pete Campbell gets a call notifying him that his father was one of some 100 passengers who perished in an American Airlines crash in New York City's Jamaica Bay shortly after takeoff. Such a crash did occur in real life on March 1, 1962, when an American Boeing 707 flipped over moments after takeoff from Idlewild (now Kennedy) Airport and crashed into the bay, killing 87 passengers and crew, including the president of Long Island University and the vice president of Union Carbide.

In *Mad Men*, while Campbell enters a state of shock and grief, a senior Sterling Cooper executive, "Duck" Phillips (Mark Moses), sees the disaster as a giant business opportunity for the agency. He tells his boss he has just talked with a friend at American Airlines, who confides that the top management needs to make an immediate change in their image, in part to survive the business fallout from the crash and its publicity. Therefore, Sterling Cooper starts its campaign to get American Airlines as a $7 million annual client, but it also realizes it has to dump the smaller Mohawk Airlines account to free itself from conflict of interest and a potential lawsuit.

While Draper makes an uncommon stand on principle and opposes dropping a loyal, paying customer in Mohawk, Phillips wins the argument. The first thing he does is draft Campbell to develop a creative campaign for helping American Airlines, even though his own father died on the company's airplane. Campbell tries to tell Draper about Phillips's end run, but Draper is in a bad mood and snubs him before Pete can give him the inside news. Irritated, Campbell shows up at the meeting between Phillips and the American Airlines executive, agreeing to head the account, and showcases his father's death as the unique things Sterling Cooper has to offer as the airline's ad agency. The man creating the ad campaign knows more than anyone else how badly the victims' relatives feel, and yet he still champions American Airlines. The show also portrayed significant events in the civil rights movement and the escalation of American involvement in Vietnam, and the men of Sterling Cooper often saw these events as advertising opportunities.

Among the cultural attitudes of the 1960s depicted in *Mad Men* is how the world of big business responded to gifted employees who were found to be gay. Like other questions of how closely the show mirrored reality, this portrayal is also the subject of some debate, although there is no question it was risky for gays to come out during this era. In the show, the issue is focused on the talented Sterling Cooper art designer, Salvatore "Sal" Romano (Bryan Batt), who is a closeted gay man. The very first episode strongly hints at his sexual orientation, set in the year 1960, when switchboard operator Lois Sadler (Christa Flanagan) develops a crush on Sal, and he resists her advances. Later he finds himself reluctantly resisting the advances of a client, Elliot Lawrence (Paul Keeley), in a hotel restaurant. When Elliot asks what he is afraid of, Sal responds: "Are you joking?" and politely leaves.

Somewhere between Seasons 1 and 2 of the series, Sal marries Kitty Romano, although it is obvious by the middle of Season 2 he has feelings for another Sterling Cooper junior executive, Ken Cosgrove (Aaron Staton). Kitty is aware of Sal's interest in Ken, but she tries not to notice the full extent of it. Sal is well liked by Draper, who sees him as a strong asset to obtaining and keeping clients happy with his creative artwork. However, Draper witnesses Sal in a compromising moment with a hotel bellhop and wonders what to do about that. To Sal's relief, Draper keeps it to himself but finds a subtle and clever way of letting Sal know he should "limit his exposure." Things go well for Sal professionally for a while, and he is even picked to direct a commercial for Pepsi, one of the agency's top clients. Ironically, it is his inner battle to "limit his exposure" that winds up costing him his job at Sterling Cooper. That occurs late in Season 3 of the show when, after resisting the advances of another client, that client is so upset he complains that he cannot work with the agency if Sal is there. Normally this might not result in his firing, but the client is Lee Garner Jr. (Darren Pettie), whose father owns Lucky Strike, one of the agency's premier clients, which brings in $25 million annually. The agency ultimately fires Salvatore Romano.

Reflecting on what it was like to be gay and working on Madison Avenue in the 1960s, David Leddick said his experience was different from Sal Romano's as depicted on *Mad Men*. Leddick worked as an agency writer in the 1950s, received a promotion, and worked as a creative director in the 1960s, saying he wound up as one of the highest-paid creative directors in the world over the next two decades.

"I beg to differ on the show's representation of the single gay character, Salvatore, who was fired by the fictional ad agency for being more open about his sexuality," Leddick said in a Huffington Post column (Leddick 2012). "There were plenty of gays who, like me, didn't bother to stay in the closet, succeeded, and thrived in this tough world. Yes, some agencies were like the one where Don Draper works. But these stuffy, old-line agencies were the big ones—not agencies like Draper's . . . they were agencies where women could only be secretaries or work in what was called the 'Women's Division' (food, fashion, and cosmetics). In those kinds of agencies, if you were gay, you were probably closeted, like that poor character on *Mad Men*. But more likely, if you were gay, you didn't stay long . . . as many of the smaller agencies were quite different—fun agencies to work for, where being gay was not an issue" (Leddick 2012).

Leddick's memories seem consistent with the depiction of another gay employee at Sterling Cooper, Kurt Smith (Edin Gali). Kurt, who is from Germany and who is hired as a young creative designer, doesn't mind telling his colleagues he is gay because it is not taboo to be gay in Europe. However, because he works at arm's-length from management in the agency, keeps sex out of the workplace, and is very talented, he does not seem at risk of losing his job.

Although New York City is often seen as the most liberal cities in America—and it seems to vie for that title with San Francisco—acceptance of gays and lesbians came slowly there in the twentieth century, and the most significant event triggering that acceptance did not occur until 1969. It happened at a gay bar called the Stonewall Inn in Greenwich Village on June 28, when New York City Police raided the bar, and the confrontation spilled over onto the street and became known as the Stonewall Riot. The event transformed what was a minor civil rights crusade into a mass liberation movement that spread across U.S. cities. But gays and their supporters had been making inroads before Stonewall in the 1960s, some of which is evidenced by David Leddick's memories. There had, in fact, been a long-standing history of gay resistance prior to Stonewall.

New Yorker George Chauncey wrote in 1994, "It would have been unthinkable 25 years ago for thousands of openly gay fans to cheery openly gay athletes at Yankee Stadium, for openly gay artists to perform to the acclaim of openly gay audiences at Carnegie Hall, or for the mainstream media to provide extensive and sympathetic coverage of it all.... But the enshrinement of Stonewall as the genesis of gay culture threatens to deny the richness and resiliency of gay and lesbian life before the late 60s and to obscure the long history of gay resistance that made the gay-rights movement possible" (Chauncey 1994).

Having a character for four seasons on *Mad Men* who represented the dilemma that all gays faced in the 1960s—keep quiet or be open—was in keeping with the realism of life in the era. When Sal Romano's character was ultimately fired, never to return to the show, executive producer Matt Weiner said the decision was meant to show the high stakes involved in working at agencies like Sterling Cooper in the 1960s. "We don't murder people on our show, but for there to be any stakes, there have to be consequences," Weiner said. "I felt it was an expression of the times that he couldn't work there anymore. It's the ultimate case of sexual harassment" (Bolcer 2010).

Regardless of these kinds of clever efforts to create verisimilitude, some former ad executives from the 1960s wish *Mad Men* would have depicted Madison Avenue advertising to be a more serious-minded profession rather than just one where discriminatory attitudes, amorality, and liquor flowed and ad men devoted so much thinking to sleeping with the secretaries. Interviewed by *The New York Times*, Weiner said he chose to make a series on advertising because "it's a great way to talk about the image we have of ourselves, versus who we really are. And admen were the rock stars of that era, creative, cocky, anti-authority. They made a lot of money, and they lived hard" (Witchel 2008).

The men who actually lived the life agree, but they are also proud of what they accomplished. "When I hear 'Mad Men,' it's the most irritating thing in the world to me. When you think of the '60s, you think about people like me who changed the advertising and design worlds," said legendary art director George Lois. "The creative revolution was the name of the game. This show gives you the impression it was all three-martini lunches.... We worked from 5:30 in the morning until 10 at night. We had three women copywriters. We didn't bed secretaries. I introduced Xerox.... You were handling millions of dollars of people's money, and no one took it lightly. Here [in the series] they're smoking, joking, ogling girls, then they think of a line" (Witchel 2008).

Others, however, like Jerry Della Femina, who has owned several agencies, said *Mad Men* was on target with its portrayal of life in ad agencies in the 1960s. "'Mad Men,' accurately reflects what went on," he said. "The smoking, the prejudice and the bigotry. I interviewed at J. Walter Tompson for the Ford account and was told, 'We don't want your kind.' It took me two years to figure out that he meant I wasn't a WASP" (Witchel 2008).

As the series progresses, the role of women at Sterling Cooper begins to change, and that change is focused on Peggy Olson. In fact, much of the buzz about the whole series is focused on Peggy and how this 20-year-old loaded with naivete, and uncertainty about herself, finds her inner courage to show her latent talent as a writer and then as a manager. From the day she arrives at Sterling Cooper as a new graduate from Miss Deaver's Secretarial School—with her hair in a long ponytail and skirt halfway down her calves—to her rise through the ranks of copywriting and managerial positions—with a more alluring hairstyle, wardrobe, and persona—Peggy's professional star is rising while Don's personal life is in decline. In the most ironic turn of the whole series, this formerly young, clueless secretary winds up becoming Don Draper's boss. Peggy's transformation is more striking than anyone else in the series.

With a couple of seasons left to go, Moss spoke about Peggy's role and what it signified about women in the 1960s workplace. "I think that when we originally started the show, that was the kind of thing people were talking about: Oh, it's called *Mad Men*, but it's actually got these really interesting female characters. Betty, Joan (Christina Hendricks), and Peggy are really complex and layered and not stereotypes. In each of their stereotypes, they're very different. That was one of the first surprises of the show, first season: Oh, there's really cool women on this" (Weintraub 2013).

Moss enjoyed playing Peggy and taking her through the arc of her career and life from ages 20 to 26. "In the '60s, in the workplace, with all of those elements . . . you just have so much to play with . . . it was when things were changing. . . . It's allowed me to change her. . . . I think that for Peggy, her problem is that she's so focused on work. She's too young to understand she's gonna have to balance that, and she's gonna have to figure out a way to have both. And I think that's a problem with women of that time as well. They hadn't quite figured that out yet" (Weintraub 2013).

Having learned how to manage from Draper, does Peggy become the same kind of boss as he has been? "What actually makes Don love her and respect her so much is that she's better than him. She has a heart, and I think it brings up an interesting kind of thing about female bosses and how they might be different than male bosses, especially at that time" (Weintraub 2013).

FURTHER READING

Adams, Tim. 2013. "Jon Hamm Interview." *The Guardian*, November 16, 2013. https://www.theguardian.com/tv-and-radio/2013/nov/16/jon-hamm-don-draper-daniel-radcliffe

Bolcer, Julie. 2010. "Gay Character Dropped from 'Mad Men'." *The Advocate*, January 27, 2010. https://www.advocate.com/news/daily-news/2010/01/27/gay-character-dropped-mad-men.

Chauncey, George. 1994. "A Gay World: Vibrant and Forgotten." *The New York Times*, June 26, 1994. https://www.nytimes.com/1994/06/26/opinion/a-gay-world-vibrant-and-forgotten.html

Ehrenreich, Barbara. 1976. "What Is Socialist Feminism?" *WIN Magazine*, June 3, 1976. http://www.feministezine.com/feminist/modern/Socialist-Feminism.html

Fraser, Nancy. 2013. "Feminism's Two Legacies: A Tale of Ambivalence." In *Revisiting the Sixties*, edited by Laura Bieger and Christian Lammert, 98. Frankfurt, Germany: Campus Publishers.

"History: 1950s." *Ad Age*, September 15, 2003. https://adage.com/article/adage-encyclopedia/history-1950s/98701

Lapovsky Kennedy, Elizabeth. 2008. "Socialist Feminism: What Difference Did It Make to the History of Women's Studies?" Gale Literature Resource Center, Fall 2008. https://go.gale.com/ps/anonymous?id=GALE%7CA193737131&sid=googleScholar&v=2.1&it=r&linkaccess=abs&issn=00463663&p=LitRC&sw=w

Lawrence, Mary Wells. 2013. "The Lady Was an Adman." *Vanity Fair*, September 4, 2013. https://www.vanityfair.com/news/2002/05/real-life-peggy-olson-mad-men-advertising

Leddick, David. 2012. "Being Gay in the World of Mad, Mad Men: What It Was Really Like." *Huffington Post*, May 17, 2012. https://www.huffpost.com/entry/being-gay-in-the-world-of-mad-mad-men_b_1519549

McShane, Larry. 2009. "Real New York Executives Fondly Remember the 1960s of 'Mad Men'." *The New York Daily News*, August 16, 2009. https://www.nydailynews.com/entertainment/tv-movies/real-new-york-executives-fondly-remember-1960s-mad-men-article-1.400302

Paefgen, Elizabeth K. 2013. "Sadnesses of the Sixties." In *Revisiting the Sixties*, edited by Laura Bieger and Christian Lammert, 317–318. Frankfurt, Germany: Campus Publishers.

Saraiya, Sonia. 2017. "John Hamm Reflects on 'Mad Men' and Don Draper at New Yorker Festival." *Variety*, October 7, 2017. https://variety.com/2017/tv/news/jon-hamm-mad-men-don-draper-new-yorker-festival-1202583633/

Stampler, Laura. 2012. "Peggy Was Not Alone: These Famous Ads Were Created by Women in the Mad Men Era." *Business Insider*, April 18, 2012. https://www.businessinsider.com/famous-ads-created-by-women-of-the-mad-men-era-2012-4

Stampler, Laura. 2015. "Forget 'Mad Men,' Here's What Women of Madison Avenue Really Looked Like in the 1960s." *Business Insider*, April 1, 2015. https://www.businessinsider.com/what-the-women-of-madison-avenue-really-looked-like-in-the-1960s-2015-4

Walton, James. 2009. "TV Review: Mad Men." *The Telegraph*, February 10, 2009. https://www.telegraph.co.uk/culture/tvandradio/4582949/TV-Review-Mad-Men-BBC4-and-In-the-Line-of-Fire-ITV1.html

Weintraub, Steve. 2013. "Elisabeth Moss Talks Mad Men." *Collider*, April 5, 2013. https://collider.com/mad-men-season-6-elisabeth-moss-interview/

Witchel, Alex. 2008. "'Mad Men' Has Its Moment." June 22, 2008, *The New York Times*. https://www.nytimes.com/2008/06/22/magazine/22madmen-t.html

Chapter 9

Selma (2014)

The Edmund Pettus Bridge in south-central Alabama was stained by violence on one "Bloody Sunday" in March 1965. When 500-some unarmed Black citizens marched across the bridge on Route 80, chaos erupted as local police troopers met the peaceable demonstrators with a brutal onslaught. The victims of that day's savage display of racism comprised a group of Black activists assembled under the leadership of Dr. Martin Luther King Jr. during a critical moment in the civil rights movement. The decisive campaign centered on the ability of African American citizens in Selma, Alabama, to secure equal voting rights, and the protest took on the form of a 54-mile march from Selma to Montgomery. The 2014 film *Selma* takes viewers back to the three months in which the action took place, following King (David Oyelowo) as well as his activist colleagues James Bevel (Common), Hosea Williams (Wendell Pierce), and John Lewis (Stephan James).

Following his personal triumph on receiving the Nobel Peace Prize in Oslo, Norway, King returns to American soil to confront the trying circumstances that compel him to visit southern territory. After holding conversations with President Lyndon Johnson (Tom Wilkinson) that can only go so far, King resorts to the only strategy he knows will work: use nonviolent protests as a platform for social reform while intentionally eliciting racist backlash—all while the TV cameras are watching. Though they recognize the high likelihood of physical harm ahead of them, the tight-knit band of civil rights leaders consider the risk well worth taking, as the stakes are high with the entire nation increasingly embroiled in conflicts linked to racial discrimination. King's fervor—and the nation backing him—would lead thousands to join the cause and march the road from Selma toward historic legislative action that same year.

Starring David Oyelowo, Tom Wilkinson, and Tim Roth, *Selma* was directed by Ava DuVernay (*Middle of Nowhere*) and distributed by Paramount Pictures. The film presents a highly accurate portrayal of King's campaign to achieve equal voting rights through the 1965 marches from Selma to Montgomery, Alabama. The movie premiered at the American Film Institute Festival on November 11, 2014, began wide release on January 9, 2015, and was re-released on March 20, 2015, to commemorate the historical march's 50th anniversary. Paul Webb wrote the screenplay, and the producers were Dede Gardner, Jeremy Kleiner, Christian Colson, and Oprah Winfrey. To paint an authentic backdrop for the story, the film was shot in Alabama and Georgia, including a few locations where the real events took place. Supporting roles were filled by Carmen Ejogo, Dylan Baker, Wendell Pierce, Common, and Winfrey. The film was shot on a $20-million budget and returned a domestic total gross of $52,076,908, finishing 61st in revenue rankings of 2014 films.

Selma widely received positive reviews from critics and garnered several film awards. At the 87th Academy Awards, *Selma* won the Oscar for Best Original Song and was nominated for Best Picture. The film also won Best Original Song at the 2015 Golden Globe Awards, where it received three additional nominations: Best Motion Picture—Drama, Best Director (DuVernay being the first African American woman to be nominated), and Best Actor.

Many film reviewers lauded the movie for its effectiveness at transferring history into a compelling storyline. Richard Roeper of the *Chicago Sun-Times* wrote, "'Selma' is an important history lesson that never feels like a lecture. Once school is back in session, every junior high school class in America should take a field trip to see this movie" (Roeper 2014). Even though the movie stuck close to its historic roots, the narrative impressed moviegoers as it communicated a strong message about America's past. "Even if you think you know what's coming, 'Selma' hums with suspense and surprise," wrote *New York Times*' chief film critic A.O. Scott. "Packed with incident and overflowing with fascinating characters, it is a triumph of efficient, emphatic cinematic storytelling" (Scott 2014).

The release of *Selma* seemed to hit its intended target at just the right time in American culture. "This is cinema, more rhetorical, spectacular, and stirring than cable-TV drama," opined *The New Yorker*'s David Denby. "DuVernay's timing couldn't be more relevant. Next year marks the fiftieth anniversary of both the Selma marches and the passage of the Voting Rights Act. Meanwhile, the Supreme Court overturned a key provision of the act last year, and Republican legislatures across the country have been deploying new voter-I.D. laws. Faced with all that—and with the recent turmoil in Ferguson, Cleveland, and New York—King would have noticed how far we have yet to go, shaken his head, and set to work" (Denby 2014). In light of national events in 2014, Scott affirms a similar notion: "It would be hard to imagine a timelier, more necessary popular entertainment in the year of Ferguson, Mo., a reminder both of progress made and promises unkept. But such relevance is hardly automatic. A timid, pious or dishonest movie about the time-burnished glories of the civil rights era—the kind of soothing fable of awakened white conscience that Hollywood has too often favored—would not do anyone any good" (Scott 2014).

Among largely upbeat critiques of the film were a few voices that called attention to historical inaccuracies scattered throughout the production. "'Selma' is a necessary film, even an essential one, with more than its share of memorable performances and vivid, compelling sequences," wrote Kenneth Turan of the *Los Angeles Times*. "But welcome as it is for being the first Hollywood production to put the Rev. Martin Luther King Jr. and his accomplishments front and center, it is also inconsistent and not always as strong as its strongest moments. This may not matter in the grand scheme of things, but it is hard to avoid" (Turan 2014). Concerning the film's character portrait of President Johnson, Joseph A. Califano Jr., Johnson's top domestic aide from 1965 to 1969, gives his blunt perspective in a *Washington Post* article: "The makers of the new movie 'Selma' apparently just couldn't resist taking dramatic, trumped-up license with a true story that didn't need any embellishment to work as a big-screen historical drama. As a result, the film falsely portrays President Lyndon B. Johnson as being at odds with Martin Luther King Jr. and even using the FBI to discredit him, as only reluctantly behind the Voting Rights Act of 1965 and as opposed to the Selma march itself" (Califano 2014).

In the grand scheme of things, *Selma* connected well with moviegoers. After the film's debut, a mix of African American business leaders and public figures contributed to a campaign in which free screenings were provided for 275,000 middle and high school students in 25 locations across America. "It's important that the civil rights struggle depicted in 'Selma' reach as many young people as possible so that the enduring lessons of the civil rights movement can be harnessed to inspire them to transform their lives and communities," said T. Warren Jackson, Senior Vice President and Associate General Counsel and Chief Ethics Officer of DirecTV (Reilly 2015). In January 2015, the cast and crew of the film also were part of a march with local Selma residents in anticipation of the historic event's 50th anniversary (Hamedy 2015).

HISTORICAL BACKGROUND

The civil rights movement of the 1960s was filled with unrest, civil disobedience, and often violence. The lasting effects of progress from that period were due in large part to the philosophy of nonviolence encouraged by Dr. Martin Luther King Jr. and the Southern Christian Leadership

Conference (SCLC). It was in this tumultuous climate for African Americans that King delivered his legendary "I Have a Dream" speech at the Lincoln Memorial during the March on Washington on August 28, 1963. Less than a month later, on September 15, four young girls were killed in the bombing of the 16th Street Baptist Church in Birmingham, Alabama, a mainly Black congregation where civil rights leaders often met. King decreed at the girls' funeral: "They are the martyred heroines of a holy crusade for freedom and human dignity. So they have something to say to us in their death. They have something to say to every minister of the gospel who has remained silent behind the safe security of stained-glass windows . . . to every politician who has fed his constituents the stale bread of hatred and the spoiled meat of racism. . . . Their death says to us that we must work passionately and unrelentingly to make the American dream a reality" (King 1992, 116). Martin Luther King Jr. was a reverend above all else and believed that every racist person could ultimately be reached through the power of love as one of God's children (Farber 1994, 74–75).

In late 1964, Dr. King flew to Oslo, Norway, where he received the Nobel Peace Prize on December 10. The prize was awarded due to his role in spearheading the nonviolent movement that had influenced the creation of the Civil Rights Act of 1964, which President Lyndon Baines Johnson signed into law on July 2, 1964. King used the award platform to focus his acceptance speech upon all—the great names and the nameless—who had joined the struggle in nonviolent protest, to those who worked to make sure that American liberty extended to all people, Black and white. "Today I come to Oslo as a trustee, inspired and with renewed dedication to humanity," King said. "I accept this prize on behalf of all men who love peace and brotherhood" (King 1998, 260).

During the months that followed, King became more concerned with the right for African Americans to register to vote unimpeded. In Selma, Alabama, and other areas of the South, African Americans faced discriminatory regulations that had restricted them from voting, such as poll taxes, voting vouchers, and literacy tests. Due to systemic racism, even the publication of an applicant's address was enough to prevent people from registering due to the fear of violent and economic repercussions. Black Americans had virtually no success in registering to vote throughout the South, and without registration, they were unable not only to elect representatives but also to participate in civil justice as members of a jury. King notes in his autobiography, "Out of 15,000 Negroes eligible to vote in Selma and the surrounding Dallas County, less than 350 were registered" (King 1998, 272).

King took up the issue of African Americans' voter rights directly with President Johnson after returning from Oslo. At that time, Johnson was working on his own Great Society program consisting of the Housing and Urban Development Act, the Law Enforcement Assistance Act, and the Voting Rights Act. However, because the Civil Rights Act was passed so recently,

Johnson did not intend to put the Voting Rights Act through to Congress in what King believed to be a reasonable and necessary timeframe. The president expressed this desire to delay the voting bill portion in order to secure votes from Southern states for the other pieces of legislation, lest they block the entire program. King exited the meeting telling Johnson, "Well, we'll just have to do the best we can" (King 1998, 270–271).

Afterward, King went with Ralph Abernathy and other members of the SCLC to Selma, where they determined that it would be the best place to demonstrate publicly for voter rights as the next step toward ensuring equality for African Americans. The Student Nonviolent Coordinating Committee (SNCC) was already working in Selma when King arrived. SNCC was originally formed from the actions of a group of four freshmen from North Carolina A&T, who held a sit-in as a form of protest at a segregated counter for whites in their local Woolworth's department store. Following their sit-in protest, SNCC formally organized as a group alongside the National Association for the Advancement of Colored People (NAACP) and the SCLC (Bloom and Breines 2011, 12–13).

Although each group worked toward the reform of voting and civil rights for African Americans, they did not always coordinate with their efforts. SNCC had already begun organizing mass voter registration days, referred to as Freedom Days, as of October 7, 1963. Local resident Annie Lee Cooper attended the first Freedom Day event organized by SNCC and attempted to register on multiple occasions thereafter in the face of increasing hostility from local law enforcement. On January 5, 1965, Dallas County Sheriff James Clark, a known racist, started to harass Cooper as she stood in a voter's registration line by jabbing her in the neck with a club. Cooper, who had successfully registered to vote in Kentucky and Ohio, had not been able to register in Selma, and as Clark continued the harassment, Cooper eventually turned around and hit him. The deputies responded by holding Cooper down while the sheriff beat her with a club before arresting her (Bernstein 2007).

Less than a month later, on February 1, law enforcement arrested Dr. King in Selma along with over 200 other protestors who had assembled to register to vote. They were charged for parading without a permit. King was released shortly after, only to be rearrested for not leaving the scene. Charles Fager, a low-level staff member of the SCLC who was also arrested, would be put into the same cell as King. Fager recalled King's practice of fasting for the first two days of imprisonment:

> Dr. King explained he and Abernathy had gone to India after the Montgomery bus boycott, and they learned Gandhi was in jail a lot, and he always tried to make the time in jail count, by making constructive use of the time. He also had religious services every day because the British tried to divide Muslims and Hindus. When they learned all of this, Dr. King and Abernathy figured they'd

end up in jail too and they ought to make the time count as much as possible. So they decided to turn that time into a religious retreat. The first two days they're in jail, they fast. (Garrison 2019)

Fager also wrote of King's demeanor when he interacted with other inmates as that of pastoral, reflecting King's identity as a Baptist minister first and foremost. King's autobiography contains notes that show how this intent to stay busy while in jail worked itself out practically as well as spiritually. These notes served as a list of 13 instructions for members of the movement; Joe Lowery, Walter Fountroy, Chuck Jones, Bernard Lafayette, and others were given specific instructions to expedite the bail process as well as keep the movement progressing during King's incarceration (King 1998, 274).

During the time that King was in the Selma jail, his wife, Coretta Scott King, met with Malcolm X, a prominent figure in the civil rights movement who had disagreed early on with King's approach of nonviolence and who had frequently spoken out not only against the method but also against its practitioners. Malcolm believed that the nonviolent leaders of the civil rights movement were wrong and criticized the "dangerous integrationist illusions put forth by Martin Luther King Jr. and his admirers" (Isserman and Kazin 2012, 40–41). During their meeting on February 5, 1965, Malcolm told Coretta King to tell her husband, "I didn't come to Selma to make his job more difficult but I thought that if the white people understood what the alternative was that they would be more inclined to listen to your husband" (Shearer 1988).

After King was released from prison, he flew to Washington to meet with Vice President Hubert Horatio Humphrey Jr., who served as a chairperson for the Council for Equal Opportunity, with Attorney General Nicholas Katzenbach also present. King and his colleagues spoke in the meeting about their desire to see that people were free to participate in voting without fear of police brutality and unnecessary delays.

Shortly after, on February 18, the people of Marion, one of Selma's neighboring cities, participated in a night march organized by Cordy Tindell Vivian of the SCLC while King was away. Without widespread media attention, they suffered from the brutal force of the local law enforcement. That night, James Bonard Fowler, an Alabama State Trooper, fatally shot 38-year-old Vietnam veteran Jimmie Lee Jackson, who was also a deacon in the United Methodist Church. Fowler was not indicted for another 40 years after the incident (Stanford University n.d.-a). This incident became the inspiration for the march from Selma to Montgomery, according to Albert Turner, a Marion civil rights worker who stated that "the idea of a march from Selma to the state capital of Montgomery came from the desire to go to the steps of Montgomery with Jimmie Jackson, take his body and lay it on the steps of the capitol" (Fleming 2015).

During this time, and throughout Dr. King's rise to prominence in the civil rights movement, the Federal Bureau of Investigation believed that King had significant ties to the Communist Party USA. The agency had begun investigating him and the SCLC in 1956. The Senate Select Committee on Intelligence's document profiling the case of Dr. Martin Luther King states, "The wiretaps on Dr. King's home telephone and the phones of the SCLC offices were authorized by the Attorney General for the stated purpose of determining whether suspected communists were influencing the course of the civil rights movement" (Church et al. 1976, 120).

Sometime in mid-November 1964, FBI Headquarters decided to send a tape recording and ominous letter in the mail made from their surveillance recordings of King to the SCLC's Atlanta office. The FBI sent these types of materials to different agencies in an attempt to destroy King's reputation throughout different levels of the government, within his own organization, in churches, and even within his family. To keep suspicion off the FBI concerning the origin of the tape, the FBI sent the material from Tampa, Florida, originally addressed to Coretta King but ultimately to Dr. King himself by way of the SCLC offices. The letter, and the recordings, spoke about King removing himself from the picture. Dr. King interpreted this to be suggestive of suicide, but the FBI claimed it was only meant as an encouragement for King to remove himself from public view (Church et al. 1976, 158–159).

As the march from Selma approached, the people of Selma and the SCLC were determined to attempt their demonstration on Sunday, March 7, 1965. King had initially planned to be in Selma for the march, arranging to be there Sunday morning, lead the march, and speak for several hours before returning home to perform an evening communion service. Instead, King stayed home at Atlanta because he was worried that the protest might lead to arrests, which would then prevent him from being available to conduct the Sunday evening service. At that point, King had already missed Sunday service twice in a row and was determined to be there for his parishioners. He later shared that he had not foreseen the potential for the level of violence that would unfold or else he would not have changed his original plans (King 1998, 278–279).

Hosea Williams from the SCLC and John Lewis from SNCC led approximately 600 people in a march from Selma that Sunday morning. Upon crossing the Edmund Pettus Bridge, local and state law enforcement blocked their passage on the opposite side. The police responded by beating and teargassing the demonstrators to drive them back into Selma—all of which was televised to a national audience. Sheyann Webb, a nine-year-old marcher on the bridge, described the police riding in on horseback with batons, whips, and ropes as though "they were driving cattle" (Webb 2011, 44). The press widely circulated images of fellow demonstrator Amelia Boynton lying unconscious on the pavement. This attack took both King and the entire SCLC by surprise and effectively spurred King into action. In press interviews and a series of telegrams, King implored clergy and others throughout the United States to come to Selma and stand up for human rights. People answered the call and flocked to Selma to support the effort.

President Johnson sent representatives Governor Leroy Collins of the Community Relations Service and acting Assistant Attorney General John Doar to meet with King and discuss the next march slated for Tuesday, March 9. At this point, the president reiterated that the passing of the Voting Rights Act would not be immediately possible because not enough people from the South would vote to approve it and he needed their votes in Congress.

Nevertheless, the second march began on March 9, 1965, two days after the first demonstration, with King accompanied by upward of 2,000 individuals. The swell consisted of hundreds of pastors and other members of the clergy who arrived quickly after King's call. As the now more formidable group approached the place of Sunday's attack, the troops were ordered to let the demonstrators through, whereupon King stopped in his tracks and bid his fellow demonstrators to kneel to the ground and pray. After a moment of prayers, the crowd rose to their feet and were promptly led back to Selma, thus evading a possible conflict with state troopers and sidestepping the issue of complying with the court order issued by Judge Johnson. According to the Stanford School of Business's report, King's unexpected course of action, which drew criticism from many marchers, kept in line with an agreement made during his meeting with the president's emissaries to avoid confrontation, and the show of restraint only served to bolster the president's support of King's cause (Stanford University n.d.-b).

Although the demonstration on March 9 went without incident, four men fatally struck Rev. James Reeb, a white clergyman who had responded to King's call to join in the march, later that evening. Rev. Clark Olsen, who was with Reeb during the attack, recounts that after he grabbed a bite at a cafe with Reeb and Orloff Miller, four men across the street began to taunt them: "We were three white men, but what I remember them saying was, 'Hey, you n—'." The four instigators then rushed the three men and started to beat them. When one of the aggressors struck Reeb on the side of the head with a club, the reverend immediately collapsed, lost consciousness, and died two days later in the hospital. This incident was considered pivotal in advancing the Voting Rights Act to an immediate signing (Schapiro 2015).

During the time between the first march and a third march that took place on March 21, 1965, President Johnson gave several addresses concerning the events occurring in Selma. On March 9, the president clearly acknowledged in a public statement that the problem in Selma stemmed from the denial of voters' rights, promising, "The best legal talent in the Federal Government is engaged in preparing legislation which will secure that right for every American. I expect to complete work on my recommendations by this weekend and shall dispatch a special message to Congress as soon as the drafting of the legislation is finished" (Johnson 1965).

The legislation was finished and put through to Congress on March 17. President Johnson understood that racial discrimination caused the problems occurring in Selma: "There is no Negro problem. There is no Southern problem. There is no Northern problem. There is only an American problem" (Johnson 1966, 282). Putting the plight of African Americans in the straightforward context of how they were being treated as American citizens was a necessary public step toward not only inclusivity but also humanization. In that same speech, Johnson announced that he would "send to Congress a law designed to eliminate illegal barriers to the right to vote" (Johnson 1966, 283).

As things moved in the White House, leaders of the SCLC pursued their own legal course of action to ensure freedom and safety in their right to assemble peacefully in protest during the planned march to Montgomery. They submitted their plan to Judge Frank Johnson, who approved the plan and who ruled against the racist policies and agendas of Governor George Wallace.

In response to the growing pressure of the social change that was about to take place in Alabama, Wallace requested a meeting with President Johnson. While Wallace's intention was the return of law and order to Alabama, his words revealed his lack of understanding regarding the true problems at hand: "Voter registration and voting rights are not the issues involved in these street demonstrations" (Fleming 2015). Wallace expected to persuade the president into using military force to curtail the demonstrations, but instead, Johnson insisted that Wallace could keep the peace in Alabama himself by protecting the marchers and granting them access to their civil right to vote (Fleming 2015).

On March 21, 1965, the march from Selma to Montgomery proceeded undeterred, with the help of the National Guard. John Lewis remembers the emotional energy of that moment: "We left Selma. . . . It was like the beginning of a holy crusade. You know, President Johnson called out the military to protect the marchers along the way, and as we walked . . . you saw the men of the Army, in their fatigues, guarding the way with their guns drawn. They stayed with us all the way from Selma" (Bearss n.d.).

The march was a 54-mile route that lasted five days, ending on March 25 outside of the state capitol building, where Dr. King spoke of the continuing advancement of civil rights, equality, and the brighter future achieved through the use of nonviolence. Recounting the spirit of the march and embodying the emotions of many of its attendees, he said, "Today as I stand before you and think back over that great march, I can say as Sister Pollard said, a seventy-year-old Negro woman who lived in this community during the bus boycott . . . 'My feets is tired, but my soul is rested.' And in a real sense this afternoon, we can say that our feet are tired, but our souls are rested" (King 1992, 120).

Yet King also knew that the arrival at Montgomery of the marchers was not the final victory in the long-fought battle, as he acknowledged that hard times lay ahead. "I must admit to you there are still jail cells waiting for us, dark and difficult moments. We will go on with the faith that nonviolence and its power transformed dark yesterdays into bright tomorrows. We will be able to change all of these conditions" (King 1992, 121). Within hours after the march, just as King foresaw, the violence against African Americans and workers in the civil rights movement would continue to manifest. Later that evening, a group of Ku Klux Klan nightriders killed white volunteer and demonstrator Viola Gregg Liuzzo while she drove marchers back to Selma.

Ultimately, through the efforts of Martin Luther King Jr., the people of Selma, and all those who answered the call to equality and freedom, President Johnson signed the Voting Rights Act into law on August 6, 1965.

DEPICTION AND CULTURAL CONTEXT

The film *Selma* is an overall faithful retelling of the events that happened in Martin Luther King's life during the early months of 1965. Sequences such as the first crossing of the Edmund Pettus Bridge resulting in "Bloody Sunday," the nonviolent assemblies outside of voter registration offices, and the final march from Selma are displayed with only minor variations due to a compression of events or to illustrate characters who were influential. Most of the historical errors in the film are accountable to this alteration of chronology. Additionally, King's heirs did not grant the filmmakers permission to use the great orator's speeches verbatim in the movie; thus, the moments evoking King's powerful eloquence are necessarily paraphrases of his original words (Scott 2014).

DuVernay commented on the perceived tension inherent in the act of telling history through works of cinema: "This is art. This is a movie. This is a film. I'm not a historian. I'm not a documentarian. I am an artist who explored history and what I found . . . this is the way that I interpreted it" (PBS NewsHour 2015). The first example of artistic license occurs early in the film as it cuts from King receiving the Nobel Peace Prize to the images of African American children walking down the stairs inside of a church building in Birmingham, Alabama. The scene's serenity is soon disrupted intensely by an explosion that takes the children's lives. The filmmakers used this juxtaposition of events with artistic license; the sequence is chronologically inaccurate, as the event occurred over a year before King arrived in Oslo. According to Winfrey, director DuVernay chose to open the film this way because the September 15, 1963, church bombing in Birmingham played an important role "as a marker for the times," encapsulating "the essence of why the need to vote, the need to have black people experience their sense of freedom and equal rights" (CBS This Morning 2014).

Another scene the film utilizes to illustrate the social tensions of the time is when Annie Lee Cooper hits Sheriff Jim Clark. The film depicts this scene as an event that would culminate in King's arrest, but the physical altercation actually happened several days beforehand. Cooper was a significant person in civil rights history who later marched on the bridge from Selma, so although the scene is not chronologically accurate, it nonetheless serves as a characterizing moment for a woman who was a large part of SNCC's efforts in Selma and is remembered for her right hook (Montgomery 2013). Winfrey said that she agreed to play Cooper in the film because of the way the real-life activist's story resonated with her. "That's why that movie means so much to me," Winfrey said, "because of what [Cooper] represents: all of those people, ancestors, all of those people who are part of my legacy, our legacy, that kept getting up and kept trying" (CBS This Morning 2014).

The largest discrepancy of the film is also the most controversial: the portrayal of President Lyndon Johnson. The controversy is related to the extent to which the movie sets Johnson as an opponent of King. There is evidence on both sides of the argument, showing first that Johnson was not an enemy who King had to convince to help, since the president was already a large proponent of civil rights. In contrast, Johnson's agenda and timeline were different from King's own, a point that the film underscores. DuVernay chose to represent this difference as an active force obstructing King from advancing the Voting Rights Act.

In *The Washington Post*'s opinion piece "The Movie 'Selma' Has a Glaring Flaw," Joseph Califano, President Johnson's chief assistant at the time, gives a full defense of what he believes was the president's actual role during that era. Califano insists that Johnson encouraged King to capitalize on the places where he could find injustices, to document and publicize them, attributing the following words to LBJ: "[I]f you can find the worst condition that you run into in Alabama, Mississippi or Louisiana or South Carolina . . . and if you just take that one illustration and get it on radio, get it on television, get it in the pulpits, get it in the meetings, get it everyplace you can. Pretty soon the fellow that didn't do anything but drive a tractor will say, 'Well, that's not right, that's not fair,' and then that will help us on what we're going to shove through [Congress] in the end" (Califano 2014).

Recorded conversations and public documents support this attitude expressed by Johnson, showing clear examples of this cooperative spirit between himself and King, available from The Miller Center and through the Lyndon Johnson Library (Johnson n.d.). These conversations between King and Johnson show not only the necessity of voters' rights being discussed but also the importance of having an African American present in the White House while still revealing the matter of Johnson's political timeline, which was not agreeable with King's.

The movie focuses on this particular disagreement in its shorter narrative, which DuVernay defends by referencing King's own impression of his meeting with Johnson as recorded in his autobiography (King 1998, 270–271). The Guardian's assessment of the film asserts that while DuVernay's portrayal might be somewhat debatable, there are indications from other eyewitnesses that support her representation, even if Johnson was not a major obstacle or a resistant force because he was slow to act (Von Tunzelmann 2015). "I'm not a custodian of anyone's legacy," DuVernay explained in a 2015 interview. "I'm not trying to maintain an image of anyone, not of King, not of Johnson, not of any of the people that we chronicle in the film. I'm trying to imbue the film and invite people into the spirit of the movement" (PBS NewsHour 2015). Jerome Christensen, a film scholar and professor of humanities at the University of California, Irvine, notes that *Selma*'s version of Johnson comes off as more of a leader navigating difficult circumstances rather than a malevolent obstructionist. In Christensen's view, most criticism of the film boils down to "a question of reputation rather than accuracy," noting that several voices railing against the movie had significant ties to the Johnson administration. "'Selma' is not education, it's mobilization—it's a movie that wants to move you. Its aim is not accuracy, but to be tragically and poignantly clever" (Buckley 2015).

Selma does represent history by illustrating that Johnson's own political timeline was incongruous to King's as well as that of other civil rights leaders. However, by making it the character-defining part of Johnson's presidency, this stylistic choice leaves out the president's own encouragements and hopes to progress the rights of African Americans. While that decision creates a more subjective depiction of Johnson, DuVernay utilizes this character to reinforce the notion of the powerlessness of Black citizens without the right to vote. In the film, regardless of Johnson's sentiments, African Americans are subject to the whim of a nonrepresentative political establishment. This depiction, contrasted with the priorities of civil rights leaders, sets the tone for the urgency that King is facing and the force of political power that, even when in agreement, is disruptive to the cause of freedom through delay.

Regarding another stylistic issue in the film, the instance of Johnson giving FBI Director John Edgar Hoover approval to leak surveillance tapes has no documented evidence to support it. This alteration of history was another instance of the film's portrayal of tension between Johnson and King. Another discrepancy, although not entirely inaccurate, is a matter concerning these same leaked FBI tapes as they were originally addressed to Coretta King. The documentation provided by the Senate Select Committee shows that they were originally addressed to Coretta at her home but were changed at the last minute to be addressed to Martin Luther King himself and then sent to the SCLC's main offices (Church et al. 1976, 158–159). So, although they were initially meant to discredit King with his wife, the tapes were ultimately not sent to her directly. The film does not show this change of routing but does show Coretta King listening to the tapes, which she did in fact according to her own testimony (Dyson 2000, 217).

As a result, the movie still maintains historical integrity even while making a stylistic compression of events to mediate the storytelling process. But the inclusion of this event in the film works to provide an explanation for King's absence from the first Selma march and also to indicate the effect that rumor or discovery had on his home. In his autobiography, King does not reference this moment but rather explains his absence from the events of "Bloody Sunday" by emphasizing his relationship with the church and his need to be there for his congregation. Even Coretta in her recounting of listening to the tapes said, "I couldn't make much out of it, it was just a lot of mumbo jumbo" (Dyson 2000). Dyson writes that the relationship between Martin and Coretta King is symbolic of "the difficulty faced by black leaders who attempted to forge a healthy life with their loved ones while the government aimed its huge resources at destroying their families" and represents the way in which "the state has often abandoned or abused the black family with cruel social policies" (Dyson 2000, 119).

Selma shows King's triumph against the strength of nonrepresentative and bigoted political forces while also setting him as a real person with his own shortcomings. DuVernay called King's story arc during the Selma campaign "so robust," for it was a timeframe "when he was firing on all cylinders, strategically, as an orator, as an organizer. But it's also some of the lowest moments that he had personally" (BlackTree Media Production 2014). "I never approached it as, 'Oh my God, I'm making a film about Dr. King,'" said the director, whose father grew up in an Alabama county located between Selma and Montgomery. "I just focused on making a film about an ordinary man doing extraordinary things in a place I know very well" (D'Addario 2014).

The filmmakers aimed *Selma*'s release into American culture at the close of 2014 to serve as both a reminder of historical progress and a call to action for contemporary struggles. "The thing about the film," said Oyelowo, who portrayed King, "is that you see the high price paid for the privileges we now enjoy, including the vote, that we really take for granted. You see here that it is something not to be taken lightly" (CBS This Morning 2014). DuVernay lamented the general lack of awareness of this particular period in civil rights history and of the relevance of King's campaign in 1965: "Some of the statements that I've heard as we've taken the film across the country [are] jaw dropping at what people don't know. . . . Selma does not resonate with people in the way that it should as being such a cornerstone for democracy in terms of what it has done for voting rights and equality" (PBS NewsHour 2015).

Figuring into the perceived timeliness of the movie's message was the fact that 13 states had passed more restrictive voter ID laws during the three years leading up to the release of the film. "This very act that was passed, that was fought for with blood, was dismantled as of last year," Oyelowo stated in a 2014 interview, referencing the 2013 Supreme Court ruling in *Shelby County v. Holder* that invalidated one central component of the 1965 legislation. "The notion being that the country has changed enough that we don't need the Voting Rights Act. Well, I think one of the things that the film does is . . . you see that the country hasn't changed enough, hasn't changed that much. So the notion that we no longer need the Voting Rights Act is criminal" (CBS This Morning 2014). Sam Walker, historian at the National Voting Rights Museum and Institute in Selma, Alabama, agrees with similar fervor: "In 2013, the United States Supreme Court stripped away what we call the 'heart' of the voting rights movement" ("Special Features" 2014). Walker, who was 11 years old in 1965 and was jailed twice because of his participation in the marches for voting rights, pointed toward the future with momentum created by the film: "And that's the part of the new movement, to get Congress to act to restore what the Supreme Court stripped away. So we're almost back to square one because we have to start a new voting rights movement. . . . No generation can expect to see the end of struggle. But each generation has a responsibility to advance the struggle. So I tell them, 'Just go out and do your part in advancing the struggle.' . . . Make the world better for the next generation" ("Special Features" 2014).

In addition to the political climate, the cultural consciousness of America also had a raw nerve exposed in relation to the issues of race and violence in the wake of 2014 newsreels. Most notable were the cases of Michael Brown in Ferguson, Missouri, and Eric Garner in New York City; both were unarmed Black men who died at the hands of white police officers. Both cases sparked public protests and unrest linked to a call for police reform. "The parallels between Selma and Ferguson are indisputable," said Oyelowo. "The way I look at it, Ferguson felt like a black problem. Once we went into Eric Garner, it became an American problem. You have the same thing with Selma. Voting rights, denial of voting rights was a black problem. The minute we had 'Bloody Sunday,' it became an American problem. We are in the same time in history" (CBS This Morning 2014). *Time* film critic Richard Corliss asserted that the words from LBJ's March 15, 1965, speech "reverberate eerily today, when police again can kill unarmed black men and face no legal punishment—and when the Voting Rights Act . . . gets effectively defanged 48 years later by the Supreme Court. So Ava DuVernay's *Selma* . . . carries a message that has lost none of its heroic, tragic relevance. If not quite in quality then certainly in import and impact, this is the film of the year—of 1965 and perhaps of 2014" (Corliss 2015).

Before the movie's NYC premiere on December 14, 2014, the cast and crew of *Selma* wore shirts displaying the words "I Can't Breathe," a phrase caught on the video footage of Garner's arrest while he was being held in a chokehold by police. Just a day before the premiere, around 25,000 individuals participated in the Millions March in New York, protesting the deaths of Brown and Garner; Wendell Pierce, who played Hosea Williams in the film, joined the marching masses for four hours that day (Dockterman 2014). These decisions did not come without controversy, of course, as *New York Times* writer Cara Buckley reflected that the filmmakers' actions may have "conveyed the sense, distasteful to some, that they were capitalizing on the politicization of the film" (Buckley 2015).

Regardless of political persuasion, the fact that *Selma* spoke directly into its surrounding cultural landscape was unmistakable. Half a century after Martin Luther King Jr. fought incessantly for racial equality in America, the same nation found itself questioning some of the nuanced issues that its citizens were confronting during the 1960s civil rights movement. Overall, the writers and the director of the movie remained fairly faithful to historicity as they portrayed a time of great cultural unrest and change in the United States. To recall the words of the great reverend himself: "Selma is a shining moment in the conscience of man. If the worst in American life lurked in the dark streets of Selma, the best of American democratic instincts arose from across the nation to overcome it" (King 1998, 289).

FURTHER READING

Adams, Noah. 2013. "The Inspiring Force Of 'We Shall Overcome'." *NPR*, August 28, 2013. https://www.npr.org/2013/08/28/216482943/the-inspiring-force-of-we-shall-overcome

Bearss, Edwin. n.d. "Determining the Facts." National Park Service. Accessed October 30, 2019. www.nps.gov/nr/twhp/wwwlps/lessons/133SEMO/133facts2.htm

Bernstein, Adam. 2007. "Ala. Sheriff James Clark; Embodied Violent Bigotry." *The Washington Post*, June 7, 2007. www.washingtonpost.com/wp-dyn/content/article/2007/06/06/AR2007060602455.html

BlackTree Media Production. 2014. "Ava DuVernay and David Oyelowo Interview for SELMA." November, 28, 2014. Video, 1:52. https://www.youtube.com/watch?v=6W9VRE-gj3s

Bloom, Alexander, and Wini Breines, eds. 2011. *"Takin' It to the Streets": A Sixties Reader*. New York: Oxford University Press.

Brown, DeNeen L. 2018. "Malcolm X Didn't Fear Being killed: 'I Live Like a Man Who Is Dead Already'." *The Washington Post*, February 26, 2018. https://www.washingtonpost.com/news/retropolis/wp/2018/02/26/malcolm-x-didnt-fear-being-killed-i-live-like-a-man-who-is-dead-already/

Buckley, Cara. 2015. "When Films and Facts Collide in Questions." *The New York Times*, January 21, 2015. https://www.nytimes.com/2015/01/22/movies/selma-questions-are-nothing-new-for-historical-films.html

Califano, Joseph A., Jr. 2014. "The Movie 'Selma' Has a Glaring Flaw." *The Washington Post*. December 26, 2014. https://www.washingtonpost.com/opinions/the-movie-selma-has-a-glaring-historical-inaccuracy/2014/12/26/70ad3ea2-8aa4-11e4-a085-34e9b9f09a58_story.html

CBS This Morning. 2014. "Oprah and David Oyelowo on New Civil Rights Film 'Selma'." December 15, 2014. Video, 4:00, 5:50, 8:43, 11:17, 11:51. https://www.youtube.com/watch?v=V_gr72m8zZ0

Church, Frank, et al. 1976. Senate Select Committee. *Supplementary Detailed Staff Reports on Intelligence Activities and the Rights of Americans: Book III.* Washington, DC: U.S. Government Printing Office. http://www.aarclibrary.org/publib/contents/church/contents_church_reports_book3.htm

Corliss, Richard. 2015. "Review: *Selma* Is the Film of the Year—But 1965 or 2014?" *Time*, January 1, 2015. https://time.com/3651009/review-selma-1965-2014/

D'Addario, Daniel. 2014. "Review: *Selma* and the Dream Worker." *Time*, November 20, 2014. https://time.com/3596996/review-selma/

Denby, David. 2014. "Living History: 'Selma' and 'American Sniper'." *The New Yorker*, December 22, 2014. https://www.newyorker.com/magazine/2014/12/22/living-history

Dockterman, Eliana. 2014. "*Selma* Cast and Crew Wear 'I Can't Breathe' Shirts to New York Premiere." *Time*, December 15, 2014. https://time.com/3633484/selma-movie-i-cant-breathe-shirts/

Dyson, Michael Eric. 2000. *I May Not Get There with You: The True Martin Luther King, Jr.* New York: Simon and Schuster.

Farber, David. 1994. *The Age of Great Dreams: America in the 1960s.* New York: Hill and Wang.

Fleming, Colleen. 2015. "Case Study: The Selma Conflict." Stanford Graduate School of Business. http://web.stanford.edu/group/instr_design/case_study/selma

Gage, Beverly. 2014. "What An Uncensored Letter to M.L.K. Reveals." *The New York Times*, November 16, 2014. https://www.nytimes.com/2014/11/16/magazine/what-an-uncensored-letter-to-mlk-reveals

Garrison, Greg. 2019. "Selma Cellmate of the Rev. Martin Luther King Jr. Recalls Civil Rights Leader Who Would Be 86." *AL*, March 5, 2019. www.al.com/living/2015/01/selma_cellmate_of_the_rev_mart.html

Hamedy, Saba. 2015. "'Selma' Cast Marches in Alabama; Free Screenings for Students Planned." *Chicago Tribune*, January 18, 2015. https://www.chicagotribune.com/entertainment/movies/la-et-ct-selma-paramount-high-school-screenings-march-20150118-story.html

Hamilton, Neil A. 1997. *The ABC-CLIO Companion to the 1960s Counterculture in America.* Santa Barbara, CA: ABC-CLIO.

Isserman, Maurice, and Michael Kazin. 2012. *America Divided: The Civil War of the 1960s.* New York: Oxford University Press.

Johnson, Lyndon B. 1965. "Statement by the President on the Situation in Selma, Alabama." *The American Presidency Project*. University of California Santa Barbara, March 9, 1965. www.presidency.ucsb.edu/documents/statement-the-president-the-situation-selma-alabama

Johnson, Lyndon B. 1966. "Special Message to the Congress: The American Promise. March 15, 1965." *Public Papers of the Presidents of the United States: Lyndon B. Johnson, 1965: Volume I.* Washington, DC: Government Printing Office. quod.lib.umich.edu/p/ppotpus/4730960.1965.001

Johnson, Lyndon B. n.d. "Conversation with MARTIN LUTHER KING and OFFICE SECRETARY, January 15, 1965." Secret White House Tapes, University of

Virginia. Accessed on November 15, 2019. https://millercenter.org/the-presidency/secret-white-house-tapes/conversation-martin-luther-king-and-office-secretary

King, Martin Luther, Jr. 1992. *I Have A Dream: Writings And Speeches That Changed The World*. New York: Harper Collins.

King, Martin Luther, Jr. 1998. *The Autobiography of Martin Luther King, Jr.* Edited by Clayborne Carson. New York: Warner Books.

Koenig, Rebecca. 2015. "'Pop up' Efforts Send Thousands of Kids to See 'Selma' for Free." *The Christian Science Monitor*, February 20, 2015. https://www.csmonitor.com/World/Making-a-difference/Change-Agent/2015/0220/Pop-up-efforts-send-thousands-of-kids-to-see-Selma-for-free

Lee, Timothy B. 2015. "The Crazy Reason Selma Doesn't Use the Actual Words from MLK's Speeches." *Vox*, January 13, 2015. https://www.vox.com/2015/1/13/7540027/selma-copyright-king-speeches

McCoy, Terrence. 2014. "How the Eric Garner and Ferguson Protests Have 'Struck a Blow to America's Image'." *The Washington Post*, December 5, 2014. https://www.washingtonpost.com/news/morning-mix/wp/2014/12/05/how-eric-garner-and-ferguson-have-struck-a-blow-to-americas-image/

Montgomery, Lucile. 2013. "Montgomery--SNCC: Circulars, Newsletters, Program Outlines, Incidents, 1963–1966 (Lucile Montgomery Papers, 1963–1967; Historical Society Library Microforms Room, Micro 44, Reel 3, Segment 48)." Wisconsin Historical Society. http://content.wisconsinhistory.org/cdm/ref/collection/p15932coll2/id/35486

PBS NewsHour. 2015. "Director Ava DuVernay on Sharing the Story of 'Selma'." January 8, 2015. Video, 3:12, 5:05. https://www.youtube.com/watch?v=XmVZReyHa-M

Reilly, Travis. 2015. "'Selma' Expands Free Screenings to Over 275,000 Students." *The Wrap*, January 16, 2015. https://www.thewrap.com/selma-expands-free-screenings-to-over-275000-students/

Remington, Alexander. 2008. "The Rev. James L. Bevel Dies at 72; Civil Rights Activist and Top Lieutenant to King." *Los Angeles Times*, December 24, 2008. https://www.latimes.com/local/obituaries/la-me-bevel25-2008dec25-story.html

Roeper, Richard. 2014. "Roeper Reviews 'Selma': History Lesson Moves Gracefully from Brutality to Tenderness." *Chicago Sun-Times*, December 30, 2014. https://chicago.suntimes.com/news/2014/12/30/18609343/roeper-reviews-selma-history-lesson-moves-gracefully-from-brutality-to-tenderness

Schapiro, Rich. 2015. "Reverend Who Flew to Selma After Bloody Sunday Massacre Recalls Watching Fellow Minister Die after Being Clubbed in Head During Civil Unrest in Selma." *New York Daily News*, March 8, 2015. www.nydailynews.com/news/national/olsen-hed-article-1.2141147

Scott, A.O. 2014. "A 50-Mile March, Nearly 50 Years Later," *The New York Times*, December 12, 2014. https://www.nytimes.com/2014/12/25/arts/in-selma-king-is-just-one-of-the-heroes.html?partner=rss&emc=rss&_r=0

Shearer, Jackie. 1988. "Interview with Coretta Scott King." *Eyes On the Prize II Interviews*. Washington University, November 21, 1988. digital.wustl.edu/e/eii/eiiweb/kin5427.0224.089corettascottking.html

Simon, Bob. 2015. "Where 'Selma' Meets Hollywood." *CBS*, February, 8, 2015. https://www.cbsnews.com/news/selma-ava-duvernay-60-minutes/

"Special Features: National Voting Rights Museum and Institute." *Selma*. 2014. Warner Home Video.

Stanford University. n.d.-a. "Jackson, Jimmie Lee." *The Martin Luther King, Jr. Research and Education Institute*. Accessed October 30, 2019. http://kinginstitute.stanford.edu/encyclopedia/jackson-jimmie-lee

Stanford University. n.d.-b. "Selma to Montgomery March." *The Martin Luther King, Jr. Research and Education Institute*. Accessed October 30, 2019. kinginstitute.stanford.edu/encyclopedia/selma-montgomery-march

Sunderland, Mitchell. 2017. "The Bizarre Reason You Rarely Hear Martin Luther King Quotes in Movies." *Vice*, January 13, 2017. https://www.vice.com/en_us/article/evgn4j/the-bizarre-reason-you-rarely-hear-martin-luther-king-quotes-in-movies

Turan, Kenneth. 2014. "Review: 'Selma' Is a Powerful Telling of the MLK Story." *Los Angeles Times*, December 24, 2014. https://www.latimes.com/entertainment/movies/la-et-mn-selma-review-20141225-column.html

Von Tunzelmann, Alex. 2015. "Is Selma Historically Accurate?" *The Guardian*, February 12, 2015. https://www.theguardian.com/film/2015/feb/12/reel-history-selma-film-historically-accurate-martin-luther-king-lyndon-johnson

Wallis, Jim. 2015. "'Selma's David Oyelowo on Playing MLK and What It Means to Be a Christian." *Sojourners*, January 8, 2015. https://sojo.net/articles/selmas-david-oyelowo-playing-mlk-and-what-it-means-be-christian

Webb, Sheyann. 2011. "Selma." In *"Takin' It to the Streets": A Sixties Reader*, edited by Alexander Bloom and Wini Breines, 43–47. New York: Oxford University Press.

Chapter 10

Hidden Figures (2016)

While the feats of male astronauts like Lt. Colonel John Glenn, the first American to orbit the earth, captured the attention of the entire nation, NASA showcased unprecedented talent in a group of African American female mathematicians who served as the brilliant minds behind the scenes and paved the way for America's pioneering presence among the stars. As the decade started to unfold and the United States was locked in an ideological battle with the Soviet Union for a dominant place in space, the diverse yet segregated Langley Research Center in Hampton, Virginia, acted as a hub of scientific activity with immense importance. Well before the first personal computer would debut, NASA's all-female "human computers" were at work, diligently perfecting the nitty-gritty calculations making humankind's journey into space possible in the first place.

The 2016 film *Hidden Figures* follows the true-to-life story of three of these women—Katherine Johnson (Taraji P. Henson), Dorothy Vaughan (Octavia Spencer), and Mary Jackson (Janelle Monáe)—whose rising careers at NASA proved to be pivotal during the beginning stages of the U.S. space program. Just as America's spacemen would test the physical limits of rapidly evolving aerospace technology, these exceptional women defied the racial and gender stereotypes still rampant in the South of the 1960s. Jackson chose to pursue the unlikely goal of becoming an engineer, Vaughan stepped up to the plate to lead the vanguard of computer programming, and Johnson pushed the limits of the unknown as she blazed a trail into "the math that doesn't yet exist." This female trio, accompanied by many others, devoted themselves to their intellectual craft and transcended cultural barriers as they successfully formed the backbone for Project Mercury, NASA's first man-in-space program. Under the leadership of Space Task Group leader Al Harrison (Kevin

Costner), Johnson and her team effectively translated the orbital flight of John Glenn (Glen Powell) from the realm of dreams into reality.

Directed by Theodore Melfi and distributed by 20th Century Fox, *Hidden Figures* premiered on December 25, 2016. To convey an authentic Southern setting, the film was shot primarily in Atlanta, with a few scenes captured on locations with historical ties to the civil rights movement. Allison Schroeder and Melfi wrote the screenplay, based on the nonfiction book bearing the same title by Margot Lee Shetterly. The story portrayed the overarching plotline of three Black mathematicians' historical accomplishments, while altering some contextual details and condensing the list of characters in the movie's dramatization. The film was shot on a $25-million budget and returned a domestic total gross of $169,607,287, finishing 14th in revenue rankings of 2016 films.

Topping the box office during its first two weekends of wide release in 2017, *Hidden Figures* received strong accolades from film critics and several award nominations, including three for the Oscars and two for the Golden Globes. The film was the domestically highest-grossing Best Picture nominee at the 2017 Academy Awards and figured among the National Board of Review's top 10 films of 2016. The movie also attained the Screen Actors Guild Award for Outstanding Performance by a Cast in a Motion Picture.

Many critics praised the film for its inspirational message and cultural relevance in modern-day America. "With the complex social forces that shaped its characters' lives still so relevant today, *Hidden Figures* is powerful precisely because it's *not* a solo portrait or a close character study," writes Lenika Cruz of *The Atlantic*. "Certainly, Hollywood will be a better industry when there are more films about the egos and personal demons and grand triumphs of black women who helped to change the world. But *Hidden Figures* shines with respect for sisterhood and the communistic spirit, and in casting its spotlight wide, the film imparts a profound appreciation for what was achieved in history's shadows" (Cruz 2017). *The Huffington Post*'s Bedatri Datta Choudhury echoes the same sentiment: "'Hidden Figures' inspires hope because it creates figures to emulate; it fills up that big, ever-growing vacuum that feeds on itself because all our heroes are gone" (Choudhury 2017).

K. Austin Collins of *The Ringer* notes the film's qualities as it provides a fresh perspective on African Americans in the 1960s. "The performances are warm and good-humored, without exception. It is absolutely an inspirational movie. . . . And it might be one of the few Hollywood movies about the civil rights era to imagine that black lives in the '60s, particularly black women's lives, were affected not only by racism but also by the space race and the Cold War" (Collins 2016). *Associated Press* writer Jake Coyle affirms that "'Hidden Figures,' punctuated by bright original songs by Pharrell Williams . . . avoids many of the typical notes of a civil rights drama and keeps its focus on its three indomitable leads and their characters' private lives. Nobody will mistake it for a deeply complicated examination of segregation and no one will wonder whether Melfi's film is going to end on a high note" (Associated Press 2017b).

While most critiques highlight the film's strong points, some reviewers were displeased with the liberties taken in the movie's portrayal of history. "It is a good movie, well-acted and inspirational. I enjoyed it even as I was exasperated by its many deviations from history, some of which are simply unnecessary," writes Michael Neufeld of the Smithsonian Institution (Neufeld 2017). Other critics found fault in the lack of depth with which the movie depicts racism. "In the end, Hidden Figures is an often-uplifting film with problematic elements and myopic framing," opines Illinois Institute of Technology historian Marie Hicks. "Though the film inserts a few scenes that hint at the indignity and terror of living as a black woman in the Jim Crow South, it oddly keeps racism at arm's length from a narrative that, without it, would never have existed" (Hicks 2017).

Overall, *Hidden Figures* seemed to strike a chord with audiences across the nation. Following the film's release, free screenings were organized in a variety of venues, including schools, nonprofits, and businesses, to promote youth awareness and accessibility to science, technology, engineering, and mathematics (STEM) careers (Muller 2017). With support from the director and key actors in the movie, these screenings took place nationally and internationally, many with the intent to benefit young female students and underprivileged families (Buckley 2017; Rainey 2017).

AMC Theatres and 21st Century Fox also collaborated to celebrate Black History Month in select large U.S. cities, holding charity screenings in February 2017 to further the film's reach in recounting the three Black protagonists' crucial place in American history (Associated Press 2017a). Liba Rubenstein, 21st Century Fox's Senior Vice President of Social Impact, said, "As we celebrate Black History Month and look ahead to Women's History Month in March, this story of empowerment and perseverance is more relevant than ever. We at 21CF were inspired by the grassroots movement to bring this film to audiences that wouldn't otherwise be able to see it—audiences that might include future innovators and barrier-breakers—and we wanted to support and extend that movement" (McNary 2017).

HISTORICAL BACKGROUND

The 1960s saw immense change across all fronts of society. Among those fundamental cultural shifts were the movements for women's rights and civil rights for African Americans, a growing acceptance of diversity, and numerous breakthroughs in technology. Within the context of an unprecedented spread of affluence across the nation, the social conscience of America was being stoked by the notion that millions of minorities were at a severe disadvantage and that something needed to be done about it. Women and Blacks had already endured more than a century of struggle for civil equality, but it was in this decade, in the wake of the unrest in society at large, that they were able to make a significant advance. Minority groups expressed their opinions with force, in an attempt to exert pressure on America's political and social power structures (Randel 1978, 197–198).

As women reshaped their roles in society, more women acquired jobs and became increasingly dissatisfied with the enormous disparities between men and women in the workplace. Around 38 percent of women worked a paid job at the start of the 1960s, but their average full-time earnings amounted to only 60 percent of the typical salary that men received (Farber 1994, 243–244). "Gradually, Americans came to accept some of the basic goals of the Sixties feminists: equal pay for equal work, an end to domestic violence, curtailment of severe limits on women in managerial jobs, an end to sexual harassment, and sharing of responsibility for housework and child rearing" (Walsh 2010). Although Congress passed equal pay legislation in 1963, the long-term problem persisted in the low-paying jobs that society classified as female work.

The political authorities of southern states had established "separate but equal" as a cultural standard for public venues, including schools, restaurants, and public transportation. The difficulty lay in the reality that the separateness that marked these facilities far outweighed any sense of equality. The civil rights movement responded to these problems by affirming the necessity of integration of Blacks and whites and strove for equal access to be granted to all public facilities.

Katherine Johnson, Dorothy Vaughan, and Mary Jackson each lived out the role of pioneers as Black women—labeled "colored computers"—in the NASA workforce of the 1960s, which mainly consisted of white men, particularly in higher positions of leadership. "The issue of equal employment opportunity (EEO) was not yet the source of difficulty it would later become [in 1965], when the imperative (for NASA) of recruiting and retaining highly trained personnel collided with the demands of blacks and women for a greater share of Federal jobs" (Levine 1982). In her book, Shetterly writes on the "surprisingly large number of black and white women who had been hiding in a profession seen as universally white and male," emphasizing the vital work they contributed to NASA's historic exploits in space navigation. "[B]efore the Supreme Court case *Brown v. Board of Education of Topeka* established that separate was in fact not equal, and before the poetry of Martin Luther King Jr.'s 'I Have a Dream' speech rang out over the steps of the Lincoln Memorial, Langley's West Computers were helping America dominate aeronautics, space research, and computer technology, carving out a place for themselves as female mathematicians who were also black, black mathematicians who were also female" (Shetterly 2016, xviii).

The first human computers joined the National Advisory Committee for Aeronautics (NACA), the precursor for NASA, in 1935. These workers were five white women who devoted all of their energies to completing mathematical calculations that supported the research of NACA engineers, who were eager to pass on these tedious responsibilities to the newly hired women. "[A]fter a few months, they realized the women were much more accurate, much faster, and did a better job—and didn't complain. And you could pay them less," explains Dr. Bill Barry, NASA Chief Historian. "That actually got put in a memo: 'Isn't this great? They do this great work and they're cheap'" (APPEL News Staff 2016).

Computers needed to have sharp minds and demonstrable talent in order to succeed at their work. The women were master organizers of mathematical work, smoothing out data and plotting and interpolating the numbers in a fast and accurate manner. Human computers reduced and analyzed data collected from wind tunnels, and they were well versed in the use of manometers, planimeters, calculators, slide rules, drafting tools, and other scientific instruments. Although the women received low salaries, their income was still higher than that of typists or secretaries. Most computers had degrees in math and were typically in their early twenties. Even though women's place in the working world was reimagined, NACA's human computers did indeed suffer from workplace bias simply because they were women (Arena 2017). Engineers, mechanics, and human computers needed to work as a team: "The engineers designed the research, the mechanics built the models, and the computers did the computation of the data. Although the development of needed aircraft (aeronautics) took priority, theoretical research into the principles of aerodynamics and designing research facilities to test these principles were also essential" (Golemba 1994, 9).

Langley expanded its workforce during a labor shortage in World War II (1939–1945) and first hired Black women as computers in 1943—one of whom was Dorothy Vaughan. West Area Computing, a segregated unit, was formed for the incoming women, who, as minorities in the South, had no other vocational options other than low-paying jobs as teachers in segregated schools. "They all had college degrees in mathematics. They were all extremely bright," said Barry. "The African American women computers were actually more qualified than their white counterparts who worked at the NACA at the time, so they naturally flourished" (APPEL News Staff 2016). The women in West Area Computing unit rapidly made their presence known as they distinguished themselves with their talent, and the department grew as capable Black women continued to learn about the prospects at NACA. These jobs gave them good pay along with the opportunity to utilize their skillsets in an engaging vocational context.

With the opportunity came challenges as well, particularly the biases based on race and gender. For instance, the "colored computers" were initially restricted to use only the bathroom and dining facilities that were designated for them (Shetterly 2017a). The women at Langley, who affirmed that they constantly received respectful and considerate treatment from their male colleagues, were always referred to as "girls," even in the organization's official reports. While it didn't seem out of place for them at the time, the computers described Langley Research Center as a "man's world" and noticed that there was "not much opportunity or encouragement for female advancement" (Golemba 1994, 93). Looking back on that timeframe, Vaughan remarked in a 1994 interview, "I changed what I could, and what I couldn't, I endured" (Golemba 1994, 43).

Despite the opposition they faced, the women kept their focus on the tasks at hand, and they excelled in their areas of expertise. "They performed," said NASA Administrator Charles Bolden. "They essentially put their heads down and did what they were asked to do. They set goals . . . and they went after those goals without paying any attention to people who said it could not be done. I think they provide a role model, or role models, for all of us" (APPEL News Staff 2016).

NACA's computers were put to the test after the United States entered an all-out crisis on October 4, 1957, at the Soviet Union's launch of the first artificial satellite, *Sputnik 1*. "This had a 'Pearl Harbor' effect on American public opinion, creating an illusion of a technological gap and provided the impetus for increased spending for aerospace endeavors, technical and scientific educational programs, and the chartering of new federal agencies to manage air and space research and development" (Garber and Launius 2005). In earnest response to the *Sputnik* dilemma, NACA was absorbed into the newly created National Aeronautics and Space Administration (NASA) on October 1, 1958. NASA now encompassed all 8,000 of NACA's employees, its $100-million annual budget, and its three main research laboratories, Langley Aeronautical Laboratory (officially renamed "Langley Research Center" at this time), Ames Aeronautical Laboratory, and Lewis Flight Propulsion Laboratory (Garber and Launius 2005). Notably, at this juncture in history, all facilities were desegregated, thus doing away with Langley's West Area Computing office entirely (Shetterly 2017a).

Within just months of its inception, NASA started to launch America's first mission into space. Project Mercury—an estimated $400-million undertaking that was the first prominent campaign of its kind—was propelled by the challenge of taking humans into the rigorous and dangerous journey of spaceflight (NASA 1961; Garber and Launius 2005). "We hadn't done this before, and so those calculations were absolutely critical to understanding how we were going to safely put people in and out of space," said Bill Barry in reference to the role of NASA's computers (APPEL News Staff 2016).

Katherine Coleman Goble Johnson was one of those computers—and one of NASA's best minds. A prodigy in mathematics hailing from White Sulphur Springs, West Virginia, she graduated from high school at the age of 14, earned her bachelor of science in mathematics and French at 18, and subsequently became one of the first three Black graduate students to attend West Virginia University. Katherine Goble (Johnson after remarriage) came to NACA in 1953 as a research mathematician, taking her place among the other Black women in the West Area Computing unit.

By this time, Dorothy Vaughan had been in charge of the group for four years—NACA's first African American supervisor and one of the generally few women to enjoy a position of leadership. Persistent in advocating the cause of the colored computers, Vaughan also supported white computers belonging to other units who merited job advancements or increases in salary. She won recognition in the eyes of the engineers, who knew that her recommendations of computers for specific projects were always spot-on—and who tended to ask Vaughan herself to tackle the especially taxing assignments (Shetterly 2017a).

After only two weeks under Vaughan's command, Goble received an assignment to temporarily fill a position in the Flight Research Division's Maneuver Loads Branch. The assignment ended up being permanent, filling her next four years with data analysis of flight tests. Goble played an integral role in the creation of the 1958 Notes on Space Technology, a collection of lectures by engineers in the Flight Research Division and the Pilotless Aircraft Research Division. When NACA transitioned into NASA that year, the same engineers with whom Goble worked became the core components of the Space Task Group, naturally bringing her along with them as they started their new space-focused endeavors. Then in 1960, Katherine G. Johnson (after marrying Colonel James Johnson in 1959) coauthored a research report with engineer Ted Skopinski, "Azimuth Angle at Burnout for Placing a Satellite Over a Selected Earth Position," which delineated equations pertaining to an orbital spaceflight with a specified landing position for the spacecraft; she was the first woman in the Flight Research Division to receive credit as an author of any such report (Shetterly 2018).

Meanwhile, at NASA's commencement in 1958, Vaughan and other women from the shuttered West Area Computing unit had been repositioned to the new Analysis and Computation Division (ACD), a group that was integrated in terms of both race and gender (Shetterly 2017a). The ACD was at the vanguard of new technology, as electronic computers were steadily being integrated into NASA's work. The IBM (International Business Machine) had gained considerable attention in preceding years, and programmers needed to learn FORTRAN, a cutting-edge programming language, in order to handle the machine. Realizing that human computers were on their way to becoming obsolete, former supervisor Vaughan decided to teach herself FORTRAN, which came "fairly easily because it used algebraic language" (Golemba 1994, 116). She then took action to prepare her colleagues with knowledge of the language as well as other relevant computer concepts, noting that the human computers were the ones who went on to teach the engineers in the use of FORTRAN (McFadden 2018; Golemba 1994, 116). A veritable authority in FORTRAN, Vaughan also made significant contributions to NASA's tremendously successful Scout Launch Vehicle Program.

Another contemporary of Johnson and Vaughan, Mary Winston Jackson, had made her way to Langley in 1951, reporting to Vaughan during her first two years in West Area Computing. Engineer Kazimierz Czarnecki then offered her the chance to gain firsthand experience in Langley's 4-foot-by-4-foot Supersonic Pressure Tunnel, "a 60,000-horsepower wind tunnel capable of blasting models with winds approaching twice the speed of sound" (Shetterly 2017b). In taking the assignment, Jackson became the first colored computer to realize integration (Golemba 1994, 44).

As Jackson conducted experiments under the engineer's guidance, Czarnecki brought up the idea of her clear potential for advancement: from the role of a mathematician to that of an engineer. The training program that would make such a move possible would require graduate-level physics and math courses, which were run by the University of Virginia. Because these afterwork classes were staged at the segregated Hampton High School, Jackson had to acquire special authorization from the City of Hampton to accompany her white classmates. She did, and after completing the coursework, in 1958 Jackson became the first African American engineer to work at NASA. At a time when one rarely saw any female engineers, regardless of race, Jackson "very well may have been the only black female aeronautical engineer in the field" (Shetterly 2017b). Also in 1958, she would become a coauthor for the first time, collaborating with Czarnecki on the report "Effects of Nose Angle and Mach Number on Transition on Cones at Supersonic Speeds."

The year 1961 was home to a flurry of activity as the space race started to heat up, with Russia taking an early lead. In March, a lifelike dummy named Ivan Ivanovich (the Russian equivalent of "John Doe") safely endured two flights of Russian spacecraft into low Earth orbit, accompanied by a dog and an assortment of other animals aboard *Korabl Sputnik 4* and *5*. Following these missions, on April 12, USSR air force pilot and cosmonaut Yuri Alekseyevich Gagarin boarded *Vostok 1* and survived a 108-minute flight that completed one orbit around the earth, making him the first human in space and an instant national hero. The fact that the budding Soviet space program succeeded in transporting a human into space before the United States only added to the mounting tension for the crews working at NASA.

Less than a month after Gagarin's flight, the United States answered back. America's first ambassador into space, Alan Bartlett Shepard Jr., realized a successful, 15-minute suborbital mission aboard his *Mercury* capsule on May 5. Katherine Johnson played a key role in preparation for *Freedom 7*'s launch, as she completed the trajectory analysis for the mission (Shetterly 2018). Then on July 21, Virgil Ivan "Gus" Grissom would follow with another 15-minute suborbital flight, whose conclusion was covered in controversy at the sinking of the costly spacecraft shortly after splashdown (Dunn 1999). Due to the hatch opening prematurely, ocean water filled *Liberty Bell 7*, forcing Grissom to escape and tread water for nearly four minutes before he was rescued (Armstrong 2007). The game continued, and

Russia responded on August 6, 1961: Soviet pilot Gherman Stepanovich Titov manned *Vostok 2*, which made an impressive 17 orbits around the planet and survived more than an entire day's worth of spaceflight.

After watching Russia send two humans into orbital space in 1961, NASA was zealously preparing for America's first orbital mission. "It was a very tense period of time between the United States and the Soviet Union," said Barry. "The space race became a surrogate for the struggle between those two countries, and so what was happening at NASA was critical to the country. President Kennedy set the goal to land on the moon in part to prove that the United States had a viable socioeconomic system—because people actually thought that the Soviet system might be better than the U.S. one because they were so successful in space" (APPEL News Staff 2016).

As a result of both technical issues and weather-related delays, Project Mercury's initial timeline for an orbital flight had been consistently pushed back—from late 1960 into the summer of 1961, then to October, December, and finally February 1962. NASA's competency and judgment were under intense scrutiny while the American public, press, and government authorities all voiced their discontent after the sequence of postponements (Shetterly 2016, 215). It was in this context in 1962 that Katherine Johnson stepped up to the plate and answered the challenge that would earn her place in history with John Glenn's *Friendship 7* mission.

"Sending a man into space was a damn tall order, but it was the part about returning him safely to Earth that kept Katherine Johnson and the rest of the space pilgrims awake at night," writes Shetterly. The mission possessed so many facets that could potentially lead to a disastrous outcome for the aspiring space traveler, not the least of which was "the notoriously temperamental Atlas rocket." Standing at 95 feet tall and boasting 3.5 million horsepower, the Atlas was essentially an intercontinental ballistic missile with modifications enabling it to take the Mercury capsule around Earth's orbit. With only a 60-percent success rate in the Atlas's first five ventures, every conceivable aspect of the forecasted flight had to undergo continual testing in order to eliminate as many elements of error as possible. For instance, the capsule needed to endure the maximum amount of aerodynamic pressure that it would face when approaching its top velocity—otherwise, a guaranteed explosion in the sky (Shetterly 2016, 213–214): "Everything rested upon the brain busters' mastery of the laws of physics and mathematics. The mission was colossal in its scope, but it required both extreme precision and the utmost accuracy. A number transposed in calculating the launch azimuth, a significant digit too few in measuring the fully loaded weight of the capsule, a mistake in accounting for the rocket's speed and acceleration or the rotation of the Earth could cascade through the chain of dependencies, causing serious, perhaps catastrophic, consequences" (Shetterly 2016, 214).

The mathematical intricacies at hand would, hopefully, ensure the survival of the soon-to-be spaceman John Herschel Glenn Jr., a 40-year-old lieutenant colonel who had an impressive track record as a pilot in the U.S. Marine Corps. This World War II and Korean War veteran acted as the charismatic spokesman for the original "Mercury Seven" astronauts, boasting the most flying experience of them all (Bond 1987, 36–38). After setting records as a naval test pilot—including the first transcontinental supersonic flight—Glenn spent three years training for this mission, incessantly aided by flight simulators and procedures trainers to sharpen his responses to any failure scenario imaginable.

To match the enormous challenge presented in realizing an orbital flight, NASA constructed an immense communications network to connect global tracking stations to IBMs positioned in Washington, D.C., Cape Canaveral, and Bermuda. The computers housed the equations linked to the orbital trajectory, ensuring the capsule's course from start to finish. However, the electronic devices were still erratic in behavior, and America's aspiring space voyagers were cautious about entrusting their future to the performance of an inanimate object. During the all-important preflight preparations, John Glenn gave the engineers a specific request: "get the girl"—referring to Katherine Johnson—to manually verify the numbers in the same equations that they had programmed into the IBM. "If she says they're good," Johnson recalls Glenn declaring, "then I'm ready to go" (Shetterly 2018). So Johnson, armed with a desktop mechanical calculator and her incredible intellect, painstakingly processed every numerical component of the framework for the orbital mission, "coming up with numbers for eleven different output variables, each computed to eight significant digits" (Shetterly 2016, 223). After a day and a half of intense concentration, the calculations were complete, and her figures equaled the computer's. Glenn was good to go.

On the morning of February 20, 1962, the skies were clear outside the Kennedy Space Center in Cape Canaveral, Florida. The Friendship 7 Mission Objective: "Place a man into Earth orbit, observe his reactions to the space environment and safely return him to Earth to a point where he could be readily found" (Dunbar 2017). At 6:03 a.m. Glenn entered the 4,200-pound, 9.5-by-6-foot *Mercury-Atlas 6* spacecraft, wearing his 20-pound pressurized spacesuit. After every gauge was checked and every bolt fastened, at 9:47 a.m. the fiery Atlas launched the bell-shaped *Friendship* 7 into the sky—as 135 million Americans held their breath, hanging on to every word transmitted from the live television and radio broadcasts.

Following an impeccable entry into orbit, the flight was smooth sailing during the first circuit, during which Glenn marveled at the unmatched vistas of the earth below and consumed a tube of applesauce while passing over Australia (Bond 1987, 43–45). At the completion of the initial orbit, he needed to improvise and switch from automatic control to manual because of a clog in one of the yaw attitude control jets (Dunbar 2017). Then at the end of orbit two, a warning light indicated that the heat shield was no longer securely fastened. Diverging from the planned course of action, Mission

Control decided that Glenn would retain the retropack during reentry as an added measure of security, just in case the heat shield had indeed loosened. When the spacecraft finished the third orbit, the retro-rockets were engaged, and Glenn prepared for the descent. "As I got into the heat of reentry, I glanced out the window, and there were big flaming chunks that were coming back by the window, back along the flight path. . . . I can still see them to this day," John Glenn recalled in a 1987 interview. "And I couldn't be certain at that time whether it was the retro-pack or the heat shield. So that caused considerable apprehension" (McCombs 1987).

During reentry, there was an anticipated gap in radio contact between Glenn and NASA due to the ionization barrier formed around the capsule. Breaking the seven-minute silence came the astronaut's declaration that all was well, exclaiming, "Boy, that was a real fireball!" (Mandel 1962). In the end, NASA discovered that a malfunction had illuminated the warning light, and the heat shield stayed intact for the entire flight. When *Friendship* 7 hit the waters of the Atlantic, the space traveler's 4-hour-55-minute-23-second journey had taken him 75,679 miles, making three passes around the planet and finally landing him 800 miles to the southeast of Bermuda (Dunbar 2017). Within 21 minutes after splashdown, America's "Ace of Space" was retrieved by the USS *Noa* and whisked back to the familiarity of solid land.

Thanks to Johnson's math and Glenn's heroics, the successful mission made history and greatly boosted America's confidence with momentum for the next round of space-bound competition. John Glenn was a champion in the public's eye, but Katherine Johnson was also a reason for celebration, albeit with less fanfare. The revelation about her significant place in supporting the triumphal space mission caught attention in local Black communities first—then in other parts of the country as the news continued to spread (Shetterly 2016, 225). It would only be after her robust 33 years at NASA, at the age of 97, when Johnson received the highest civilian award, the Presidential Medal of Freedom, awarded by President Barack Obama in 2015 in recognition of her career's many remarkable achievements. Then in 2017, Langley Research Center solidified the legacy even further, naming its newest building after her: The Katherine G. Johnson Computational Research Facility (Gillard 2017).

DEPICTION AND CULTURAL CONTEXT

Author and executive producer Margot Lee Shetterly noted the expected discrepancies between the facts in her book and the commercialized version of history as portrayed in the film: "For better or for worse, there is history, there is the book and then there's the movie. Timelines had to be conflated and [there were] composite characters, and for most people [who have seen the movie] have already taken that as the literal fact" (Pearlman 2016).

While history underwent simplification to give audiences an easier-to-digest storyline, the underlying historical takeaways came through with clarity. "When I look at the final version of the movie, they really took a lot of my feedback into consideration," said Shetterly. "What was very true was that everybody wanted to get the story right, and they wanted to do honor to these women" (Tinubu 2016).

Director Melfi commented on the tension between historicity and artistry in cinematic storytelling. "I say this all the time, but the movie is not a documentary. We were painfully aware and very careful with how we portrayed the women and the things they accomplished," he affirmed. "There are little liberties taken here and there to dramatize, but the crux of the story is true." The filmmakers had invited a group from NASA, including chief historian Bill Barry, to weigh in on the script for *Hidden Figures*. "They wanted to get the atmosphere of the film correct," Barry said. "I think that the movie is true to the stories of the main characters. On the whole I was very happy with the outcome" (Pearlman 2016).

The real Katherine Johnson, a centenarian now constantly flooded with attention from the likes of dignitaries as well as everyday citizens, saw the film three times within the first month of its release and gave her approval. "I'm glad that I'm young enough still to be living and that they are, so they can look and see, 'That's who that is,'" Johnson said. "And they are as excited as I am." For as much inspirational momentum her life story has gained in recent years, Johnson maintains a down-to-earth perspective on it all: "There's nothing to it—I was just doing my job," she told *The Washington Post* during an in-home interview in Hampton Roads, Virginia, in 2017. "They needed information and I had it, and it didn't matter that I found it. At the time, it was just a question and an answer" (St. Martin 2017).

Independently of race, Katherine Johnson has captured the most recognition among all of NASA's human computers, and her story is such an outlier in popular history that her legacy has tendency toward legend. "The power of [Johnson's] story is such that many accounts incorrectly credit her with being the first black woman to work as a mathematician at NASA, or the only black woman to have held the job," Shetterly writes. "She is often mistakenly reported as having been sent to the 'all-male' Flight Research Division, a group that included four other female mathematicians, one of whom was also black. One account implied that her calculations singlehandedly saved the Apollo 13 mission. That even Katherine Johnson's remarkable achievements can't quite match some of the myths that have grown up around her is a sign of the strength of the vacuum caused by the long absence of African Americans from mainstream history" (Shetterly 2016, 250).

The film's version of history leans in that direction as it sprinkles several anachronisms throughout NASA's work environment, likely with the intentions to reinforce the overpowering sense of segregation in the South. The movie portrays Langley Research Center as having segregated facilities in

1961, including the West Area Computing unit. Although the audience sees Dorothy Vaughan as a stand-in supervisor seeking official recognition and fair compensation for her position, Vaughan actually received the promotion as supervisor of West Computing 12 years before the events in the film took place. When NACA turned into NASA in 1958, all of Langley's facilities were no longer under the effects of segregation, and the West Computing office was accordingly abolished. By 1961, the former West Computers were already part of a desegregated working environment in the Analysis and Computational Division (Shetterly 2017a).

Another misrepresentation of history are the running sequences when Johnson is shown making multiple half-mile treks per day to a "colored" restroom, which only existed on the opposite end of Langley's campus in the movie. In reality, it was Johnson's colleague Mary Jackson who had to go out of her way to find a colored restroom, though still on the East Side. In an interview, Jackson noted that "even after they began to integrate the computers, one still had to 'know' which restrooms were for which race" (Golemba 1994, 43–44). Johnson, however, was not even aware of the segregation of the East Side restrooms, and several years transpired as she used the unmarked, technically "whites-only" restrooms before any complaint was recorded. She chose to ignore the complaint, and any concern soon fizzled out (Shetterly 2016, 129).

Although strategically positioned in the film, the elements conveying an overwhelming sense of discrimination at Langley were perhaps misleading for the NASA of 1961. Katherine Johnson shared during an interview with WHRO-TV that her experience at NASA was not tainted by feelings of inequality. "I didn't feel the segregation at NASA, because everybody there was doing research. You had a mission and you worked on it, and it was important to you to do your job . . . and play bridge at lunch. I didn't feel any segregation. I knew it was there, but I didn't feel it" (WHRO-TV 2011). Similarly, Dorothy Vaughan and Mary Jackson both expressed this paradox: They felt somewhat bitter about the segregation they experienced, but without any resentment toward their white colleagues or complaints about their treatment from the engineers. White and Black computers went on record that personnel of both races "worked well together without any problems" (Golemba 1994, 43). Overall, the segregationist atmosphere and unequal working conditions depicted in the movie were more representative of the long-standing racist and sexist attitudes pervasive in the South and a small reflection of NACA's former days, rather than the particulars of Langley in 1961 and 1962.

Outside of NASA, scenes in the film that show protesters decrying the effects of segregation—while surrounded by police and barking dogs—are indicative of the mood that permeated many southern states in the early 1960s. The sit-ins at the Woolworth's lunch counter in Greensboro, North Carolina, which managed to enact desegregation after the six-month protest in 1960, were fresh in the minds of Black citizens of Virginia and appropriately received mention in the movie's first church scene. Later in the film, Mary Jackson's husband burns with anger as the family watches the television broadcast telling of the May 14, 1961, bus bombing that targeted the civil rights activists known as the Freedom Riders.

While *Hidden Figures* keeps racial tensions constantly in the backdrop for the protagonists, the film does not delve too deeply into the increasing violence and the demonstrations that were building momentum nationwide. The story's focus remains on the individual trajectories of the three women at NASA, intermittently reminding the audience of the larger picture in American culture with clips of President John F. Kennedy, Martin Luther King Jr., and various space missions. The movie shows heartwarming depictions of middle-class Black families, who go about their daily lives with a sense of both camaraderie and resolution to make it through trying circumstances.

> Scientific progress in the twentieth century had been relatively linear; social progress, however, did not move in a straight line, as the descent from the hopeful years after the Civil War into the despairing circumstances of the Jim Crow laws proved. But since World War II, one brick after another had been pried from the walls of segregation. The Supreme Court victories opening graduate education to black students, the executive orders integrating the federal government and the military, the victory, both real and symbolic when the Brooklyn Dodgers signed Negro baseball player Jackie Robinson, were all new landings reached, new corners turned, hopes that pushed Negroes to redouble their efforts to sever the link between separate and equal decisively and permanently. (Shetterly 2016, 140)

From society at large to the specifics at NASA, *Hidden Figures* consistently weaves in historical recordings to the narrative to heighten a sense of authenticity. The shuttle launches consist of a blend of archival footage, computer-generated imagery, and original acting to represent the events that took place. Additionally, the writers took most of the communication between John Glenn and Mission Control directly from historical NASA transcripts. The film similarly includes accurate mathematical equations on the chalkboards that the actors were required to memorize for each individual scene. In the scenes involving the newfangled IBM, the cast was able to make use of a genuine model owned by a collector (Melfi and Henson 2016).

While casting a historical backdrop, the filmmakers created fictional composite characters in Space Task Group leader Al Harrison, manager Vivian Mitchell, and engineer Paul Stafford, in an attempt to simplify the complex and often fluctuating arrangement of personnel at Langley during the early 1960s (Loff 2017). "You might get the indication in the movie that these were the only people doing those jobs, when in reality we know they worked in teams, and those teams had other teams," Shetterly explained.

"There were sections, branches, divisions, and they all went up to a director. There were so many people required to make this happen. . . . Even though Katherine Johnson, in this role, was a hero, there were so many others that were required to do other kinds of tests and checks to make [Glenn's] mission come to fruition. But I understand you can't make a movie with 300 characters. It is simply not possible" (Pearlman 2016).

Since Costner's character was fictional, his presence in the story lent itself to more criticism than there might have been otherwise. The scene showing Harrison destroying the "Colored Ladies Room" sign never took place, as well as the scene in which he let Johnson into Mission Control to witness the *Friendship 7* launch (all while the real-life Mercury Control Center was stationed in Cape Canaveral, Florida). Dexter Thomas (2017) of *Vice News* and Megan Garber (2017) of *The Atlantic* both criticized Costner's robust role in the storyline, accusing the writers of employing a "white savior" trope. Melfi commented on the addition of the scenes involving Costner, "There needs to be white people who do the right thing, there needs to be black people who do the right thing, and someone does the right thing. And so who cares who does the right thing, as long as the right thing is achieved?" (Thomas 2017). Despite the accusations of "whitewashing" the story, Melfi defended his adaptation as a form of entertainment that, in the end, represents history, albeit with artistic license. "The fact is this: NASA was desegregated by a white male. NASA was not desegregated by a black male. NASA was not desegregated by white women," Melfi asserted (Blay 2017).

Although the film met an audience removed from the immediacy of the social inequalities of the 1960s, tensions still exist in the ongoing narratives concerning gender and race in America. The story was released into American culture at a time when women's rights are lauded in the national spotlight, amid growing intolerance for any type of discrimination, as well as heightened awareness of the closing gap in pay between men and women. The filmmakers attuned *Hidden Figures* to the growing emphasis on giving women an edge in the workplace, as young female students are encouraged to pursue the previously "all-male" STEM careers. "The story and the contributions that these women, black and white, made to mathematics and to our advancement in technology and to the space race—I wanted to be a part of that storytelling," said Octavia Spencer, who portrayed Dorothy Vaughan. "This is important, not only for women of color, but for all young girls to know that they have value" (20th Century Fox Belgium 2017). "I hope this film shows kids of all races and sexes that there's more opportunity and success to be had than in a Kardashian kind of world," director Theodore Melfi said. "To see a different dream about their mind is so desperately needed" (Lee 2016).

Janelle Monáe, who played Mary Jackson in the film, commented on the protagonists' visionary journeys throughout the trials of the early 1960s.

"They didn't allow race and gender to get in the way of them achieving this goal: get the Americans into space. This movie shows us all working together—white men, white women, black women—knowing we all bleed the same color. And when we're together, we achieve extraordinary things. I hope this serves as a reminder that we did it then and we can do it now" (FOX 5 DC 2017).

Many of the cast members were intended for the movie to serve as inspiration for a brighter future in American society. "It can be very frustrating when we're still talking about equal pay for women, and we're still talking about inclusion," Monáe said. "So, what I am inspired by, though, is that these women—although they may have expressed their frustrations amongst each other—when they went into work, they worked hard, they fought for what was rightfully theirs, and they won. They didn't allow it to affect them mentally" (FOX 5 DC 2017). Spencer noted the timeliness of the story's release. "I think our country *then* was at the precipice of redefining itself, and we find ourselves there now," she opined. "And the beautiful thing about being able to see history in hindsight is how we can influence the future" (20th Century Fox Belgium 2017).

In an interview with *The Hollywood Reporter* at the film's premier, Melfi recounted an anecdote from a trip to one of the film's screenings: When Octavia Spencer entered the first-class lounge at an airport, more than 10 minutes went by without anyone waiting on her. But when Melfi came into the room, someone offered him coffee right away. "I could've cried at that moment," he said. "I want to dedicate this film to everyone in the world who has ever experienced that, who has sat through unconscious bias their whole lives, who has not gotten a cup of coffee or a promotion or been paid properly because of the color of their skin or their gender" (Lee 2016).

The real-life problem that the movie addresses can be summed up, in Melfi's words, as "unconscious bias": "The movie is about 'colored bathrooms' and 'colored coffeepots' and not getting promotions, not getting paid what you're worth. Not being a supervisor when you're qualified to become a supervisor. Not being able to go to a school to get a degree like Mary Jackson's character. . . . Or having the same degree as a man, but that degree is good for a man to be an engineer but not good enough for a female to be an engineer" (NASA 2016). While the events in *Hidden Figures* took place decades in the past, the biases still covertly operating in American society hold relevance for modern-day audiences to address. Melfi continued, "All those things that are not overt, per se, but they permeate every aspect of civil rights, and NASA, and the struggles this country had back then and the struggles we see today" (NASA 2016).

The reasons the stories of Katherine Johnson, Dorothy Vaughan, and Mary Jackson remained "hidden" for so long are multifaceted. Shetterly explains that sexism and racism were two key factors, in addition to the fact that the women in question led full lives with their families outside of their careers at NASA. She affirmed that this story provides an outlet "to shine a light on a lot of women who have not been talked about. None of these women really got the recognition they deserved and . . . now an entire group of women are being recognized for the work that they did" (St. Martin 2017). Troy Hylick, Katherine Johnson's grandson, commented on the remarkable qualities of all of the women in the book and the movie: "Because of all of the roadblocks that were put in their place, and they had to get over and get around and get under . . . they became superhuman because all of those things that they had to do, just to do the job they were in there to do" (St. Martin 2017).

While a forerunner in her own right, Johnson was, in fact, only one of the many women tucked away in NASA's history. Besides Vaughan and Jackson, who are seen as stars in the movie, NASA was also home to Dorothy Hoover, who published theoretical research on Robert T. Jones's delta wings in 1951; Marge Hannah, a white mathematician who became the first supervisor for the Black computers; and Doris Cohen, the first woman to author a NACA report in 1941 (Shetterly 2016, xvii). With representations in both the book and film, the stories about these outstanding women "are destined to change our national narrative about the space program and the people who contributed to it" (Neufeld 2017).

Following two terms under the nation's first Black president and a presidential campaign run by the first female candidate backed by a major political party, it is evident that much change has taken place in American society since John Glenn's first venture into space. With *Hidden Figures*, the filmmakers expressed a desire to remind America of the path the country has traversed, with the hope to avoid repeating the same mistakes of the past but instead to receive inspiration from pioneering figures in American history. The diligent female mathematicians in NASA's budding space program solidified an intellectual legacy for the following generations. An unassuming but brilliant group of "hidden figures" catalyzed a future that would differ drastically from the confines of their immediate experience: one of exploration leading far into the recesses of space—and one of freedoms transcending the social injustices that many women like them endured.

In 1962, American hero John Glenn was 40 years old when he took to the skies in *Friendship 7*. In his portrayal of the astronaut, the actor Glen Powell was in his late twenties, more than a decade younger than the true Glenn, who was indeed an outspoken, congenial figure as depicted in the film.

Although John Glenn did request for Katherine Johnson to check the computer-based calculations, he did not make a last-minute call from the launch pad as the film shows. While vitally important to the mission, the request was not related to any emergency situation, and Johnson worked on the math for a solid day and a half (Shetterly 2016, 216–223).

FURTHER READING

APPEL News Staff. 2016. "NASA's Hidden Figures Helped the Agency Make History." NASA, December 21, 2016. https://appel.nasa.gov/2016/12/21/nasas-hidden-figures-helped-the-agency-make-history/

Arena, Jenny. 2017. "Hidden Figures and Human Computers." Smithsonian Institution, January 26, 2017. https://airandspace.si.edu/stories/editorial/hidden-figures-and-human-computers

Armstrong, Dennis. 2007. "Mercury-Redstone 4 (19)." NASA, November 16, 2007. https://www.nasa.gov/mission_pages/mercury/missions/libertybell7.html

Associated Press. 2017a. "Free Screening of 'Hidden Figures' Offered for Black History Month." *NBC Southern California*, February 14, 2017. http://www.nbclosangeles.com/news/local/Hidden-Figures-Free-Screening-413750893.html

Associated Press. 2017b. "Review: 'Hidden Figures' Is a Feel-Good History Lesson." *Detroit Free Press*, January 4, 2017. https://www.freep.com/story/entertainment/movies/2017/01/04/hidden-figures-movie-review/96172684/

Blay, Zeba. 2017. "'Hidden Figures' and The Diversity Conversation We Aren't Having." *The Huffington Post*, February 23, 2017. https://www.huffingtonpost.com/entry/hidden-figures-and-the-diversity-conversation-we-arent-having_us_58adc9bee4b0d0a6ef470492

Bond, Peter R. 1987. *Heroes in Space: From Gagarin to Challenger*. New York: Basil Blackwell.

Buckley, Eileen. 2017. "'Hidden Figures' to Inspire City Students to Pursue STEM Careers." *WBFO*, February 1, 2017. http://news.wbfo.org/post/hidden-figures-inspire-city-students-pursue-stem-careers

Choudhury, Bedatri Datta. 2017. "'Moonlight' and 'Hidden Figures' Give Us Radical Hope When We Need It Most." *The Huffington Post*, March 5, 2017. https://www.huffingtonpost.in/bedatri-datta-choudhury/moonlight-and-hidden-figures-give-us-radical-hope-when-we-ne_a_21805844/

Collins, K. Austin. 2016. "Queens of the Space Age," *The Ringer*, December 27, 2016. https://www.theringer.com/2016/12/27/16037254/hidden-figures-film-review-950967fc9abd#.p55gnm5d1

Cruz, Lenika. 2017. "What Sets the Smart Heroines of Hidden Figures Apart." *The Atlantic*, January 9, 2017. https://www.theatlantic.com/entertainment/archive/2017/01/hidden-figures-review/512252/

Dunbar, Brian. 2017. "Friendship 7." NASA, August 7, 2017. https://www.nasa.gov/mission_pages/mercury/missions/friendship7.html

Dunn, Marcia. 1999. "Liberty Bell 7 Yields Clues to Its Sinking." *Los Angeles Times*, December 12, 1999. articles.latimes.com/1999/dec/12/news/mn-43115

Farber, David. 1994. *The Age of Great Dreams: America in the 1960s*. New York: Hill and Wang.

FOX 5 DC. 2017. "HIDDEN FIGURES Interviews—Taraji P. Henson, Octavia Spencer, Monae Pharrell Costner Parsons." January 3, 2017. Video, 3:06, 3:52. https://www.youtube.com/watch?v=QUGBFhKWKHM

Garber, Megan. 2017. "Hidden Figures and the Appeal of Math in an Age of Inequality." *The Atlantic*, January 18, 2017. https://www.theatlantic.com/entertainment/archive/2017/01/hidden-figures-and-the-appeal-of-math-in-an-age-of-inequality/513434/

Garber, Steve, and Roger Launius. 2005. "A Brief History of NASA." NASA, July 25, 2005. https://history.nasa.gov/factsheet.htm

Gillard, Eric. 2017. "NASA Langley's Katherine Johnson Computational Research Facility Officially Opens." NASA, October 5, 2017. https://www.nasa.gov/feature/langley/nasa-langley-s-katherine-johnson-computational-research-facility-officially-opens

Golemba, Beverly E. 1994. *Human Computers: The Women in Aeronautical Research*. Unpublished manuscript, NASA Langley Archives. https://crgis.ndc.nasa.gov/crgis/images/c/c7/Golemba.pdf

Hicks, Marie. 2017. "Hidden Figures Is a Groundbreaking Book. But the Film? Not so Much." *The Guardian*, February 13, 2017. https://www.theguardian.com/science/the-h-word/2017/feb/13/film-hidden-figures-nasa-black-women-mathematicians-book

Lee, Ashley. 2016. "'Hidden Figures' Director Theodore Melfi Recalls 'Unconscious Bias' Incident Involving Octavia Spencer: 'I Could've Cried'." *The Hollywood Reporter*, December 12, 2016. https://www.hollywoodreporter.com/news/hidden-figures-director-recalls-unconscious-bias-incident-involving-octavia-spencer-955411

Levine, Arnold S. 1982. "Managing NASA in the Apollo Era (NASA SP-4102)," NASA. https://history.nasa.gov/SP-4102/ch5.htm

Loff, Sarah. 2017. "Modern Figures: Frequently Asked Questions." NASA, August 3, 2017. https://www.nasa.gov/modernfigures/faq

Mandel, Paul. 1962. "The Ominous Failures that Haunted Friendship's Flight." *Life*, March 2, 1962.

McCombs, Phil. 1987. "John Glenn at Liftoff Plus 25 Years." *The Washington Post*, February 20, 1987. https://www.washingtonpost.com/archive/lifestyle/1987/02/20/john-glenn-at-liftoff-plus-25-years/e201be00-f395-429b-b09b-e92b471806e6

McFadden, Christopher. 2018. "Dorothy Vaughan: NASA's 'Human Computer' and American Hero." Interesting Engineering, March 11, 2018. https://interestingengineering.com/dorothy-vaughan-nasas-human-computer-and-american-hero

McNary, Dave. 2017. "'Hidden Figures' Set for Free Screenings in 14 Cities for Black History Month." *Variety*, February 14, 2017. https://variety.com/2017/film/news/hidden-figures-free-screenings-black-history-month-1201988170/

Melfi, Theodore, and Taraji P. Henson. 2016. Audio commentary. *Hidden Figures*. 21st Century Fox. DVD.

Muller, Marissa G. 2017. "The Hidden Figures Effect Is Real: How It's Inspiring Young Women to Seek Careers in Science and Technology." *Glamour*, January 30, 2017. http://www.glamour.com/story/hidden-figures-inspiring-young-women-science-and-technology

NASA. 1961. "Mercury-Atlas 6 at a Glance." January 21, 1961. Archived from the original (PDF) May 25, 2009. https://web.archive.org/web/20090525123504/https://mira.hq.nasa.gov/history/ws/hdmshrc/all/main/DDD/16286.PDF

NASA. 2016. "NASA Invites Media to Talk with Cast of Hidden Figures." December 12, 2016. Video, 2:29. https://www.youtube.com/watch?v=YWuo8bcIXiM

Neufeld, Michael. 2017. "Katherine Johnson, Hidden Figures, and John Glenn's Flight." Smithsonian Institution, February 20, 2017. https://airandspace.si.edu/stories/editorial/glenn-johnson-hidden-figures

Pearlman, Robert Z. 2016. "'Hidden Figures': 'The Right Stuff' vs. Real Stuff in New Film About NASA History." Space.com, December 27, 2016. http://www.space.com/35145-hidden-figures-right-stuff-history.html

Rainey, James. 2017. "Free Screenings of 'Hidden Figures' Go Wide: From L.A. to Australia." *Variety*, January 27, 2017. https://variety.com/2017/film/news/hidden-figures-free-screenings-1201971825/

Randel, William Pierce. 1978. *The Evolution of American Taste*. New York: Crown Publishers.

Shetterly, Margot Lee. 2016. *Hidden Figures: The American Dream and the Untold Story of the Black Women Mathematicians Who Helped Win the Space Race*. New York: William Morrow and Company.

Shetterly, Margot Lee. 2017a. "Dorothy Vaughan Biography." NASA, August 3, 2017. https://www.nasa.gov/content/dorothy-vaughan-biography

Shetterly, Margot Lee. 2017b. "Mary Jackson Biography." NASA, August 3, 2017. https://www.nasa.gov/content/mary-jackson-biography

Shetterly, Margot Lee. 2018. "Katherine Johnson Biography." NASA, August 16, 2018. https://www.nasa.gov/content/katherine-johnson-biography

St. Martin, Victoria. 2017. "'Hidden' No More: Katherine Johnson, a Black NASA Pioneer, Finds Acclaim at 98." *The Washington Post*, January 27, 2017. https://www.washingtonpost.com/local/hidden-no-more-katherine-johnson-a-black-nasa-pioneer-finds-acclaim-at-98/2017/01/27/d6a6feb8-dd0f-11e6-ad42-f3375f271c9c_story.html

Swenson, Loyd S., James M. Grimwood, and Charles C. Alexander. 1966. *This New Ocean: A History of Project Mercury*. Washington, DC: National Aeronautics and Space Administration.

Thomas, Dexter. 2017. "Space So White: The Oscar-Nominated 'Hidden Figures' Was Whitewashed—But It Didn't Have to Be." *Vice News*, January 25, 2017. https://news.vice.com/en_ca/article/d3xmja/oscar-nominated-hidden-figures-was-whitewashed-but-it-didnt-have-to-be

Tinubu, Aramide. 2016. "'Hidden Figures' Author Margot Lee Shetterly Talks Uncovering a Rich & Powerful Story." Hollywood.com, December 21, 2016. http://www.hollywood.com/movies/hidden-figures-author-margot-lee-shetterly-talks-uncovering-a-rich-powerful-story-60668763/

20th Century Fox Belgium. 2017. "Hidden Figures | Featurette: Achieving the Impossible." January 20, 2017. Video, 2:29, 20:02. https://www.youtube.com/watch?v=XiwBpkyjrmQ&t=1112s

Walsh, Kenneth T. 2010. "The 1960s: A Decade of Change for Women." *U.S. News*, March 12, 2010. https://www.usnews.com/news/articles/2010/03/12/the-1960s-a-decade-of-change-for-women

WHRO-TV. 2011. "What Matters—Katherine Johnson: NASA Pioneer and 'Computer'." February 25, 2011. Video, 11:20. https://www.youtube.com/watch?time_continue=2&v=r8gJqKyIGhE

Select Bibliography

Amos, Jim. 2019. "Rev Up The Harley, 'Easy Rider' Celebrates Its 50th Anniversary By Rolling Back Into Cinemas." *Forbes*, May 8, 2019.

Biskind, Peter. 1998. *Easy Riders, Raging Bulls: How the Sex, Drugs, and Rock 'n Roll Generation Saved Hollywood*. New York: Simon & Schuster.

Bloom, Alexander, and Wini Breines, eds. 2011. *"Takin' It to the Streets": A Sixties Reader*. New York: Oxford University Press.

Blount, Kirven. 2005. *What's Your Poison? Addictive Advertising of the 40s–60s*. Portland, OR: Collectors Press.

Bond, Peter R. 1987. *Heroes in Space: from Gagarin to Challenger*. New York: Basil Blackwell.

Bringgold, Gary. 2014. *99 Observations about the Advertising Business in the 1960s and 1970s*. Old Fashioned Press. Kindle book.

Bromell, Nicholas Knowles. 2002. *Tomorrow Never Knows: Rock and Psychadelics in the 1960s*. Chicago: University of Chicago Press.

Buckbee, Ed, and Wally Schirra. 2005. *The Real Space Cowboys*. Burlington, Canada: Apogee Books.

Buckley, William F., Jr. 2017. "The Playboy Philosophy." *The National Review*, September 28, 2017. Originally published October 1, 1966. https://www.nationalreview.com/2017/09/hugh-hefner-dies-playboy-philosophy-william-f-buckley-jr-criticism-sexual-revolution/

Burgess, Colin. 2011. *Selecting the Mercury Seven: The Search for America's First Astronauts*. New York: Springer.

Callan, Jim. 2005. *America in the 1960s*. New York: Facts on File.

Canby, Vincent. 1983. "Film: 'Right Stuff,' On Astronauts." *The New York Times*, October 21, 1983.

Carlson, Darren K. 2001a. "Most Americans Believe Oswald Conspired with Others to Kill JFK." Gallup, April 11, 2001. https://news.gallup.com/poll/1813/most-americans-believe-oswald-conspired-others-kill-jfk.aspx

Carlson, Michael. 2001b. "L. Fletcher Prouty: US Officer Obsessed by the Conspiracy Theory of President Kennedy's Assassination." *The Guardian*, June 21, 2001.

Chang, Justin. 2017. "Commentary: 50 Years after 'The Graduate,' Restless Benjamin Braddock Still Speaks to Young Men—and Women." *Los Angeles Times*, April 20, 2017.

Clash, Jim. 2017. "Chuck Yeager, Who Tweets, Says Sam Shepard's 'Right Stuff' Character Was Right-On." *Forbes*, January 23, 2017. https://www.forbes.com/sites/jimclash/2017/01/23/chuck-yeager-who-tweets-says-sam-shepards-right-stuff-character-was-right-on/#5fdc83ff2874

Clayborne, Carson. 2001. *The Autobiography of Martin Luther King, Jr.* New York: Warner Books.

Cohen, Lizabeth. 2003. *A Consumer's Republic: The Politics of Mass Consumption in Postwar America*. New York: Vintage Books.

Cohen, Robert. 2009. *Freedom's Orator: Mario Savio and the Radical Legacy of the 1960s*. New York: Oxford University Press.

Didion, Joan. 1967. *Slouching Towards Bethlehem*. New York: Farrar, Straus, and Giroux.

English, Ilene. 2019. *Hippie Chick: Coming of Age in the 1960s*. Berkeley: She Writes Press.

Farber, David. 1994. *The Age of Great Dreams: America in the 1960s*. New York: Hill & Wang.

Femina, Jerry Della. 2010. *From Those Wonderful Folks Who Gave You Pearl Harbor: Front-Line Dispatches from the Advertising Wars*. New York: Simon & Schuster.

Fraser, Nancy. 2013. "Feminism's Two Legacies: A Tale of Ambivalence." In *Revisiting the Sixties,* edited by Laura Bieger and Christian Lammert. Frankfurt, Germany: Campus Publishers.

Girgus, Sam. B. 1998. *Hollywood Renaissance: The Cinema of Democracy in the Era of Ford, Capra, and Kazan*. New York: Cambridge University Press.

Hamilton, Neil A. 1997. *The ABC-CLIO Companion to the 1960s Counterculture in America*. Santa Barbara, CA: ABC-CLIO.

Hastings, Max. 2018. *Vietnam: An Epic Tragedy: 1957–1975*. New York: Harper.

Heimann, Jim. 2005. *The Golden Age of Advertising: The 1960s*. Cologne, Germany: TASCHEN.

Howard-Pitney, David. 1964. *Martin Luther King, Jr., Malcolm X, and the Civil Rights Struggle of the 1950s and 1960s*. New York: Bedford/St. Martin's.

Isserman, Maurice, and Michael Kazin. 2012. *America Divided: The Civil War of the 1960s*. New York: Oxford University Press.

Kael, Pauline. 2011. "The Bottom of the Pit." In *The Age of Movies: Selected Writings of Pauline Kael*. New York: Library of America.

King, Martin Luther, Jr., and Jackson, Jesse. 2000. *Why We Can't Wait*. New York: Signet.

Leddick, David. 2012. "Being Gay in the World of Mad, Mad Men: What It Was Really Like." *Huffington Post*, May 17, 2012.

Maas, Jane. 2013. *Mad Women: The Other Side of Life on Madison Avenue in the 60s and Beyond*. New York: St. Martin's Griffin.

McAdams, Frank. 2005. *The American War Film: History and Hollywood*. Los Angeles: Figueroa Press.
McGilligan, Patrick. 2015. *Jack's Life: A Biography of Jack Nicholson*. New York: W. W. Norton & Company.
McKeen, William. 2017. *Everybody Had An Ocean*. Chicago: Chicago Review Press.
Moretta, John Anthony. 2017. *The Hippies: A 1960s History*. Jefferson, NC: McFarland & Company, Inc.
New Yorker Staff. 2016. *The 60s: The Story of a Decade*. New York: Random House.
Nicholson, Virginia. 2015. *Perfect Wives in Ideal Homes: The Story of Women in the 1950s*. New York: Viking.
Nicholson, Virginia. 2019. *How Was It for You? Women, Love, Sex, and Power in the 1960s*. New York: Viking.
Olson, Wyatt. 2013. "40 Years after Release, POWs at Hanoi Hilton Reflect on Experience." *Stars and Stripes*, February 10, 2013.
Perry, George C. 2001. *San Francisco in the Sixties*. London: Trafalgar Square.
Rasmussen, Karen, Sharon D. Downey, and Jennifer Asenas. 2003. "Trauma, Treatment, and Transformation: The Evolution of the Vietnam Warrior in Film." In *War and Film in America: Historical and Critical Essays*, edited by Marilyn J. Matelski and Nancy Lynch Street. Jefferson, NC: McFarland & Company, Inc., Publishers.
Riley, Sylvia. 2019. *Winter at the Bookshop: Politics and Poverty, St. Ann's in the 1960s*. London: Five Leaves Publications.
Seitz, Matt Zoller. 2017. *Mad Men Carousel: The Complete Critical Companion*. New York: Harry N. Abrams.
Toland, Jim. 2014. *Fire and Fog: Sex, Drugs, Rock 'n' Roll, Murder in 1960s San Francisco*. Chicago: Rico Press.
Witchel, Alex. 2008. "'Mad Men' Has Its Moment." *The New York Times*, June 22, 2008.
Zorach, Rebecca, and Romi Crawford. 2017. *The Wall of Respect: Public Art and Black Liberation in 1960s Chicago*. Evanston, IL: Northwestern University Press.

Index

Abernathy, Ralph, 149
Acheson, Dean, 107, 118
advertising, 129–142; *Advertising Age*, 130; agencies, 129; campaign of VW Beetle, 127, 138; campaigns, 130, 134; and cars, 130; changes in 1960s, 131–132; creativity, 138; expenditures in 1950s, 129; marketing techniques, 130; in the 1960s, 129–132; pitches, 130; product demonstrations, 130; and TV quiz shows, 129–131; women in, 133, 136–137, 142
Anderson, Maj. Rudolf, 112–113, 115
Apollo 1 fire, 68
Armed Forces Vietnam Network, 47

baby boom, 6
Beatles, 21
Bell X-1 rocket, 55, 58
Berlin Wall, 110–111
Bernbach, Bill, 133
Bevel, James, 145
Black cinema, 79
Black Panthers, 8
Bloody Sunday, 145, 156
Bonnie and Clyde, 25
Braniff Airlines, 133

cable TV, 121
Camelot, 94
Campbell, Pete, 126
Castro, Fidel, 90–92, 110–111
"the center was not holding," 11
civil rights, 8, 20
Civil Rights Act of 1964, 7, 79–80, 95, 148
Civil Rights Movement, 144, 147–148, 166
Clark, James, 149, 155
cocaine, 28
Cold War, 59, 107, 108, 111, 114
communes, 24–25
Congress on Racial Equality (CORE), 77
Connally, John, 96
Costner, Kevin, 89, 104, 107–108, 118–119, 163, 177
critical discourse analysis, 116
Cronkite, Walter, 63, 121
Crosby, David, 28
Crossfire, 90
The Courting of Marcus Dupree, 85
Cuba, 107–108, 110

Dealey Plaza, 89, 91–92
Deer Hunter, 37–52; box office, 38; cast, 37; Cimino, Michael, 37, 45–49; critical response, 38, 44–45; De Niro,

Deer Hunter (*Continued*)
  Robert, 37–38, 46; depiction and cultural context, 44–52; historical background, 39–44; Russian Roulette scenes, 38, 47–49; Savage, John, 37; Streep, Meryl, 37; Tet offensive, 42–43; Vietnam, 39–43; Walken, Christopher, 37
Didion, Joan, 11
Donaldson, Roger, 108
"Don't trust anyone over 30," 7
Doyle Dane Bernbach, 133
DuVernay, Ava, 146, 154
Dylan, Bob, 21

Easy Rider, 17–37; box office, 17–18; cast, 17–18; counterculture, 27; critical response, 25–26; depiction and cultural context, 25–37; Fonda, Peter, 17–18, 27–28; historical background, 19–35; Hopper, Dennis, 17, 27–28; inside audience, 18; meaning of title, 19; Nicholson, Jack, 18, 27
Edmund Pettus Bridge, 145, 154
Edwards Air Force Base, 56
Eisenhower, Dwight D., 112
episodic anthology, 125
Equal Employment Opportunity Act, 166
EXCOMM, 107, 111–112, 116
Explorer 1, 59

fallout shelters, 109, 112
feel-good decade of 1950s, 9
FORTRAN, 169
Fowler, James Bonard, 150
Freedom Summer, 82
free love, 23
Free Speech Movement, 7–8, 20, 132

Gagarin, Yuri, 62, 170
Gaither Report, 112
Garlett, Marti Watson, 80–81
gay rights, 140–141
gender equality, 166
gender stereotypes, 163
generation gap, 7
Gentle Thursdays, 132
German Democratic Republic (GDR), 110

Gitlin, Todd, 6
The Graduate, 1–17; Bancroft, Anne, 1–3; box office, 1–2; Braddock, Benjamin, 1–5, 11–15; cast, 1–2; depiction and cultural context, 11–15; final scene, 5; Henry, Buck, 2, 11–12; historical background, 6–11; Hoffman, Dustin, 1–2, 5; Nichols, Mike, 1, 2, 5, 11, 12; "plastics" scene, 2; Robinson, Elaine, 3–5; Robinson, Mrs., 3–4, 12–13; Ross, Katharine, 1, 2; sexual revolution, 9; youth estrangement, 18
Great Society Program, 148
Green, Paula, 133
Greensboro sit-ins, 20

Hanoi Hilton, 42
heat shield danger, 64–65
Hefner, Hugh, 9
Helm, Levon, 55
Heyser, Maj. Richard, 114
Hidden Figures, 163–179; analysis and computation unit, 169; box office, 164; cast, 164–165; "colored computers," 167; critical response, 164–165; depiction and cultural context, 173–179; Harrison, Al, 163, 176; Henson, Taraji P., 163; historical background, 165–173; human computers, 163–166; Jackson, Mary, 163, 166, 177; Johnson, Katherine G., 163, 166, 168, 170–174; Monae, Janelle, 163, 177; oppression of women, 132–133; Project Mercury, 163, 168, 171; Spencer, Octavia, 163, 177; Vaughan, Dorothy, 163, 166, 169, 175, 177; West Area Computing Unit, 169; women's gender roles, 166
Hill, Jean, 91, 100
hippies, 17, 21–24
Ho Chi Minh, 42
Ho Chi Minh City, 44
Hoover, J. Edgar, 78, 86, 155
House on Un-American Activities Committee (HUAC), 110
Human Be-In, 23–24
Humphrey, Hubert H., 150
hypocrisy and the 1960s, 10, 12

integration, 79
Irish Mafia, 118
Iron Curtain, 110

Jackson, Jimmie, 150
JFK, 89–107; Banister, Guy, 91, 94; Bay of Pigs, 90, 92, 94; box office, 90; cast, 89–90; Costner, Kevin, 89; critical response, 89, 97–99; depiction and cultural context, 97–107; Ferrie, David, 91, 99; Garrison, Jim, 89, 91, 92, 100–101; grassy knoll, 94, 100; historical background, 93–97; Jones, Tommy Lee, 89; Kennedy, John F., 89, 90, 107; Oswald, Lee Harvey, 89, 91, 95–96, 98, 101; Ruby, Jack, 95–96; Shaw, Clay, 89, 91–92, 99, 100; Stone, Oliver, 90, 97–98, 100–101, 103; Sutherland, Donald, 101; Texas School Book Depository, 89, 92, 96; Tippit, J. D., 96; 25th anniversary, 102; Warren Commission Report, 90–91, 96–97; Warren, Earl, 95; "X," 91–92, 101–102
Jim Crow Laws, 79
Johnson, Judge Frank, 152
Johnson, Lyndon Baines, 42, 90–91, 98, 108, 145–146, 148, 153, 155

Kennedy, John F., 26, 63, 107, 111–112, 115, 119, 120; approval ratings, 94; assassination, 26, 89–90, 93, 98, 121; Assassination Records Collection Act, 103; conspiracy theories, 89–90, 93, 98; Gallup Poll on Kennedy assassination, 98; House Select Committee on Assassinations, 93–94, 97; magic bullet, 97; rifle shots, 93, 97; second shooter theory, 97; Zapruder film, 97
Kennedy, Robert F., 26, 107, 113
Killen, Edgar Ray, 87
King, Coretta Scott, 150, 156
King, Martin Luther, 8, 10, 80, 145–151, 159; and Black churches, 105; FBI wiretaps of King, 151; "I have a dream" speech, 148; and LBJ, 155–156; and Nobel Peace Prize, 148; in Selma jail, 150
Ku Klux Klan, 77, 83–84, 86, 154

Langley Research Center, 163, 167–168
Lardner, Ring, 98–100
L.A. sound, 21
Leary, Timothy, 23
LeMay, Gen. Curtis, 107, 118
Lewis, John, 145, 151, 153
Liberty Bell 7 (rocket), 63, 68, 170
Liuzzo, Viola Gregg, 154
Lovelace Air Force Base, 60
LSD, 23–24
Luna 2 spacecraft, 62

Maas, Jane, 133
Mad Men, 125–144; and alcohol, 127; awards, 125; depiction and cultural context, 135–142; Draper, Betty, 126; Draper, Don, 126–127, 142; and gays, 135, 139, 140–141; and gender roles, 126–127; Hamm, Jon, 126; Hendricks, Christina, 126, 142; historical background, 129–135; Holloway, Joan, 126–127; Jones, January, 126; and Judaism, 126; and Madison Avenue, 125; Moss, Elizabeth, 126–127, 142; Olson, Peggy, 126, 136, 142; ratings, 128; real-life clients, 138; and sexism, 127; Slattery, John, 126; and smoking, 127; Sterling Cooper Draper Price, 125, 130; Sterling, Roger, 126; Weiner, Matthew, 125, 128, 138; women in workplace, 135–136
marijuana, 23
McCann-Erickson, 130
McCarthy, Joseph, 110
McNamara, Robert, 107, 109, 112, 116–117
Melfi, Theodore, 164, 177–178
Mercury Seven astronauts, 61, 65, 69, 71, 172
Mercury Seven media circus, 70
Meredith, James Howard, 81
military industrial establishment, 90
The Missiles of October, 119
Mississippi Burning, 75–88; Anderson, Rupert, 75–77, 82, 83, 84–85; box office, 75; cast, 75–76; Chaney, James, 75, 77–78, 81–82; critical response, 77, 86; Dafoe, Willem, 75, 77, 85–86;

Mississippi Burning (*Continued*)
  depiction and cultural context, 81–88;
  Dourif, Brad, 76; Goodman, Andrew,
  75, 77–78, 80, 82; Hackman, Gene,
  75, 77, 85; historical background,
  77–81; McDormand, Frances, 76;
  Neshoba County, Mississippi, 80–82;
  Parker, Alan, 75, 81; Pell, Clayton, 76,
  83–84; Pell, Mrs., 75, 83–85; Schwerner,
  Michael, 75, 77–78, 80, 82; Ward,
  Alan, 75–77, 82–83
Mitchell, Jerry, 87
Montgomery, Alabama, 145–146, 153

NAACP, 149
NASA, 56, 59, 61, 163, 176, 177
National Advisory Committee for
  Aeronautics, 166–168
New Journalism, 57
Nixon, Richard, 43

O'Keefe, Willie, 91, 99, 100
Oliver, Beverly, 100–101
On the Trail of Assassins, 90, 97
Operation Frequent Wind, 44

The pill (birth control pill), 9
playboy philosophy, 9
Plessy v. Ferguson, 79
Polykoff, Shirley, 133
Port Huron Statement, 20
Presidential Medal of Freedom, 173
Prouty, L. Fletcher, 101–103
public displays of affection, 132

quiz show scandals, 131

racial stereotypes, 163
Redstone 3 rocket, 63
Reeb, Rev. James, 152
Richardson, Robert, 103
The Right Stuff, 55–74; "Ace of Space,"
  65; astronaut selection process,
  60–61; Carpenter, Scott, 65; Cape
  Canaveral, 56–57; cast, 55–56;
  chimpanzee test, 62; Cooper, Annie
  Lee, 149, 155; Cooper, Gordon, 55,
  66, 68–69; critical response, 66–67;
  depiction and cultural context, 66–74;
  first orbital flight, 64; Glenn, John,
  56–57, 62, 64, 69, 163–164, 171–173,
  179; Glenn, Scott, 55; Grissom, Gus,
  55, 63, 68, 170; Harris, Ed, 55–57;
  Hershey, Barbara, 55; historical background,
  57–66; Mach 1, 58; manned
  space flights, 55–56; NASA, 56, 59,
  61; Pancho's Happy Bottom Riding
  Club, 58; Project Mercury, 55, 57, 59,
  62; Quaid, Dennis, 55; Schirra, Wally,
  66, 69–70; Shepard, Alan, 56–63, 170;
  Shepard, Sam, 55, 67; Slayton, Deke,
  55, 65; sound barrier, 57; sub-orbital
  flights, 63; Ward, Fred, 55; Wolfe,
  Tom, 55, 57, 67–68; Yeager, Chuck,
  55, 57–58, 66–68, 71
Roth, Tim, 146
Rusk, Dean, 107, 114
Russia, 107–110

Salinger, Pierre, 118
Sanford, Otis, 80
segregation, 78–79
Self, David, 108
Selma, 145–159; box office, 146; cast,
  146–147; critical response, 146–147,
  154–155; depiction and cultural context,
  154–159; historical background,
  147–154; march on Selma, 151–153;
  Oyelowa, David, 145, 158; Sixteen
  Street Baptist Church bombing, 148;
  Southern Christian Leadership Conference,
  147–148, 151–153; Student
  Nonviolent Coordinating Committee,
  149; Winfrey, Oprah, 146, 154–155
Separate but Equal Doctrine, 79
Shetterly, Margot Lee, 164, 166, 173–174
Sixties, 6–10; counterculture, 18–19,
  25; drugs, 23; sadness, 137; suburbia,
  130; protest songs, 21
socialist feminists, 132, 134
Soviet Union, 108–109, 111
space race, 171
Spiesel, Charles I., 99–100
Sputnik, 56, 19, 108
states rights, 78
STEM careers, 165, 177

Stone, Oliver, 90, 97–98, 100–101, 103
Stonewall riot, 140
Students for a Democratic Society (SDS), 8, 20
Summer of Love, 23

Thirteen Days, 107–124; Bay of Pigs, 111; box office, 108; critical response, 108, 115–117; Cuban Blockade, 109, 112, 116; Cuban invasion, 120; Cuban missile crisis, 197, 112, 113–114, 120; Culp, Stephen, 107; depiction and cultural context, 114–121; Dobrinyn, Anatoly, 107, 113; Greenwood, Bruce, 107–108, 115; historical background, 109–114; interrelated texts, 117; Kennedy, John F., 107, 111–112, 115, 119, 120; Kennedy, Robert F., 106, 113; Kruschev, Nikita, 108, 111, 113, 117, 120; missiles in Turkey, 113, 120; O'Donnell, Ken, 107–109, 111, 115, 118–119; Russian missiles, 107, 112; spy planes, 108, 111; U-2, 111
Thompson, J. Walter, 130
Twenty-One, 131

University of California at Berkeley, 8

VanDoren, Charles, 131
Vietnam, 8, 13–14, 20, 39–41, 94, 131–132; college students, 13; cruelties, 41; deaths, 13; fall of Saigon, 44; and Kennedy, 94; military draft, 8, 13, 40; My Lai, 43; POWs, 42–43, 59; PTSD, 50–52; public opinion, 42; ROTC, 13; search and destroy missions, 40, 44; soldiers' experiences, 40, 44; volunteers, 40
Vietnam Veterans Against the War, 38, 43
Voter Registration Act, 149, 152, 157
Voting Rights Act, 7, 79–80, 95

Wallace, Gov. George, 153
Weatherman, 8
Webb, Charles, 11
Wells, Mary, 133
Wells Rich Lawrence Ad Agency, 134
white male supremacy, 132
Williams, Hosea, 145, 151
Willingham, Calder, 2, 12
Woolworth's sit-in, 149

Yeager, Chuck, 55, 57–58, 66–68, 71
Young & Rubicam, 130
Z, 102

About the Authors

JIM WILLIS is a veteran journalist, author of 16 books, and professor emeritus of journalism at Azusa Pacific University in Southern California. He holds a PhD in journalism from the University of Missouri, and he is married to gifted musician Anne Willis and has two sons and three stepdaughters.

MARK MILLER is a freelance writer, editor, and translator. He is a summa cum laude graduate in journalism and Spanish at Azusa Pacific University, and he lives in Duarte, California.

www.ingramcontent.com/pod-product-compliance
Lightning Source LLC
Chambersburg PA
CBHW052340230426
43664CB00041B/2571